THUNDERBIRD
ON GLOBAL
BUSINESS STRATEGY

The Faculty of Thunderbird,
The American Graduate School of
International Management

Edited by Robert E. Grosse

John Wiley & Sons, Inc.

New York • Chichester • Weinheim • Brisbane • Singapore • Toronto

ISBN 0-471-32606-2

Printed in the United States of America.

10 9 8 7 6 5 4 3 2 1

Acknowledgments

We would like to acknowledge the thoughtful guidance of Melvyn Copen, under whose leadership this project was launched at Thunderbird. Without his support and encouragement, the project would never have taken place. We would also like to thank Ms. Georgia Lessard, graphic artist extraordinaire, for her help on many of the figures, tables, and other artwork associated with this project.

Contents

Part III
Key Concerns of the
Global Manager   247

Introduction

In the twenty-first century, successful managers must have a global perspective on their businesses, whether or not they work in international companies. The competition of this century, in addition to moving through the Internet, crosses national boundaries at will, leaving inward-looking companies at risk of being overwhelmed by their global competitors. The corner grocery store is competing with products from the next corner and even from the rest of the world, via telephone-based home shopping, Internet-based purchasing, and other new delivery services. Managers must understand the risks and opportunities raised by foreign competitors, foreign markets, and foreign suppliers, since they are now only a keystroke away.

Our focus is on the particularly global and international aspects of business that managers need to be worrying about and need to understand. Our purpose is both to raise awareness of these issues and to provide guidance on how to deal with them. Whether it is management of a global supply chain or use of global financial markets, the availability of these options has to be in the thinking of successful managers today.

This book is written entirely by current and former Thunderbird professors. Thunderbird is the recognized leader in graduate international management education in the United States, ranking first in every *U.S. News and World Report* survey since 1995. Thunderbird has offered an international management degree since 1946, the first such program in the United States. It is the only U.S. business school focused completely on global business, requiring all students to master at least two languages, to develop extensive knowledge of at least one region of the world, and to complete MBA core requirements and international business studies. Thunderbird's 120 faculty members are leaders in their fields of international business, international studies, and language for business. A selection of Thunderbird authors have assembled their thinking on key global business issues to create this book.

This book marks the initiation of a strategic alliance between Thunderbird, The American Graduate School of International Management, and John Wiley & Sons Publishers. The goal of the alliance is to present a series of books that explore key issues in global business management, so that managers and analysts can better understand the problems and opportunities facing companies at the beginning of the twenty-first century.

The studies offer a wide-reaching set of perspectives on global business strategy, aimed at senior managers whose decisions need to take a wholistic view and to consider this broad array of conditions and concerns. The current volume highlights one of Thunderbird's two core areas of competence: global business strategy. The other area of research and teaching leadership that Thunderbird pursues is cross-cultural management. Both of these fields are the subjects of books to be published in the Thunderbird-Wiley partnership.

Global Strategy Perspectives

The book is divided into three parts, starting with five analyses of global strategy itself. Part I is initiated with a study by John C. Beck on "Responding to Global Crises Using the Change Cycle." Beck looks at the Asian crisis of 1997–1998, and he shows the reactions of companies that experienced the crisis as well as a set of recommendations about how companies *should* react to such situations. The change cycle is a concept introduced by Beck to organize thinking about crises and company responses. In a two-dimensional structure, he argues that a firm may make large or small changes, and respond to internal or external pressures. The costs and risks of responding to internal problems/opportunities with small changes are low; the costs and risks of responding to external pressures with large changes are enormous; and many additional situations lie in between. The goal of management is to understand the need for change in response to all kinds of pressures, and to evaluate proposed responses along the two dimensions of the change cycle. Beck presents tools for crisis response in each of the four quadrants of the matrix, and demonstrates how they could be used or were used in dealing with the Asian crisis.

Robert E. Grosse lays out a view of Transformational Management, in which companies are faced with dramatically changing markets, technology, and other competitive challenges. Responses of several leading corporations demonstrate both positive and negative outcomes of undertaking these transformations. One of the key findings is that, while companies need to take such a forward-looking view to survive in the competition of the new century, the final step of implementation can completely make or break the strategy, as evidenced in the negative outcome for Motorola Corporation with its Iridium project.

Grosse's idea of Transformational Management involves a four-step process: (1) identifying the future technological and competitive conditions in an industry; (2) positioning the firm to be a leader in that context; (3) informing clients of the vision; and (4) finally implementing the strategy to make this future a reality. An outstanding example of a firm that has gone through a successful transformation is Monsanto Corporation, formerly a chemicals company and now a life sciences company with activities in pharmaceuticals, agricultural chemicals, and food ingredients.

This view is quite challenging, since it posits a wrenching and time-consuming change process that does not allow an easy transition for any firm that takes up the transformation. But in more and more instances, Grosse asserts that firms are going to face such a challenge, as markets mature, subdivide, and redefine themselves as the result of technological, regulatory, and other changes in the world economy. Transformational Management is a basis for coping with this newly arrived reality.

Alan I. Murray offers another view of global strategy, focusing specifically on knowledge competition, that is, competition in contexts where knowledge creation and management are key drivers of company competitiveness. His 5^3 model lays out a strategy framework based on five *constraints* that all firms face (such as competition and capabilities), which lead to five strategic *choices* (such as the domain in which the firm wants to compete and the design or organizational configuration selected to pursue the strategy) and finally to five *considerations* that must be dealt with under each choice.

Murray's perspective focuses on knowledge-based competition, the central basis for competitive survival in most industries of the future and of many industries today. He tries to identify the key questions that all firms must ask in this kind of competition, and then he provides a systematic and detailed analytical structure for answering each question in turn. This fascinating model provides ample ground for debate by decision makers, and, above all, provides a structured way to identify the really crucial questions that a firm needs to answer, along with the tools to develop the answers.

Andrew C. Inkpen then moves the discussion into the realm of networks of companies that cooperate to build on their internal strengths and to take advantage of the strengths of other firms. His study on managing global strategic alliances describes a wide variety of cooperative arrangements and offers guidance to managers on taking the best advantage of these relationships. He argues that, although there is no single best way to manage an alliance, there are common principles that should contribute to alliance success. These principles include things such as viewing the alliance partner as a true ally, in seeking to maximize joint benefits from the alliance rather than disregarding the partner's interests.

The use of strategic alliances is virtually necessary in today's competition, with huge capital costs and expensive, risky research required in many businesses, as well as distribution channels that can be shared if partners can devise sensible arrangements for mutual benefit. Inkpen focuses particularly on international alliances and on the kinds of advantages that the partners can bring into such situations. These advantages include access to new markets as well as opportunities for learning about different cultures and business practices from the foreign partner firm.

Inkpen argues that a key reason for alliance failures is that firms fail to explore the organizational compatibility of their partners, and, related to this point, that they fail to take the partner's goals into account in pursuing the alliance. This unwillingness or inability to look at the alliance as a source of joint benefit, and to design organizational mechanisms for incorporating the alliance and supporting it, causes breakdowns in communication and trust between partners and can lead to breakdown of the alliance.

Inkpen then presents a series of steps that firms can take to reduce this problem. For example, design organizational links between parent firms before launching the alliance; make sure that there is organizational fit at more than one level of the organizations; maximize communication between partners and be always ready to change alliance structure to better meet organizational goals. He concludes that there are a handful of key considerations—most of which are manageable if the firm explicitly recognizes them—that frequently make the difference between success and failure in international strategic alliances. Not surprisingly, these keys are not different from the ones needed for successful domestic alliances—careful planning and investigation of the partner before beginning the alliance, to ensure commitment and organizational fit; flexibility in operating the alliance to take account of changes in the venture and the environment; and constant consideration of the partner's interests, to make sure that the alliance really is a win–win deal.

Anant K. Sundaram and his colleagues study the issue of corporate governance, comparing the systems that have developed in the three leading economies of the world: the United States, Germany, and Japan. They define corporate governance as, "the top management process that manages and mediates value creation for, and value transference among, various corporate claimants (including the society-at-large), in a context that simultaneously ensures accountability toward these claimants." Thus, at issue is the way in which corporations are managed, for whose interests, and under what rules.

This fundamental set of questions is answered somewhat differently in each of the three countries. Sundaram et al. explain these differences and their implications in a fascinating overview of the situation today. For example, they compare *external* mechanisms for corporate control in each country, such as labor unions, government regulatory structures, and financial markets in which company shares (ownership) are traded. In the United States, the stock market permits rapid and widespread opportunities for changing corporate control via purchase of controlling shares in a company, when one investor (or group) views the company's value as being higher or potentially higher than what the market shows. This situation is quite different in Japan, where corporate control seldom changes hands through open stock market transactions, since ownership is often held by tightly-linked groups of investors (*keiretsu*). And in Germany, the situation likewise is much less open, with large financial institutions holding controlling interest in many companies, again not permitting the open market to shift control easily.

They also look at *internal* mechanisms for corporate control, such as the structure and role of the board of directors and the way in which compensation is used to motivate performance. For example, U.S.-based firms use the board of directors, including outside directors, as an overall policymaking guide, where German firms have a management board that includes labor representatives and that focuses on day-to-day management. Japanese firms tend to have boards made up of almost all inside directors, along with a *keiretsu* bank representative.

Compensation of top executives is far higher relative to lower level employees in U.S. firms, while in Germany it is much less skewed, and in Japan even less. The use of stock options to motivate performance is widely used in the United States, while seldom occurring in German or Japanese firms. Perhaps as a consequence, there is more bidding for U.S. top executives between firms, and thus shorter tenure by U.S. executives at their firms. The Japanese system of permanent employment with one firm, while no longer so widely followed, still exemplifies the low level of executive job-hopping in that country, and the German system falls somewhere in between.

Sundaram et al. conclude from their review of the three corporate governance systems that there is a tendency worldwide for convergence toward the U.S. system. This system seems to be best at resolving the *agency problem,* namely aligning managers' interests with those of owners. The Japanese and German systems are much more similar to each other than to the U.S. system. (They are based on *communitarian* governance, in which stakeholders such as employees, customers, and other members of society have more say in corporate decision making.) The *contractarian* system of governance that characterizes U.S. corporations seems to be better able to produce more transparent decision making, stimulate investment in R&D, and provide other outcomes that make it most suitable for business at the beginning of the new century.

Part 2 moves the discussion from broad strategy questions to a focus on functional areas such as marketing and finance.

Managing the Functional Areas at the Global Level

Sundaresan Ram explores the idea that simultaneous product development for multiple markets is no longer an option—it has become a necessity for corporate survival. Firms today must use global product development to maintain their competitiveness by realizing key development cost savings and by taking advantage of new ideas that occur in different markets around the world. Markets are no longer segmented in time such that products can be sequentially introduced over extended periods, but rather business is now globally linked to the point where cost savings from global product development *must* be realized just to compete.

Even with a global perspective on product development, different strategies may serve different firms better. When customer pressures for tailoring products/services to local needs dominate, differentiation is needed. When scale economies of centralized production are very important, this factor may dominate and lead to less product/service adaptation to serve local preferences. This issue is analogous to the marketing debate between standardization and adaptation of products, prices, promotion, and so on, across national boundaries.

Ram also argues for companies to establish an Innovation Charter to maximize the number of good product ideas that end up getting into production. An innovation charter is a clear, concise statement of the company's philosophy regarding product development. Once the charter is clearly defined, communicated, and assimilated by each and every opinion leader in the firm, the quality of ideas that enter the first phase of the product development cycle are likely to be higher. This idea provides a useful new tool for firms to consider for optimizing product development in an era of hyper-speed competition.

William E. Youngdahl turns to a very visible topic of the 1990s, the management of a global supply chain. (For non-initiates, supply chain management involves planning, sourcing, making, and delivering.) He describes how companies often move through stages of globalization of their supply chain management, from optimizing relationships with suppliers and integrating communications with them on a global basis, to achieving a "virtual" supply chain, with integration of owned and contracted supply sources, flexible creation and elimination of temporary supply chains as needed, and substitution of information for inventory.

This picture may seem like a dream for futurists, but in fact many companies are developing global, virtual supply chains as telecommunications and transportation costs and efficiency have improved dramatically in the 1990s. Youngdahl gives ample illustrations of firms such as Hewlett-Packard that are integrating their global supply networks, to utilize plants around the world as nodes of innovation and production for the firm's global needs. He also points out that the use of virtual supply chains, in which much of the activity is contracted out, brings with it tremendous risks of losing control of the business, as happened with IBM in personal computers, losing control to its two key suppliers Intel and Microsoft.

Youngdahl traces the steps that firms follow to achieve fully-integrated global management of their supply chains, starting from functional competence optimization in the four areas of the supply chain. This stage is followed by a process of rationalizing at the global level the various supply chain activities, such as standardizing products, sourcing production in global low-cost locations, developing suppliers that can deliver to the firm's locations around the world, and so on. A third stage is the optimization of this system, to cut costs and manage risks. This may involve redistributing production to achieve faster delivery times or more responsiveness to key markets and paring down the number of suppliers to focus on top-tier strategic partners. And finally, the last stage is to create virtual, global supply chains, with a minimum of the firm's own capital committed to the maximum efficient supply, production, and distribution network. Achieving this final stage requires outsourcing of activities that can be better supplied by unrelated firms, along with putting the firm's own capital into activities that can best leverage it into adding value. This kind of supply chain structure implies the use of strategic alliances, and reminds us to focus on the issues raised earlier by Andrew Inkpen in designing and managing those alliances.

Raj Aggarwal and Robert E. Grosse present a view of the global finance function, explaining the various instruments and markets that now exist for cross-national financing and investing, as well as managing risks. This chapter illustrates the phenomenal proliferation of instruments that have arisen largely in response to the opening of financial markets to global competition and capital flows. Futures, options, forwards, financing facilities, and many more instruments have become commonplace around the world in the 1990s, as most countries permit foreign investors to come in and domestic investors to take part of their wealth overseas. Senior managers in corporations around the world need to be informed about the opportunities that now exist for gaining access to funding through instruments such as euro-commercial paper, ADRs, and asset-backed financing facilities, as well as the investment vehicles that exist, from country funds to bonds and bond funds around the world, to treasury instruments, and finally about the risk-management instruments, from exchange-traded ones to highly specialized and individually-designed hedges.

Aggarwal and Grosse move systematically through the finance function to describe the global elements of each area, from capital budgeting to portfolio management, and so on. They highlight some of the problems in current international finance, such as the volatility of capital flows that can cause emerging market crises overnight when confidence drops and speculators sell off financial instruments in any given country. This has certainly been evident in the Asian financial crisis of the late 1990s, and in the contagion effect of the Mexican "tequila" crisis of 1994, which spread rapidly around Latin America. Their conclusions are that the financial markets are probably best left alone to adjust to such volatility, but that the global financial system needs to offer protection instruments such as forwards and futures, to ensure that those who want to avoid these risks can do so efficiently.

This chapter concludes by suggesting that financial managers today need to think global but act "Glocal," that is, with due regard to balancing both global and local needs and conditions. They need to take advantage of the financing, investing, and hedging markets and mechanisms that exist globally, and at the same time they need to manage local operations in conformance with local requirements and needs. While the instruments are largely global, the rules of the game and the cultural practices are largely local, and must be taken into account in financial decision making. This is not a very different conclusion from what we see in the other functional areas analyzed here.

Shoshana B. Tancer analyzes the legal function and shows how ethnocentricity can lead firms into major mistakes when they operate overseas. She then explains steps that can be taken to avoid such pitfalls and to recognize the cultural differences that are embodied in the different legal systems around the world. Three basic legal systems are described: those based on common law, civil law, and Islamic law.

Countries with a common law tradition, including the United States and Great Britain, rely on customary law and precedents that are established in the judicial system. Civil law-based countries rely on legislative codes that are interpreted by scholars and judges, and they do not follow prior court decisions as a fundamental basis for legal interpretation. And finally, Islamic law countries base legal decisions on the teachings of the Koran, as interpreted by the judicial system.

Tancer points out some of the kinds of mistakes that managers can make by assuming that legal systems function similarly across countries, when in fact there are fundamental differences. For example, the use of a notary in the United States is a minor event, principally for asserting the validity of a person's signature on a legal document. In civil law countries, the notary is a legally trained person qualified to prepare contracts and to verify not only the identity of individuals, but also clear title to property, and to authenticate documents, among other things.

Tancer goes on to explain a number of contexts in which the law differs significantly in company affairs among the three kinds of legal traditions, from the right of establishment to personnel policies to antitrust law. For example, most countries use some form of requirement to register foreign-owned investments such as subsidiaries of multinational firms, where in the United States there is no such limitation. (The registration process has become much more of a formality in many countries, where in earlier decades it was used as an entry barrier around which only selected firms were allowed to pass—such as those accepting partial local ownership.) Also, most countries have more strict lay-off policies than does the United States, so that surplus employees in times of slow-down in demand for the company's products or services cannot be let go without mountains of red tape and enormous severance payments. These examples illustrate some of the many legal differences that are presented. Managers will find both entertaining reading and valuable suggestions on avoiding the consequences of failure to pay adequate attention to legal aspects of international business.

Key Concerns of the Global Manager

The final part of the book explores a series of topics that arise in cross-border business and that have become especially significant in the 1990s. Each author has taken on a different topic, so that the section presents an overall panorama of the kinds of issues that are facing the global firm at the end of the century.

D. Lance Revenaugh looks at the enormous challenge of harnessing information technology to successfully run a global firm today. He argues fundamentally that the key resource for making this work is flexible people, not the most advanced machines or computer programs. By keeping up with the machinery or programming innovations that characterize twenty-first-century business, a firm will still not be able to compete successfully, unless its human resources are able to work successfully with this technology and to put it into good use in carrying out their tasks.

Revenaugh also asserts that competing globally and using new technologies are both becoming crucial competitive imperatives, rather than the earlier key advantages of product quality and cost, which are becoming more commoditized. That is, a firm must be able to rapidly assimilate new technology to stay ahead or stay even with respect to quality and cost, and a firm must use global markets to find an adequate customer base and to realize scale economies.

He points out the important failing of some companies that seek to keep up with the latest technological shifts without preparing their people resources adequately to utilize them. He uses the example of SAP and other Enterprise Resource Planning systems, which can overwhelm companies unless careful attention is paid to training and motivating staff to use them. The global scale economies and other information and efficiency gains can be lost when personnel are not able to utilize the system successfully, or become opposed to the system's rigidities that appear to decrease their productivity.

In all, Revenaugh makes a strong case for putting people first in the information technology field. That is, he argues that in looking at IT's new role in strategy development a manager needs to include a broader base of inputs. The assertion here is that IT and Human Resources will be the key contributors to the strategy development process, letting management know what constraints exist and what opportunities can be exploited.

Robert S. Tancer explores the subject of intellectual property protection, a huge issue for firms whose competitive strengths derive from knowledge of patented processes or copyrighted written works. The chapter is structured to follow the issues raised in the Trade-Related Aspects of Industrial Property Rights (TRIPS) Agreement that was part of the negotiation of the World Trade Organization, which replaced GATT in 1995. The TRIPS Agreement seeks to promote "effective and adequate protection of intellectual property rights." Because all members of the World Trade Organization have agreed to accept the terms of the TRIPS Agreement, its coverage provides a useful set of issues for consideration here.

The two main types of intellectual property that are protected under the agreement are patents and copyrights, though trademarks and some other forms of intellectual property are covered as well. Tancer begins with a brief historical look at intellectual property protection in the United States and Europe. He notes that patents and copyrights were given protection by the U.S. Constitution, whereas in Europe, such protection came from the concept of "natural law," under which fair and just treatment was due to intellectual property creators. These ideas became codified internationally in the 1880s with the Paris Convention (patents) and the Berne Convention (copyrights), respectively.

Tancer explains the problems and limitations of obtaining adequate protection of patents in many countries, even though the trend is for countries to implement legislation consistent with the TRIPS Agreement. Likewise, he points out the problems companies face in upholding their rights to copyrighted materials, which are sometimes copied and distributed illegally in countries with weak copyright laws and/or weak enforcement. He gives several examples of problems experienced by U.S. multinational firms in protecting their intellectual property, from CD makers' dispute with China, where bootleg music CDs have become widely available in huge quantities, to pharmaceuticals manufacturers, whose patents are often not protected, particularly in less developed countries who make the argument that medical advances should be shared with poorer nations at reduced prices.

Tancer presents a perspective on intellectual property protection that gives managers a good sense of the key issues and some recommendations on how to deal with the problems that arise when adequate protection exists. He also leaves the reader with some optimism concerning the global harmonization of laws on intellectual property protection that is occurring, largely in the TRIPS context.

Christine Uber Grosse takes on the subject of cross-cultural management, looking at ways that companies can prepare their managers to handle foreign assignments and also to deal with clients, coworkers, and governments from a different culture. She starts with the observation that companies with important overseas business activities recognize the need for training or otherwise preparing their executives for dealing with these situations, but almost none of them follow through with programs to accomplish this task.

Grosse asserts that there are five ways to prepare executives for cross-cultural assignments. It can be through travel and work experience, training, cultural informants, hiring practices, and/or diversity policy. The first of these strategies looks suspiciously like a do-nothing strategy—just dropping managers into cross-cultural experiences without prior training or background. This sink-or-swim process is likely to produce some successful managers, who can then be assigned to other such tasks. However, it is costly and probably foolish to court failure by those not able to swim instantly, and to ignore the availability of prior preparation through training, use of cultural informants, or other planned preparation. Actually, this first category of strategy does include preplanned activities such as assignment of the person/people to multicultural environments within the firm itself, and travel to overseas affiliates or clients to gain some knowledge of their culture.

She notes that an increasing (though still small) number of companies are attempting to provide prior training before overseas or even domestic cross-cultural assignments. Training programs may be developed in-house, but because of the relatively small number of people assigned overseas, it is often more efficient to contract with an outside provider of training services. In discussions with more than 100 executives in international firms, Grosse found that almost two-thirds provided some kind of pre-assignment training before an overseas assignment, and that the majority of them used in-house programs for the training.

The rest of the chapter describes additional methods used by companies to try to prepare their managers for cross-cultural dealings. The details presented give a good understanding of the whole range of possibilities, plus their strengths and weaknesses. Grosse favors cross-cultural training as one key method in whatever package of pre-assignment support a company decides to offer its managers, but she also gives a balanced perspective on the costs and benefits of all of the alternatives.

John C. Beck concludes the book with a look at the impact of the Internet on global business. The fundamental premise (or simply the current reality) is that new competitors who master the Internet as a marketing and supply chain vehicle are taking over markets from traditional competitors, and even creating new markets for their goods and services. Successful firms in almost any business, from petroleum to banking, from computer software to shoes, will have to respond directly to the Internet challenge in order to survive.

Beck argues that the World Wide Web has been almost two-thirds a U.S. phenomenon in the 1990s, while in the next decade more than two-thirds of the users will be from non-North American locations. This point alone demonstrates the crucial need for global firms to stake out their claim on the net. It also highlights the problem of developing *trust* between users of the Internet, since people from different cultures and countries have historically faced a huge barrier of mutual suspicion or at least lack of trust. The Internet does not eliminate this barrier, but as new methods are found to ensure quality of goods/services delivered, and to guarantee payment, the barrier is very likely to diminish in importance.

Likewise, the role of governments as gatekeepers is challenged in the extreme with the Internet, since it is currently almost impossible for a government to restrict access by a country's people to anything that is available on the Internet. New rules are being developed to give governments some degree of access to information, and thus to potential regulatory power, but these rules are far from clear at this point. Thus, the role of governments in international business is really in a tremendous upheaval, and government-business relations are being dramatically redefined.

Another traditional concern of international business—crossing language barriers—is vividly highlighted by commerce on the Internet. As Beck notes, today most of the language appearing on the Internet is in English, and most of the users are English speakers. But in a few short years, as web use really becomes global, the largest number of users will be non-English speakers, or at least those for whom English is not the native language. How will this affect global business? At the least it will cause a boom in the demand for translation services. It may push further for English to be adopted as the lingua franca of the world. And it may produce a boom in the use of multilingual Internet pages, to serve the needs of key global language target audiences (certainly the Chinese-speaking audience, among others). These are really major concerns of the globalization of the Internet and of e-Commerce.

The picture that emerges from Beck's essay is thought provoking. While he is able to sketch some of the elements of the revolution in business practices and global trends, what is coming remains to be seen. No one can know the future, but Beck has given us some very useful pieces of the puzzle to mull over and fit together as we all see the Internet economy develop.

Overall, the ideas in this book give a very useful panorama of Thunderbird's view on global strategy. The broad perspective of global business strategy that permeates the Thunderbird curriculum and concerns of the faculty is well represented here. At the same time, the contents of this book provide a very up-to-date picture of global business strategy, both in the area of general management strategy as well as in the various topical areas that constitute Parts II and III of the work. When a manager thinks about surviving in the hypercompetitive, global environment of today and the future, these analyses will provide ample tools for designing strategies for success.

ROBERT E. GROSSE

Global Strategy Perspectives

1 | Responding to Global Crises Using the Change Cycle

JOHN C. BECK

In our fast-paced, electronically-connected world, not only do evolutionary changes in our immediate environment occur more often, but revolutionary changes that result in "crises" are much more common as well. From the stories of companies coping with financial crises of the twentieth century, we can draw some lessons for coping with change and model of change that may be useful when next faced with a potential crisis.

The events starting with the devaluation of the Thai baht in July 1997 are the most significant economic upheavals in the Asian region since World War II. National governments toppled, companies folded, and entire industries have been imperiled. One study estimated that the Thai economy alone lost over five trillion baht (between US$150 billion to $200 billion depending on whether you set the exchange rate at pre- or postcrisis figures) between January 1996 and December 1997—and Thailand was not the worst hit. In early 1998, it would have been possible to buy the entire South Korean financial industry for $4 billion (about the amount Bill Gates makes on a good day for the U.S. stock markets). While much of the analysis in this chapter can apply to both countries and industries, our emphasis is at the corporate level. How are specific companies responding in Asia? How can they take advantage of opportunities inherent in crisis situations?

We begin by describing the ways in which many companies in Asia reacted to catastrophes or took advantage of opportunities inherent in the Asian crisis. Next we consider a model known as the *Change Cycle,* showing how it applies to companies. Finally, we explore ways in which organizations move through Change Cycles, whether they are responding to crisis or some other catalytic event.

The Asian Crisis

In 1996, almost $100 billion dollars in capital flowed into Indonesia, Thailand, Malaysia, the Philippines, and South Korea. In 1997, nearly $20 billion exited those same countries. This dramatic shift marks one of the most significant economic reversals in modern history (see Figure 1.1). It is estimated that even before the Indonesian riots, the crisis had led to the loss of over five million jobs in the region. Bankruptcies in South Korea—arguably the worst hit country

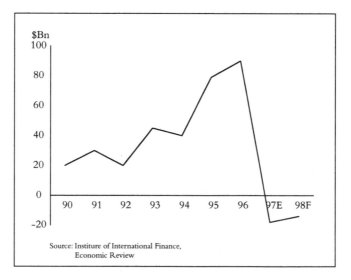

Source: Institute of International Finance, Economic Review

Figure 1.1   Capital flows to Asia have reversed.
Indonesia, Malaysia, Phillipines, S. Korea, Thailand

for company closures—ran at up to 100 companies a day. (By contrast, only two Malaysian firms officially went bankrupt in the first nine months of the crisis.) Furthermore, Thomson BankWatch Asia, a credit rating agency that monitors 1,200 banks in 82 countries, found 150 banks in India, China, Indonesia, and South Korea to be "technically bankrupt."

In all of the press coverage of the Asian financial crisis, there has been a notable lack of specific information about the behaviors of companies. There are many anecdotal reports of specific company reactions, but very little broad data. To understand the effects of the Asian crisis on both Western- and Asian-headquartered firms in the region, we conducted a survey of 66 companies in 7 countries. Our sample included leading companies from financial services, industrial and consumer products, telecommunications, and energy. All of the companies we interviewed were impacted by the crisis. And, as expected, the hardest hit were banks and financial services companies, who are struggling to manage increasingly bad debt and tightening liquidity.

The Asian crisis has been perceived as truly foundation-breaking only in certain industries. Respondents from the financial sector and both consumer and industrial product markets experienced major ramifications. But in resources and communications sectors, negative effects were much less dramatic. It may actually be possible for companies in these less-affected sectors to stay their pre-crisis strategic courses for much longer. For them, the most likely change catalyst may be opportunity, rather than crisis. (See Figure 1.2.)

Given the relatively low impact of the Asian crisis in some sectors, it is perhaps not entirely surprising that many companies remain optimistic about Asia's prospects, and the new opportunities the crisis could create. Nearly 60% of all the firms we surveyed claim to view the Asian crisis as an opportunity. The remaining firms are virtually paralyzed and are focused mainly on short-term survival tactics.

Views of crisis versus opportunity vary significantly by the location of the headquarters of companies. Over two-thirds of Western multinational firms (MNCs) with operations in the region viewed the Asian crisis as an opportunity. Only about half of Asian-headquartered companies were similarly optimistic (Figure 1.3).

There were also some large differences in the level of damage experienced by respondents from different countries. We divided Asian

	Falling Sales	Contracting Profits	Liquidity Crunch	Debt Servicing
Financial Services	●	●	●	●
Consumer Products	◑	◑	●	◑
Industrial Products	◑	◑	◑	◑
Resources	○	◑	◑	○
Communications	◑	○	○	○

○ Low impact ◑ Medium impact ● High impact

*Limited sample size
Source: AC Analysis

Figure 1.2 Crisis impact by industry.

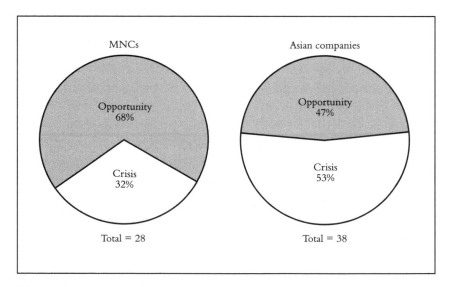

Figure 1.3 View of crisis: MNCs versus Asian companies.

nations into two groups, based on the lost value in the stock market and readjustment of their exchange rates. The "wounded tigers" were those that were hurt most: Thailand, Indonesia, South Korea, Malaysia, and the Philippines. Countries less affected by the crisis were China, Taiwan, Singapore, and Hong Kong—the "scared tigers." These countries have had little or no foreign intervention in their banking or regulatory systems. And while stock market values in these countries have dropped, they have not suffered as much as their "wounded" counterparts. Still, all of these countries—except China and Hong Kong—have experienced currency devaluation.

Companies from the wounded tigers and the scared tigers reacted in very different ways to the crisis. Not surprisingly, companies in the wounded tigers were much less likely to see the situation as an opportunity (26%), as opposed to 62% of those in the scared tigers (Figure 1.4).

Any analysis of these data leads to the same conclusion: In most companies, in most industries, in most countries in Asia, companies perceive the financial crisis as a powerful motivation to *change*. None of our respondents expected to be conducting "business as usual" in the future.

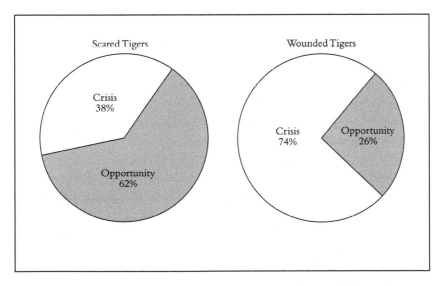

Figure 1.4   View of crisis: Scared Tigers versus Wounded Tigers.

The Change Cycle Model

To help make sense of companies' reaction to the Asian crisis, we applied a model of change referred to as the *Change Cycle*. This model provides a descriptive framework for understanding reactions to the Asian crisis, but it is also powerfully prescriptive. The Cycle allows corporate leaders to know how they should react and which managerial tools they should use, at every stage in the process of change. It enables companies to respond proactively and efficiently to either crisis or opportunity.

Organization versus Environment

The Change Cycle is based on two axes. The X-axis has to do with the focus of the change. Is the focus organizational or environmental (or in less academic terms, focused on the internal processes of the organization or focused outside the firm on customers, competitors, and market forces)? Most managers can influence only change inside their organizations, but there are times when the focus of their attention must be on external factors to make effective internal decisions (Figure 1.5).

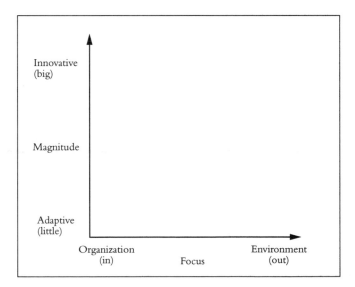

Figure 1.5   The change cycle axes.

Innovation versus Adaptation

The Y-axis in Figure 1.5 shows how the Change Cycle relates to the level of change taking place. An organization with large-scale change is at the top of this axis; while an organization where no change is taking place would be located at the bottom. Most organizations function between these two extremes most of the time.

There are some theorists who argue that the only way to succeed in a competitive industry is to maintain continual, revolutionary change. A company cannot sustain indefinite revolutionary change, however, without depleting its employees and its resources. Such change entails tremendous energy, time, and money. In reality, then, most companies are experiencing some revolution and some evolution at any given time, though usually they are doing more of one than the other. The Y-axis captures the scale of change as it moves between the extremes of revolution and stagnation.

The Axes Combined

These two axes are continua. A company making *only* organizational changes would fall on the far left-hand side of the chart, while the far right-hand would show a company in which attention is focused *only* on the environment. Most firms, however, have a focus on *some* organizational and *some* external issues. The same holds true for big and little changes. At the bottom of the Y-axis, there would be no change taking place in the organization. At the top, everything would be in flux (100% change). With the possible exception of a brand-new venture which is doing everything new for the first time, we can think of no organizations in which either one of these extremes is fully realized.

The two axes combined create a four-part matrix (Figure 1.6). We have labeled the four areas Squares I through IV. Lines intersecting the two axes indicate only that the focus has shifted slightly. On the X-axis, the line signifies a change from being a bit more internally focused to a bit more externally focused. On the Y-axis, the line indicates the point at which 50% of the organization is in flux and 50% is quite stable. If one forgets that these axes are continua, and thinks of the squares as completely distinct, the Change Cycle model loses some of its power.

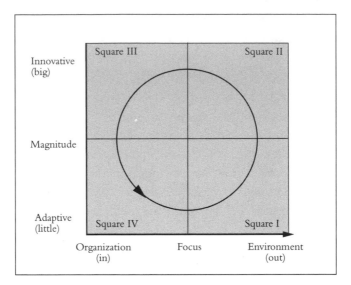

Figure 1.6   The best path through change.

The Cycle

There is a best path through any change process and even widely dissimilar changes follow this same course. That "best" path is indicated in the Change Cycle model by a circle. The path combines a circular and linear process: transition through one cycle of change moves the company forward to a higher level of success, while also bringing it back to the beginning of the cycle.

This integration of circular and linear logic represents a marriage between a modern, Western cultural viewpoint, and a worldview more typical of traditional and Eastern cultures. Western religion and philosophy are grounded in the idea of linear progress toward perfection, while most Eastern thought is based on the idea of cyclical patterns: rebirth into another lifecycle as opposed to perfection in Heaven, the re-creation of a mythical Golden Age rather than historical "progress" toward an idealized future. The Change Cycle accommodates the reality of repetitive cycles of change, while charting a course through these cycles that moves companies forward. Each successive cycle is made easier by incorporating the knowledge gained from the last.

The skills needed to move effectively through the Change Cycle are similar to a good golf swing. Golfers who focus on a consistent, full, rounded swing are those most likely to play an even, low-handicap game. Some golf greats, like Arnold Palmer and Lee Trevino, were champions even though their swings were less than perfect. In the Change Cycle, too, sometimes the exception will yield surprisingly good results. But in the vast majority of cases, following the cycle is the optimal path to change.

The "Optimal" Square IV

Perhaps the best place to begin our discussion of the Change Cycle is in the "optimal" Square, Square IV (Figure 1.7). This is the phase in which the focus is largely inside the organization, and the level of change is small. It is optimal for two reasons:

1. Small changes are quicker and cheaper than large ones.
2. Responses to factors within the organization are less costly than responses to outside factors.

There are transaction costs involved in moving the focus of managers' attention from internal to external. It requires more time and money to understand what is going on outside of the company than inside the company. Internally, a manager can pick up a phone, ask

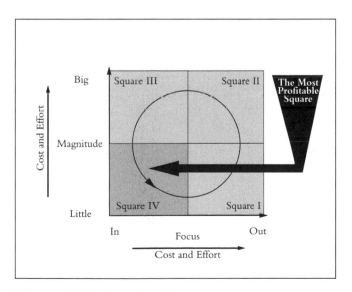

Figure 1.7 The optimal Square IV.

the company operator for the phone number of someone else in the firm, and be immediately connected. If the person is not in, the manager can leave a message on an internal voice mail system. There is no need to explain why information is needed or how it will be used—both parties belong to the same organization, making the flow of information freer than it is when the connection crosses company boundaries.

It is more complicated, costly, and draining to focus on the external world. Getting information from outside the organization may involve figuring out who has that information, tracking down phone numbers, getting past subordinates, and convincing strangers that you will use the information honorably. We are not suggesting that the effect is not worth the cost and effort. It is impossible to survive without external information. But there is a cost; and companies and individuals who do not acknowledge that cost are fooling themselves.

Left to their own devices, companies would prefer to stay in Square IV, where costs are lower because very few changes are taking place. In fact, anyone who sat in an MBA class 15 to 20 years ago was probably taught that rationalization, routinization, and moving down the experience curve were the basic elements of good business. The very foundation of management theory in the early 1900s was Fayol's work on rationalization and Frederick Taylor's time-motion studies. The objective of these works was to make every employee's actions as efficient as possible. Profitability would improve as efficiency improved. Through most of the twentieth century, great management theory was predicated on the concept of a firm "buffering" itself from the environment. In other words, managers were taught that Square IV should be the destination of choice for any organization.

This idea substantiated natural human inclinations. We have an innate need for routine and the security that accompanies routine. We would all prefer to avoid change. Square IV does entail the kind of predictable, well-honed operation that allows a business to prosper—but only in times of relative stability.

Catalytic Events

The problem with Square IV is that just about the time a company has been lulled into a sense of peace and found its place in a benevolent world, something comes along to move a company out of its comfortable situation. Whether change comes in the form of violent upheaval or gradual entropy, it is inevitable. Companies that are too committed to their Square IV ways may be unable to respond effectively to a volatile environment.

Catalytic events are the engines of the Change Cycle. They can take a number of forms. Most obvious are "Shock" events. These events, like the oil crisis or the Asian financial crisis, dramatically force companies to reconsider their approach to business, and consider new, innovative ways of coping with the world. Other catalytic events include transitions, such as growth or the development of more sophisticated ideas or technologies, and opportunity.

An event can be considered catalytic only if it shifts the external world in some significant way. There are many changes that do not affect the fundamental operation of firms; companies simply ride out most environmental changes and go back to business as usual. Truly catalytic events must be (1) foundation-breaking and (2) irreparable.

By foundation-breaking we mean that a change alters the strategic foundations on which a company's operations are built. If an environmental shift (whether shock, opportunity, or transition) is not significant enough to require drastic action, there is no reason the organization should go through the cost and effort of a new cycle. To be irreparable, the catalytic event must be such that simple patching will not work—otherwise, the company could maintain its status quo with only minor adaptations.

Tools for Assessing the Catalytic Event

There are a number of tools to help a company assess whether or not a catalytic event (either one that has already occurred or one that appears imminent) is foundation-breaking and irreparable. Companies that are particularly good at this assessment can begin making effective changes earlier than other firms in the industry, gaining a *first mover* advantage. (There is substantial literature on whether or not first mover status is really advantageous. Some later movers are able to watch the early movers to see what works and what does not, then implement the effective moves quickly and efficiently to make the trip around the cycle very quickly.) Tools for assessing change include:

- *Benchmarking.* While not exclusively a catalytic event tool, benchmarking can be used to understand how other firms (competitors and noncompetitors alike) are positioning, organizing, and optimizing themselves for competitive advantage in the marketplace. This insight into a set of other companies can often help managers decide if there is a compelling business case for change.

- *Competitor analysis.* A constant and watchful eye on competitors can give industry-specific warnings of environmental change. When two or three competitors begin to restructure or reposition at about the same time, this a good indication they may be responding to catalytic events in the environment. Such a repositioning of competitors may constitute a catalytic event in and of itself.

- *Environmental scanning.* All companies should be scanning the environment for potential opportunities and threats. Most will say they do. But relatively few companies have policies and procedures in place for elevating the information from these scans to a decision-making level quickly. Those that do can turn environmental scanning from a rather static tool (like a hoe) to a competitive weapon (like a howitzer).

- *Tracking similar or related markets.* Companies can usually gain some insight into potential catalytic events by observing other markets or industries. This is because different national economies and product markets tend to be more tightly interrelated than is generally thought. For example, companies in the scared tigers (e.g., Hong Kong) could have learned from the wounded tigers that extremely overvalued markets cannot avoid a readjustment indefinitely. While stock and currency values in Thailand, Indonesia, and South Korea took the first hit, it was not long until investors shifted their attention to Hong Kong's overvalued property and equity prices. This interim period (between the market crashes in the rest of Asia and when it hit Hong Kong) was a period of opportunity in which Hong Kong companies could have positioned themselves more effectively to insulate and/or take advantage of the coming changes in their own environment.

Square I: Survive

After any catalytic event, the affected company moves into Square I. This is a period in which the company should be making little changes that are focused outside the organization. The reason for being focused outside should be fairly intuitive—a major crisis (in the environment) has just occurred, or opportunity (in the environment) has been identified. The company enters Square I like a soldier landing in alien territory and must focus its first change efforts on understanding the new environment.

In most cases, a company that has been in Square IV for some period of time has culturally (and in many cases structurally and organizationally) come to be accustomed to the small changes characteristic of Square IV. It is difficult to rapidly shift such a culture to one that makes radical changes. There is a natural tendency for any period following a crisis or opportunity identification to be one of small changes.

This tendency is a good one. The period immediately following a catalytic event should not entail large changes, because the company docs not possess enough data about the new environment to make sound choices about large-scale change. Unfortunately, crisis tends to create panic in managers, who may consequently react with an immediate and drastic makeover of the organization. Too often, such responses are ill-considered and reactive.

Following the Black Monday stock market crash in October 1987, many speculated that the U.S. economy would face sure recession and possibly even depression. Lee Iacocca, then CEO at Chrysler, announced in the press that the company might have to lay off most of the employees it had gained as part of its recent acquisition of American Motors. As it turned out, the U.S. economy recovered amazingly quickly and Chrysler might have lost market share and competitive strength had it decided to make this rash move following the crisis.

Years should not be spent in Square I activities following a catalytic event. In a large organization, months are probably the optimal unit of measurement. A company in Square I needs to regroup, analyze the environment, organize for a major change effort, and go through a period of trial and error to understand what will work (and what won't) in a world that is very different from its accustomed environment.

Square I is about surviving the catalytic event that has just occurred. Certainly in the case of the first year or so following the onset of the Asian financial crisis, most companies were mostly in survival mode.

Samsung in Square I

Samsung is a good example of a company that has experienced a significant catalytic shock and is now working its way through the survival behaviors of Square I. A visit to Samsung's headquarters in Seoul reveals a company in crisis. Two out of every three light bulbs in the headquarters building have been loosened or removed from the sockets to save energy. Executives work long hours without the traditional perks of company-sponsored drinking and dinner parties. The corporation has sold major assets—its construction equipment business went to Volvo and U.S.-based Clark Material Handling Company bought its forklift division.

One good example of Samsung's reaction is the shift that took place in its elite Global Strategist Program. This program, first envisioned in the late 1980s, finally got its start in the fall of 1997 when Samsung hired a dozen non-Korean MBAs from the top business schools in the world. This internal consulting group reported to the president's office. It was charged with determining the future of the new global Samsung Group. Initially, these elite employees were working on projects that had to do with acquisitions, new product and division launches—creative, nontraditional plans for the medium- to long-term future of the firm. But in January, these projects were reformulated. In reaction to the Asian crisis, the teams were redeployed on projects concerning cost-cutting, employee rationalization, and divestiture.

Such refocusing of the firm's strategic direction was certainly consistent with other changes taking place in Samsung. In the spring of 1998, the *chaebol* owed domestic and overseas banks $23.4 billion in debt (the equivalent of 267% of equity). Samsung had sold $300 million in real estate and other assets and had decided to cut global investments by 30%. The Asian crisis was taking an even bigger toll on the many companies making up the Samsung Group.

Samsung was clearly in a crisis of over-borrowing and currency instability. Significant financial evidence suggested that Samsung was actually quite structurally sound. Samsung's sales increased after the onset of the crisis, from $11 billion in 1996 to $13 billion in 1997, yet its net profit dropped from $111.3 million in 1996 to about $84 million in 1997. Actual year-on-year operating profits were up at Samsung in 1997, but currency losses cut the earnings severely as the Korean Won depreciated 55% in value against the U.S. dollar in the first few months of the Asian crisis.

What we see in Samsung is typical of Square I firms—reacting to crisis, but needing to find opportunities that point to the future. This split between backward-looking crisis management and forward-looking opportunity seeking is one of the fundamental dilemmas facing a company in Square I. Any firm that is able to skillfully navigate from one to the other is well on its way to a successful turn through the Change Cycle.

Some Square I Tools

Companies faced with crisis or opportunity, like Samsung, find themselves in Square I looking for a set of behaviors that will help them to deal more effectively with their situation. Some of the most successful companies use one or more of the following activities:

- *Corporate grieving.* Employees in the organization need to go through a period of grieving: denial, anger, and finally acceptance that a change has taken place. If they do not have a chance to grieve, change will occur more slowly and less effectively.
- *Brainstorming.* List-creation or free-form association helps managers identify ways in which the new environment will be different from the old one.
- *Scenario planning.* Development of best- and worst-case scenarios allows a firm to envision the range of possible futures. Scenario development is useful only if it results in a plan. Ideally this plan is one that can lead a company to flourish in the best case and minimizes negative outcomes if a worst-case scenario actually develops.
- *Five-forces analysis.* When a five-forces analysis on the old environment and the new environment are compared, obvious areas of opportunity and weakness for the company can immediately be identified.
- *Visioning.* Helps managers understand what the company's future might be in the post-catalytic event world. This tool leads companies naturally into Square II activities.

Late Square I: What It Looks Like, What to Do Next

If after a period of observation, trial-and-error, and survival behaviors in Square I, the company decides that there was no real catalytic event (the changes were not significant enough to warrant a move around the cycle), a company might backtrack along the change cycle, retreating to the safety and profitability of the previous Square IV. This was not true for Samsung. The company's position during the Asian financial crisis made deep change advisable for several reasons. For one thing, key institutions and practices throughout Asia were likely to change as a result of the financial crisis. Moreover, Samsung had a chance to seize opportunities under the guise of crisis. Some analysts suggested that the crisis might provide the perfect cover for Samsung to abandon its ill-conceived venture into automobile manufacturing. In a time of crisis, companies which are basically sound (but caught in an environmental maelstrom) might want to question some of the premises and assumptions on which the previous cycle was built. Are there businesses that the company wanted to off-load even before the crisis? Are there business practices that could not be changed before the crisis because they were politically incorrect, but which will be accepted now as part of survival?

Transition to Square II: Revive

If a company has entered Square I as a result of environmental change, survived the initial chaos, and determined that innovative change is necessary for the company to thrive in its new milieu, then it is time to move into Square II. In most cases, the readiness to move into this phase will be evidenced by the emergence of a new attitude on the part of employees. An organization is ready to move on when the attitudinal tumult of the grieving phase is complete and a more forward-looking, optimistic mindset becomes apparent.

The acceptance of the new environment in which the organization must function after the catalytic event comes partly through time, and partly through the active acquisition of information. Organizational leaders who have done their work well in Square I should be very familiar with the new environment by the time they move to Square II. And it is in Square II that the leaders will bear the burden of turning research and ideas into clear positions and strategies for which they will be fully accountable. In Square II, the organization will be making big changes with regard to the outside world. Managers must be willing to return to gathering data—going "back to Square I" any time they become aware of a gap in their understanding of the new environment.

Square II is the time for leaders to take the general knowledge about the environmental changes and translate that into an action plan (or big change) for the organization. This is when the ideas that are beginning to emerge in the survival period of Square I are expanded, and true *revival* takes place.

Square II might be compared to a revival meeting for the company, in which a spokesperson riles the audience much as a preacher or organizational leader who has begun to envision a successful future in a post-crisis environment, must coax, cajole, and ultimately convert the congregation (organization) to that vision. The congregation (employees) are at different stages of wanting to believe, which should influence the way the preacher delivers the message. Those employees who are most willing to stand up and be counted as adherents of the emerging plan are those who are most likely to be called to take the work forward. This is a high-voltage phase of the change process.

The entire point of Square II is to be as visionary and innovative as possible, but in such a way as to elicit buy-in from the rest of the organization. During this time of revival, the company is creating its new future in the changed environment. Clear and distinct positioning are crucial during this period. If the environment for one company in an industry has changed, then chances are it has changed for others in the industry as well. Companies that can analyze and capture a strong position in the new environment are those that are most likely to profit in the long run.

Kroger during the Depression

Some companies that have responded to economic crises in the past have managed to reposition themselves in the new environment for long-term profitability and growth. A good example of this kind of repositioning is Kroger Company. At the onset of the Depression, Kroger was a struggling grocery store operator with over 5,000 stores, mostly in urban locations. To appeal to a clientele that was increasingly price-conscious because of the high unemployment rates accompanying the Depression, Kroger decided that they needed to reduce costs in any way possible. Managers sought out locations with lower real estate prices for larger consolidated stores. The concept of the suburban supermarket came out of the reaction to this crisis. To service these new stores efficiently, Kroger developed a new hub-and-spoke distribution and purchasing model. This helped to increase Kroger's buying power, economies of scale, and operating efficiencies.

By 1935, six years after the stock market crash, the corporation had 50 supermarkets in place and had recovered financially with its new channel strategy—a strategy that allowed them to gain market share and profitability advantages over companies like A&P, which stuck with more traditional crisis management responses to the Depression. Today Kroger is one of the United States' largest retail grocery chain, with over 2,200 stores and $28 billion in sales in 1998.

Some Square II Tools

As in Square I, organizations in Square II can utilize a set of tools to help them make the correct choices in this phase of the change cycle. Many of the tools of traditional strategic positioning can be used in Square II. Companies may conduct value chain, generic strategies, SWOT, competitor maps, and other forms of analysis to determine exactly where the company needs to "play" with regard to competitors. Companies should use the following tools to "revive" in their new competitive contexts:

- *Generic strategies.* A company in Square II needs to decide which kind of competitive strategy (low-cost leadership or differentiation) will lead to a profitable future.
- *Strategic positioning.* Through competitor mapping, the company can create a strategy that will position it differently from any competitors in the industry.
- *Portfolio analysis.* The most famous example of this type of analysis is the Boston Consulting Group growth-share matrix. A multibusiness firm needs to understand which businesses are the most important to the company's ongoing success. Those businesses that are less likely to succeed should be shed, others beefed up, and new businesses acquired.
- *Core competencies.* A corporation should focus on businesses and activities that are supported by its strongest competencies or skills.

- *War gaming (competitive simulation).* This is a way for the company to begin operationalizing ideas that have come up during the brainstorming of Square I.
- *Red teaming.* The term *red team* comes from American military war gaming, where the blue team was traditionally the United States and, during the Cold War, the red team was the Soviet Union. In this context, red teaming is defined as teams of executives "playing" the "enemy" to understand what the competitive context (and competitor moves) will be in some potential future.

Coca Cola in Asia: Square II

Analysts suspected that Coca Cola would be one of the U.S. corporations hardest hit by the Asian crisis. After all, the company gets 70% of its sales and 80% of its profit from international markets. The analysts were surprised when Coke (which had reported sales growth of 9% in the first quarter of 1997, before the crisis), claimed 14% growth for the same period in 1998—and the geographical group that includes Southeast Asia expected to see sales increases of 17% to 18%.

Coca-Cola executives claimed that their response to the crisis is in some ways responsible for the growth their company experienced in Asia. Michael Bascle, president of Coca-Cola Company's Southeast and West Asia Division, said, "Where others see crisis, we see opportunity. While others cut back on spending, we continue to invest. When others plan for no growth, we build for acceleration."

Coca-Cola had drawn on its experiences with the Mexican peso crisis to deal with Asia. During the Mexican peso crisis, Coke actually increased its advertising spending in the country and, as a result boosted market share from 57% in 1994 to 64% in 1996.

In Asia, too, the company increased advertising budgets by over 50%, while others were cutting back, and media space costs decreased, yielding almost three times as much advertising coverage. Coke claimed to have added market share in the Philippines, Malaysia, and Thailand. And unit case volume growth in the region grew by 5% in Thailand (despite a drop in the Thai soft drink market of 0.4%), 7% in Singapore, 11% in Malaysia, and a whopping 99% in Vietnam during 1997.

Coca-Cola used this crisis in Asia as an opportunity to adopt a more aggressive strategy with regard to bottling operations as well.

The company invested US$500 million to take 100% ownership of its Korean bottler, and increased its stake in its Thai bottler from 44% to 49%. In China, Coke opened 21 bottling plants in the last half of the 1990s making China Coke's sixth largest market in the world. Since the crisis began, Coke opened the largest plant in the country—a US$50 million facility—and announced plans to build three more during 1999.

Square III: Go Live

After the plans for a new strategic change have been finalized in Square II, it is time to implement those changes. This moves us into Square III. The magnitude of change is still very large—the company will be implementing new systems and structures that have probably never been in place before. But now, having determined their strategic plan with regard to the environment, leaders should be ready to begin implementing that strategy *in* the organization.

Square III is known as "Go Live"—a term used by systems engineers and consultants to describe the completed implementation of large information systems in an organization. The phrase can be heard in any company that is installing Enterprise Resource Systems (increasingly the information backbone in large organizations). Vendors like SAP, Peoplesoft, and Oracle create systems that can connect each piece of information generated in an organization to one central hub. The people and process changes that accompany these technology system changes are tremendous.

This is the kind of large, innovative change, focused on the internal operation of the organization, that exemplifies Square III. Such change may take some time: for example, the change to bring the entire worldwide operations of Compaq up to a standard system could take five to six years. Along the way, local operations—Houston headquarters, Glasgow, Singapore—will all come online, or "go live" over a period of months or years. But no one can really know how well the system works until the entire worldwide grid is connected and ready to function in concert. In a change project like the implementation of these large systems, it is this final worldwide go-live to which thousands of people devote years of work.

Whether it is a technology implementation or any other form of strategic change implementation, Square III is a time in which ideas developed in Square II are put into practice.

The events that are undertaken in this Square can be compared to those in epics like *The Odyssey, The Illiad,* or even *Huckleberry Finn* that we were all required to read. These stories are all about journeys—but most of us cannot even remember where Odysseus or Huck were trying to go. Epics are not about the destination, but the complexities of the journey—as writer Lawrence Block puts it, "one damn thing after another." That phrase—one damn thing after another—summarizes most companies' experience of Square III.

Employees at every level work harder in Square III than at any other phase of change. The straightforward work of strategy implementation is accompanied by highly charged political manuevering as the organization is re-arranged. Members of the company must be brought to a common point-of-view and enthusiasm to implement the new strategy. This is much easier if Square II is successful and the entire tent-full of worshippers are "converted" to the new strategy. Japanese corporations have been characterized as slow to make decisions (Square II) but very fast in implementation (Square III). This is because the Japanese decision-making system ensures that *every* member of the organization is "on-board" before moving to the next step. In most Western companies, the opposite is true—decisions are made quickly, with plans to co-opt employees during the implementation stage. Neither the Japanese nor the Western model is necessarily more effective—they are just different. But if you are in a Western firm, you can expect to do much of the political work of the Change Cycle in Square III.

Most reengineering activities take place in this quadrant as well. But reengineering, as defined by the pioneers in this field Hammer, Champy, and Davenport—is different from other Square III activities. In the classic examples of reengineering work, all of these authors discuss companies that are sound in terms of their strategic positioning in the marketplace, but can be made more efficient by utilizing new information technologies. The question of reeningeering is not how to serve a different set of customers or compete in a changed marketplace. The question is how to better serve current customers through enabling technologies. The whole point of reengineering is that the system had been "engineered" once already. In a reengineering Change Cycle, the catalytic event would be the emergence or competitor acceptance of a new set of technologies. For a firm to most effectively serve the chosen client-base, a set of environmentally focused Square I and Square II behaviors will result in a implementation of these new technologies known as reengineering. In some cases, the surviving and reviving stages can be passed through quickly because the new technologies do not necessitate a changed strategic positioning. But in others, reengineering requires (or enables) a new positioning that will be of greater financial benefit to the firm.

Pratt Whitney needs to reduce its cost structure to remain competitive with GE jet engines. After it saw its market share cut in half by competitors through the late 1980s, the firm embarked on a complete overhaul of its manufacturing process. While the reengineering was necessary to remain cost competitive, the activities did not change the basic strategic positioning of the firm.

Some Square III Tools

In addition to reengineering, there are a number of tools that are useful and relevant in Square III. Any of the tools related to organizational design can be used here, as can the others listed. At some point in this "go-live" stage, most of the tools listed should be explored if not utilized completely.

- *Organization design.* Designing the company's structure to deliver the chosen strategy.
- *Value chain.* By looking at each activity in the process of value creation in a corporation, the cost/differentiation tradeoff can be made as part of the implementation of a strategy.
- *Information systems.* Today information systems are one of the most important tools for creating efficiency and effectiveness in an organizational structure. With these systems as a backbone, a company is able to utilize human and physical resources more effectively than ever in the past.
- *Internet/e-Commerce.* The Internet and other electronic systems can be put into place to deliver the product or services to market and to enable low-cost procurement.
- *Supply chain management.* Designing and controlling the entire system of procurement, logistics, and supplier relationships.
- *Balanced scorecard.* A system for setting and tracking financial, human development, customer satisfaction, and operational targets

for a business. The targets are meant to help the company meet its strategic goals. When units and employees achieve the targets, they are rewarded financially.

Merrill Lynch in Japan in Square III

Following the crisis, Japan's financial sector was through its most difficult straits since World War II. Executives and politicians were indicted, some committed suicide, and everyone was losing money—so much that a couple of Japanese securities firms went belly up, and of those surviving only two big firms—Nomura and Kokusai—made a profit in 1997. Yamaichi Securities, Japan's fourth largest firm, declared bankruptcy in November 1997; a true crisis for the company, its employees, and customers.

Merrill Lynch began operations in the early 1960s in Japan and has built a strong institutional and a growing asset management business. The decision to acquire Yamaichi Securities assets was part the company's decade-long quest to get into the retail side of the securities business. In the late 1980s, Merrill Lynch decided to set up its own wholly-owned retail network throughout Japan. It was a great time to be in the financial sector in Japan. The Dow Jones-Nikkei Index reached 39,000 in 1989, and in the same year Japanese bought over $338 billion in mutual funds.

The problem was that this was also a period of extreme Japanese nationalism. American companies found it difficult to crack the Japanese retail market, and in 1993 Merrill Lynch shuttered its six Japanese retail branches.

In 1998, with a much less attractive market—the Nikkei Index at 16,000 and only $77 billion in mutual funds being sold a year— Merrill Lynch found a way into the market through crisis. Executives at headquarters hoped that the same forces that helped mutual funds sales drive the Dow-Jones Index to over 9,000 in the United States would fuel similar growth in Japan. One big difference between the early 1990s and 1998 was that the Japanese government actually supported the buyout, with no less a figure than Prime Minister Ryutaro Hashimoto making a public statement encouraging Merrill Lynch to conclude the talks with Yamaichi in favor of a partnership. Such institutional approval would not have been imagined in the early 1990s.

The Road to Partnership

When Yamaichi officials and government bureaucrats realized that their firm was close to bankruptcy, they unsuccessfully approached CSFB and some other Western firms as buyout partners. There were actually many interested buyers, but they were put off by the insistence that all of the employees be retained. Merrill Lynch was among the firms that rejected the idea of acquisition as too risky.

But rumors persisted that Merrill Lynch was more than just passively interested in Yamaichi. Before Christmas of 1997, a team of top Merrill executives went to Japan, returned home for the Christmas holidays, and then went back to Tokyo for more a more intense series of negotiations, preparations, and due diligence. They were making certain that Merrill Lynch understood the regulatory environment, could remain insulated from the liabilities of the old Yamaichi, and would be able to secure the backoffice capabilities of the Yamaichi data center.

As Merrill Lynch Chairman and Chief Executive Officer David Komansky said in an interview with *Yomiuri Shimbun,* "The worst thing in the world would have been to have done this prematurely and then found out that we misunderstood or underestimated the challenge. We wanted to be certain we knew what we were doing."

Since the official announcement of a buyout agreement (and not a traditional buyout, as Merrill Lynch was taking only the best employees and offices that Yamaichi had to offer), Merrill executives interviewed 4,000 Yamaichi employees during a three-week period. They decided to employ just over half of them. Merrill also took over the leases of 31 branch offices across Japan, removing the Yamaichi logo from buildings and replacing it with the Merrill Lynch bull.

Merrill Lynch & Co. was gearing up for the July 1998 launch of a new firm, provisionally known as Merrill Lynch Japan Securities, that would cater to individual clients in Japan. In anticipation of this "go-live" date, the former Yamaichi employees were trained to an American standard. That meant ridding them of a few bad habits. For instance, in Japan it was a normal practice to give company funds to a favored client when that client lost money. The brokers for the new firm learned that they could not do that in an American firm.

All of this interviewing, training, reorganization, office preparation, and so on, was an expensive proposition. By April 1998, Merrill Lynch had poured $100 million into what will be Merrill Lynch Japan Securities. And the firm expected to devote an additional two to three years on Square III behavior before turning a profit.

The return on this cycle of investment could be tremendous. Merrill Lynch set a goal of capturing 200,000 to 300,000 accounts by the end of 1999—meaning that each salesperson will need to open 11 to 16 new accounts per month over an 18-month period. At the end of that first 18 months, the firm hopes for 4 to 5 trillion yen of assets under management. Analysts believed Merrill Lynch had a good chance of succeeding in their goals, since some 60% of between $9 trillion and $10 trillion in private savings was still stashed away in low-yield bank accounts or worse still, in mattresses.

Merrill Lynch's biggest competitors in the near future may be non-Japan-based firms. In 1996, foreign firms accounted for less than a quarter of the turnover on Tokyo's stock exchange; by the end of 1997, they accounted for a third of it. Merrill is not alone in thinking about the Japanese retail market. As of early 1998, U.S. fund managers such as Fidelity and Putnam were going after the same retail market that drove Merrill into a relationship with Yamaichi. Fidelity had been investing heavily in building a retail distribution network in Japan, and Putnam struck an alliance with the insurance company Nippon Life.

As to the future of the institutional markets in Japan, Takuma Amano (an independent investment banker who has worked for CSFB and Yamaichi Securities, and was managing director of SBC in Japan until 1990), has said that he believes that by 2003, the new Big Four institutional players in Japan will be Merrill Lynch, Morgan Stanley, Goldman Sachs, and Nomura Securities—with foreign firms holding a 50% share of the Japanese institutional market.

With so much competition from foreign as well as domestic securities firms, it was important that Merrill Lynch move quickly to shore up its base of name recognition in Japan. The Yamaichi "acquisition" is also a tremendous advantage. In an annual survey of popularity of potential employers conducted in early 1998, Japanese university graduates ranked Merrill Lynch ahead of Nomura Securities for the first time in history.

Square IV: Take Five

By the time a firm makes its way through the trials of Squares I through III, everyone involved is probably worn out. Square IV is welcome relief; the Shangri-la, Nirvana, or Promised Land the company has been seeking. This period will probably never be as wonderful as everyone expected it might be; employees will be able to rest more once they reach this phase. And rest they should. However, they should not relax to the point of unconsciousness, unless they wish to lose the war after winning most of the battles. The idea is not to fall asleep, but to "take five"—put on a Dave Brubeck recording, sit back, and relax, but not too calmly. As with any "break," Square IV is a breather from a period of tough work in the past, and a preparation for tough work in the future.

This quadrant is where a company can expect to make money (Figure 1.8). Much of it will be earned by reducing costs, increasing expertise, and capitalizing on experience in this marketplace. As a company shifts from Square III to Square IV, it moves down the experience and cost curves. Square IV is the place for housekeeping; tweaking the system that has been put in to make sure that it runs as smoothly as possible; making the organization as profitable as it can be. In other words, as a company "takes five," it makes adaptive changes focused inside the organization.

Remember that we have already described Square IV as the optimal place for any corporation. Companies should get to this stage as quickly and stay here as long as possible. But they must be ready to move on should the need arise, resisting the natural bureaucratic pull toward the bottom left-most corner of the diagram. There is only one absolute about Square IV, and that is that another Square I will eventually follow. Companies need to position themselves at the place marked by the X in Figure 1.8. This positioning will allow companies to survey the environment regularly, while making relatively small changes as part of constant cost and quality improvements.

In our survey of companies reacting to the Asian crisis, we found that most of these companies, whether they claim to see this period as an opportunity or a crisis, are firmly set in their Square IV ways. They are cost-cutting, rationalizing, and reserving judgment on future market moves. They run the risk of getting so focused on maintaining their Square IV position that they lose their capacity

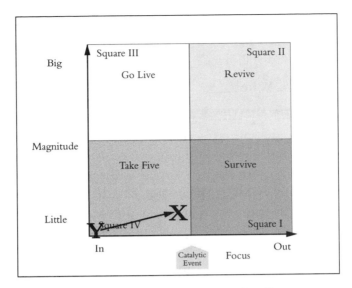

Figure 1.8   The change cycle "takes five."

for adapting to, and operating successfully in, the post-crisis environment.

Some Square IV Tools

- *Continuous improvement.* Reducing cycle time and waste in the production process. This set of tools—including flowcharts, Ishikawa diagrams, scatter plots, histograms—gives significant empowerment to operating personnel to make improvements in their working environment.
- *Sourcing and purchasing rationalization.* Global purchasing, rationalization of overheads to reduce costs.
- *Six sigma.* A measure defining the quality level of a product, service, or process. It basically calls for zero defects, although literally it allows for up to 3.4 defects per million opportunities.
- *Customer care.* Creating customer satisfaction and loyalty through a set of tools which emphasize meeting individual customer needs.
- *Rewards structure.* Creating rewards that measure increasingly specific output goals.
- *Process management.* Involves the creation of a formal process team with responsibility for the maintenance and enhancement of

the organization's processes. This team can support the processes with a methodology and seek opportunities to add software automation where appropriate.

The Cycle as a Whole

Citibank in Latin America

Citibank, during the Latin America debt crisis in the early 1980s, offers a case of a company that in the face of crisis actually developed a very forward-looking strategy for coping with the downturn (Figure 1.9, #1). Citibank, with the highest credit exposure of any foreign bank in Latin America at the onset of the debt crisis, considered withdrawing from the region like their competitors Bank of America and Chase Manhattan (Figure 1.9, #2). But, even with its huge debt exposure in the region, Citibank remained committed.

They wisely forged closer ties with governments by working with them to resolve the debt crisis (Figure 1.9, #3). More importantly,

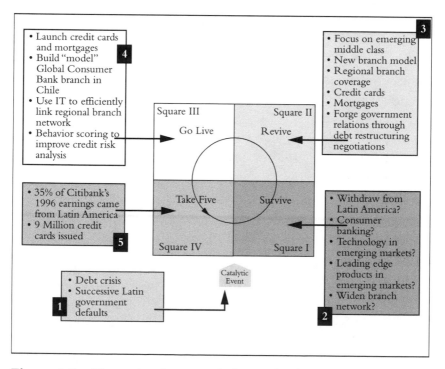

Figure 1.9   The entire change cycle for Citibank.

Citibank began to rewrite the retail banking rules. Citibank aggressively expanded its regional branch network, launched new products and services (both credit card and mortgage products), and introduced new technologies to link all of the branches across Latin America; all at a time when its competitors were exiting the region (Figure 1.9, #4).

Today, Citibank is positioned as one of the region's leading consumer banking institutions with nearly 35% of the bank's earning (US$1.3 billion) coming from Latin America. By 1997, the bank was the leading foreign financial institution in Latin America with 9 million credit cards in circulation (Figure 1.9, #5).

Using the Change Cycle to Make a Difference in Asia

Being able, as Kroger and Citibank were, to find strategic responses that reshape industry game rules and create competitive opportunities, is critical for companies wishing to emerge as winners from the Asian crisis. Already Coca-Cola and Merrill Lynch have made bold moves to improve their positioning in the region. Others, like ABB, the large European engineering group, announced that they would add about 50 more manufacturing sites to the current 100, transferring to over 10,000 jobs to the region.

But foreign institutions are not alone. DBS, a Singaporean Bank, is accelerating its regional presence by acquiring stakes in financial institutions in Thailand and the Philippines. Kian Joo Can Factory Berhad, a major Malaysian canning and packaging company, acquired its ailing competitor, Carnaud Metal Box at a bargain price. This move has allowed it to boost its market share in Malaysia from 42% to 55%. Finally, Core Pacific, a Taiwanese finance company, purchased the Hong Kong arm of Yamaichi securities for $80 million. This allowed it to quickly expand into the Hong Kong financial market.

Once companies make these decisions (and in the above cases, announce them in the press) they still need to be able to drive through the entire cycle as quickly as possible. Decisions of this caliber are only arrived at when the catalytic event demands a new strategic positioning. And we believe that many companies operating in Asia (both Western and Asian firms) need to move around the cycle. In moving around the cycle, speed is of the essence; there are only a limited number of alliance/acquisition candidates—those who get to the best ones first win; relationships with the governments in the region have to be established and managed—and again the victory often goes to companies that can form these relationships early and exclusively; and finally, any time a company is not in Square IV its costs are higher than if in Square IV—companies that can get to Square IV first and stay there the longest (while maintaining relevance to the marketplace) are those that have competitive advantage.

All of this effort on achieving speed will be wasted, however, if it is not "smart speed." This is the reason that each square of the Change Cycle needs to be approached carefully and conscientiously, albeit with some measure of dispatch.

Conclusion

The Change Cycle provides a model of change that can help companies to react to crisis or to take advantage of an opportunity. Companies that can understand that the stages follow each other in a logical order and move through the cycle quickly are those that will be best positioned for success in the marketplace.

Companies, whether Asian or Western, that have shown early success in dealing with the Asian financial crisis are those moving through the Change Cycle to take advantage of opportunities. As those in crisis are able to comprehend the new environment and work to revive under the rules of a new environment, they will more quickly be able to gain a viable position in post-crisis Asia.

2 | Transformational Management

ROBERT E. GROSSE

Corporate strategy for survival into the twenty-first century requires an ability to look forward at the competitive, technological, and regulatory environments and to create a path for the company to build and thrive in that context. The company must transform both itself and the competitive environment to build a position of strength into the century ahead. The vast majority of companies are not able to mobilize this kind of effort. The peril for them is the competitor that does. Without the ability to carefully consider the future and act on it, companies will be competing in the past.

Transformational management is management that carefully considers the competitive context in which a company finds itself, and that identifies the characteristics of competition in the future in business activities that the firm wants to pursue. It does not say: here are our products/services, now where can we sell them—but rather: we see the world going in a new direction, here are our current strengths, here is what we will position ourselves to do in the future. Now let's tell the rest of the world what that future looks like and how we will be the provider of choice in that context.

I would like to thank Val Pavlov, Francis Nzeuton, and Pari Thirunavukkarasu for their excellent research assistance on this project.

Monsanto Corporation offers a clear illustration of this way of thinking. Monsanto was historically a midsized chemical company, with sales in various sectors including agricultural chemicals, pharmaceuticals (after the purchase of GD Searle in 1985), and industrial chemicals. The company produced nylon carpet, polyurethane, pesticides, and various and sundry other chemical products. Its two most successful consumer products were Roundup herbicide, introduced in 1974, and Nutrasweet artificial sweetener, introduced in 1965. Even with these two important products, Monsanto experienced slow growth during the 1980s and early 1990s. Despite a boom in the stock market since 1987, Monsanto's stock price was languishing behind competitors and the market in general. Top management recognized the need to make a change.

The company had been involved in biological research for more than a decade at the time, with a breakthrough product—Roundup-resistant tomatoes—ready for launch in 1992. The product pipeline was not full at that point, but it was promising, and certainly more promising than the company's efforts in chemical products. Monsanto sized up its situation, decided that the future held great promise for genetic engineering of seeds for Roundup-resistant crops, and similar biology-based innovation in other product lines, and chose to dramatically refocus its efforts in this direction. Instead of a chemical company, Monsanto chose to become a biotech leader in crop protection, food-product seeds, and pharmaceuticals—what they are calling a life sciences company.

Similar strategy has been demonstrated by Williams Corporation, a Fortune 500 operator of natural gas pipelines. Williams built a multibillion dollar business in natural gas pipelines and other related oil and gas activities, largely concentrated in the Midwest United States. Given the truly dramatic ups and downs of the oil and gas industry, in the late 1980s the firm looked to diversify its business into alternative activities.

One possibility that was considered to take advantage of Williams' existing infrastructure was to utilize decommissioned pipelines for transporting other kinds of products besides oil or natural gas. The solution was fiber-optic telecommunications cables, that could be channeled through the used pipelines! In 1986, Williams launched a fiber-optic cable venture, which by 1993 had become the nation's fourth largest long-distance network. Williams redefined itself as an infrastructure company, looking to offer services ranging from oil and gas transportation to operation of gasoline stations to provision of telephone service in regions of the United States where its pipelines are located.

Williams went through a wrenching stage of decision making in the early 1990s, when it sold the telecommunications business to LDDS (in 1994) and signed a noncompete agreement for the following five years. Reconsideration of this business during the interim led Williams to re-enter telecommunications service in 1998, immediately after the five-year period expired—and it has proven an enormous success because the price of oil dropped at about the same time, leaving Williams' core natural gas and oil business in a very weak position in 1998–1999.

Another similar situation occurred at Motorola Corporation in the early 1990s—though in this case the results have been far from successful. Motorola was finding increasingly fierce competition for its cellular telephones from Nokia and others, and decided to break out of the slump by following a course of Transformational Management. The Motorola leaders examined their core business of providing wireless telephone instruments and service to customers, considered the technological alternatives for moving the business into the twenty-first century, and designed a strategy for creating a worldwide telephone access system with a single phone number and limitless access to target phones through satellite signals.

This plan, discussed more later cost Motorola more than $5 billion of investment in development of a telephone instrument that could receive and utilize the satellite-reflected signal from anywhere around the world, along with the 66-satellite network that had to be built, launched and maintained in orbit around the earth. It required that Motorola convince the market that this kind of service is desirable, and it demanded that Motorola be ready to offer the service soon enough to beat out potential rivals and to recoup the huge investment. Many of these steps were taken boldly and with full commitment; a major slip in implementation has turned the venture from a potential great success story into a lesson in strategic failure.

Geographic Scope

While *transformational management* may not appear necessarily international, given the competition that is developing at the beginning of the twenty-first century, a transformational strategy must contain a global element. Motorola's global telephone strategy clearly does contain that fundamental basis for competing. Monsanto concentrated initially on the U.S. market, but it subsequently has applied its biological research to products such as rice that are not even produced in the home market; the global context is clearly the right one in this case, too. Global markets imply the application of core strengths to the broadest array of potential customers possible. The logic for realizing the benefits of transformational management also calls for spreading the costs of transforming the firm over the largest market possible, thus the global application of such strategy is compelling.

Williams clearly defined its strategy as domestic, with a focus on regions in the United States where it operates natural gas pipelines. Nevertheless, Williams also has identified the opportunities for leveraging its knowledge of both energy and telecommunications in other countries, and today the firm has operations from Brazil to Australia. Other companies may not find that overseas markets play such a large role in their strategies, but at the same time they may face foreign competitors in their home country markets, or opportunities to produce some or all of their products in foreign locations. If these conditions are not urgently calling for a response today, they easily may be in the near future.

The second basic logic for pursuing a global strategy based on transformational management is to amortize the costs of building the strategy over a larger market area. In every case discussed (except for Motorola), the firm can pursue its forward-looking strategy in a domestic market without necessarily looking abroad. The challenge is to repay billions of dollars of expense in moving to the new strategy; and the solution is to spread the expense over a wider terrain.

In all, for both competitive and cost reasons, transformational management requires a global view.

The Four-Phase Sequence of Transformational Management

Transformational management is the process of corporate strategy determination that calls for a firm to project its domain of business activity into the future, to identify mechanisms for competing successfully in that context, and to educate the market about that future and the company's ability to provide the services/products that will be needed in that future. It requires an active effort to define the technological and regulatory environments that will prevail in the future, as well as to anticipate the competitors who will populate the market. And finally, it requires a clear and timely implementation plan to take advantage of rapidly moving opportunities and to focus the firm's efforts on completing the cycle from identification of the strategy to its realization (Figure 2.1).

The firm must first assess its core strengths, that enable it to exist profitably. Without some competitive strengths, or the possibility of developing them, there would be no basis for projecting a future competitive position. Second, the firm must undertake a process of futurism. Its leaders must decide on the kinds of business activity that the firm wants to pursue, and the technological and regulatory environments that will characterize that activity during the coming 3 to 5 years. This does not have to be "high-tech," necessarily, but just forward-looking. Monsanto achieved this step of looking forward in its strategic planning for years in its chemicals businesses. Senior management saw the opportunities in biology-based research and products, but could not take the final step to

Envisioning the future

Designing a strategy to meet that future

Selling that future

Implementing the Plan

Figure 2.1   The four phases of transformational management.

concentrate on those businesses for more than a decade. Moving beyond the envisioning process was traumatic.

As another example, if the business in question is a management consulting firm, the future may call for the firm to offer services on a wider geographic basis, to keep existing clients happy. Or it may require a move into greater focus in one or more areas of management consulting such as information technology or organizational design/corporate restructuring (as with Andersen Consulting). This competitive domain need not extend out into the far-away future, but just long enough to make sense for the key investments that are needed to keep the firm competitive for a planning horizon such as three to five years.

Once the broad outline of the firm's intended competitive domain and the key challenges in that domain have been sketched, the firm must design a set of steps to position itself as a leader. These steps include investment in R&D to enable the firm to produce the new products or services that will be demanded in the unfolding environment. In the case of Monsanto, this implied the continuous process of investing in research and development of new genetically altered seeds for producing Round-up resistant crops. In the case of Motorola, this required the development of both the satellite network and the telephone instruments that can send and receive the signal around the world. For Williams, this required obtaining skills in telecommunications and learning the ropes of customer/provider relations in this sector, when the firm's historical base had been in natural gas, a decidedly different kind of industry.

The crucial next step is for the firm to commit to pursuing the R&D and other expenses needed to achieve the vision. As much as may be said for the analytical part of the equation, the *implementation* of the chosen strategy may be the hardest step to take. In the case of Andersen Consulting, this required a wrenching breakaway from the parent accounting firm, Arthur Andersen. For Monsanto, it meant betting the company on the life sciences (largely agricultural chemicals and pharmaceuticals) business.

With the firm's own direction clearly defined, the task remains to educate the public about the conditions that are coming and the way in which the firm's products or services offer superior qualities in that future. This step has been particularly vexing for Motorola, since the

Iridium system of cellular phones and satellite communication has been slow in reaching the public (first coming to market in October 1998), and the product has seen two major competitors step forward with presumably competing instruments and service—though neither of them had yet reached the market by December 1999.[1]

Monsanto on the other hand has easily established a position as a biotechnology leader worldwide and has educated the public about the benefits of its biotech products. Monsanto's transformational management process is described in Figure 2.2.

Monsanto's largest recent problem is a global concern about genetically-altered crops, which critics claim may hold unknown risks for consumers. During 1998, the European Union considered limitations on the sale of genetically-engineering foods such as tomatoes, corn, and other vegetables. This debate was highly visible and rancorous, with consumer protection groups staging protests and politicians taking passionate stances against these foods. Monsanto got much more than it bargained for in its effort to inform the public about the future of its business.

Andersen Consulting has built a world-leading consulting practice in the area of information systems. While the firm has been careful to emphasize its intent to provide solutions to clients' information management problems, one of the main bases of that information is the accounting data that is used in recordkeeping. Andersen Consulting has moved away from Arthur Andersen in focusing on

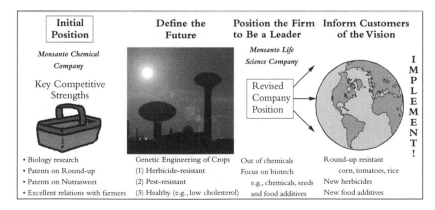

Figure 2.2 Monsanto transformational management.

the technology-based aspect of information management, rather than on the traditional recordkeeping and financial reporting aspects of the accounting data. There is a huge overlap in the two activities, but Andersen Consulting has positioned itself as a provider of corporate management consulting, based on information systems, rather than as a provider of auditing and financial recordkeeping. This message has come out clearly to the public, with Andersen Consulting's advertisements appearing worldwide in newspapers, magazines, and billboards. Figure 2.3 depicts Andersen Consulting's transformational management process.

Note that the transformation here began with the split between the old Arthur Andersen company's two halves, the auditing group versus the consulting group. This is different from the Monsanto case, in which the firm moved sequentially from chemicals into pharmaceuticals and bioengineering, but it is similarly cataclysmic, since the firm is forced to reject one of its historically fundamental bases (in this case, accounting/auditing).

Andersen Consulting defined the future largely as being a world in which information systems consulting, from designing computer systems to implementing SAP software for clients, would be the centerpiece of the business. This is dramatically different from Arthur Andersen's traditional business, that is still pursued by the accounting experts in that separate firm.[2]

Based on its definition of the relevant market space, Andersen Consulting has gone on a rampage of recruiting consultants and building an

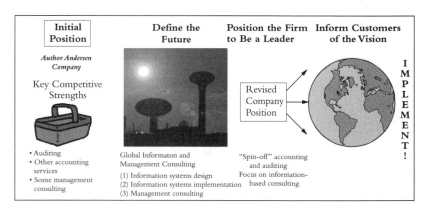

Figure 2.3   Andersen consulting transformational management.

enormous practice worldwide in information systems and management consulting. The firm has undertaken a massive public relations campaign to inform existing customers and potential future customers that Andersen has the skills for the task, and that information systems is a major source of competitive advantage, and so on. Time will tell if this bet has been a good one, but thus far in its short life, Andersen Consulting has become a major player in global management consulting and a leader in information systems consulting.

Problems of Implementing a Transformational Strategy

The greatest barrier to all of these firms that have pursued a strategy of transformational management is their need to jettison the prior business activity or way of doing business. Monsanto took more than a decade to decide to leave the chemicals business. The chemicals activities had to be reorganized and spun off into a new company. For Arthur Andersen, the decision was even more traumatic, leading to a highly contentious and visible legal battle between factions, which ultimately resulted in the creation of two separate firms. For Motorola, the Iridium business was ultimately spun off into a joint venture with suppliers and other strategic allies. None of these was an easy or pleasant experience for the firm involved.

Another company that typifies the huge paradigm shift needed to implement a transformational strategy is Rockwell International. Rockwell historically has been a manufacturer of high-tech electronics and machinery, with a major business segment serving the defense industry. During the course of 1996 and 1997, Rockwell sold off its aerospace and defense businesses, which had developed the Space Shuttle and the B-2 bomber, to Boeing, and then spun off its automotive components business. These had been the previous core activities that had been supplemented over time with activities in automation, semiconductor systems, and avionics and communications.

Rockwell's vision of the future was for a continually consolidating and relatively slow-growing defense sector. The firm's view was that the only strategy in the defense sector that would permit the double-digit annual earnings growth that it sought was to expand dramatically. This would mean becoming totally a defense company, which was not supported adequately with Rockwell's key competitive advantages that could better be applied elsewhere. Rockwell also saw slower growth in its automotive parts business, with great cyclicality in the business and possibly global excess capacity as well. On the positive side, the firm saw the probability of rapid growth in several sectors that depend heavily on the electronics technology that has been underlying Rockwell's competitiveness overall.

Back in 1986, Rockwell had moved into industrial automation equipment with the purchase of the Allen-Bradley Company for more than $1 billion. Over the following 10 years, this business was built, and in 1995 with the addition of Reliance Electric, Rockwell became the leading manufacturer of industrial automation equipment. By the early 1990s, it was clear that commercial electronics would be a better focus than military or aerospace, so this business was built to the current level where it is Rockwell's largest (Figure 2.4).

The focus on avionics and communications was not as striking a shift, since this business was part of Rockwell's military and aerospace activities. With the decline in demand from some market segments, the natural direction was to keep the avionics which serves commercial aviation, as well as land- and sea-based vehicles. And communications is becoming a part of this business just as is computing. Rockwell's experience as the leading producer of Global Positioning Systems (GPS) led naturally to pursue satellite-based communications and other telecom applications. Rockwell's core electronics technology fit this segment ideally. The semiconductor

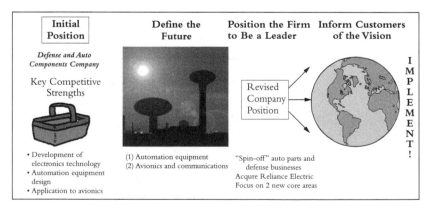

Figure 2.4   Rockwell International transformational management.

systems segment utilized Rockwell's technology from the earlier military and aerospace activities, but it was not viewed as sufficiently vital to the new strategy, and it was spun off in early 1999.[3]

A lesson to be learned from these experiences is that transformational management has a high organizational cost, which typically works itself out over a period of several years. This process often results in the difficult creation of a new firm, independent of the previous business, to pursue the new strategy.

New Entrants into Transformational Management

Another similar situation occurred for Xerox Corporation, which encountered a sales slowdown in the 1980s and early 1990s causing it to underperform the U.S. stock market by 17% for the past entire decade. The company was losing market share in its copier lines to Canon and Ricoh, while other technologies (such as electronic mail) were replacing some of the paper copying business as well.

The company has taken stock of its situation, considered the technological advances that were undermining its success, and begun to launch an initiative to take back leadership in the document processing business. Xerox has improved the quality of its copiers and the functions that they can perform. It has regained technological leadership or at least parity in its traditional copier activities.

The problem for Xerox is to define the business accurately. Will the next decade rely on paper documents to the extent needed for Xerox to maintain a solid growth path? Or will documentary materials become increasingly electronic, with less emphasis on copying and more on storing and transferring the knowledge that they contain? Unquestionably, the "paperless society" that was promised by computers has not arrived and shows no sign of overwhelming the use of paper. By the same token, the growth of electronic information storage and transfer is much more rapid than that of paper documents. For Xerox to thrive in the new environment, the company must define the medium that clients will want to use for their knowledge management and transfer, and then make sure that Xerox provides that kind of medium. It is not obvious that Xerox has achieved that goal.

An example of a company's effort to make the transformation across several failed attempts is that of Olivetti. This Italian industrial giant was long known as a typewriter and office machine company, which almost failed in the 1980s. Carlo de Benedetti took the reins in 1978 and transformed Olivetti into a personal computer and office products company, which took the leading position in the European market for several years. With the entry of several U.S. competitors in the late 1980s, Olivetti again found itself in trouble, being outcompeted by IBM, Dell, Toshiba, and Compaq.

The solution was not obvious, though one business that Olivetti entered in the 1980s, telecommunications, has turned out to be the one in which the company is trying to bet its future. With the bold bid for Telecom Italia in 1998, Olivetti launched one of the first major hostile takeover bids in Europe. After successfully overcoming the strong opposition of Telecom Italia's board and an attempt to recruit Deutsche Telekom as a white knight, Olivetti did take control of the telecommunications company. Now it remains to be seen if Olivetti really can remake itself as a leading telecommunications company moving into the twenty-first century. It is not obvious that the firm's existing competencies are sufficient as a base to develop the skills and knowledge needed to compete successfully in this sector in the new century.

Lessons from the Transformational Management Experience

The costs of undertaking a transformational management process are unquestionably high. It is organizationally wrenching to drop an earlier focus and way of doing things to rocket off in a new and unproven direction. Realistically, the firms that have done so have not jumped off a cliff to start the new business, but rather have agonized over it for years before making a break with the previous direction.

This could be viewed as simply good business—considering the competitive environment, thinking about the firm's strengths and ability to compete in the future, and then moving aggressively to establish a leadership position. However, there are many barriers to making such a move, and most companies have not been able to do so. Also, the problem of implementing a transformational management strategy is just as critical and difficult as defining one—and more firms fall by the wayside by not focusing on this step. For these reasons alone, the names in the Fortune 500 change dramatically over the years. Only the next few years well demonstrate whether

Monsanto, Motorola, Andersen, and Rockwell really have succeeded in transforming their management and their sectors to survive in the new competitive environment.

References

Barney, J. (1991). Firm resources and sustained competitive advantage. *Journal of Management, 17,* 99–120.

Hamel, G., & Prahalad, C.K. (1994). *Competing for the future.* Boston: Harvard Business School Press.

Slywotsky, A. (1996). *Value migration.* Boston: Harvard Business School Press.

Notes

1. Both Globalstar (a consortium of Loral, Brasilstar, and Qualcomm) and ICO Global Communications have announced plans to launch competitor satellite networks and global phone access. Globalstar has already put 8 satellites into orbit toward their overall system of 48 satellites, with operation of the service scheduled for late 1999. In early 1999, ICO was in the process of raising the capital needed to support its 12-satellite network; the firm asserted that its target date for initiating phone service is in mid-2000.

2. Arthur Andersen has also pursued a major consulting business, though focused on management consulting and not on information systems.

3. In this case, Rockwell's management was not completely decided on the disposition of semiconductors, and there has been some debate in the company as to whether or not that spin-off was a good decision.

3

Strategic Choice under Knowledge Competition

ALAN I. MURRAY

Strategic Choice When Competition Is Knowledge-Based

This chapter lays out a comprehensive framework for designing a global strategy in any knowledge-based company. This structure is presented in the form of the "5-cubed" or "5^3" model. The 5^3 model builds on the traditional SWOT (strengths, weaknesses, opportunities, and threats) analysis, and it allows managers to overcome the glaring disadvantages of that analysis.★

SWOT Analysis: Advantages and Disadvantages

The strategy any business chooses to pursue and the means adopted for its pursuit are constrained by factors external to the business. For

---

★SWOT analysis gives interesting insights for thinking about strategy, but it does not illuminate the relative importance of the strengths and weaknesses, etc., nor does it indicate how firms should proceed to build strategy from the items that are identified. In contrast the 5^3 model provides much more detailed planning guidelines for constructing competitive strategy.

this reason, any sound model of business strategy and organization design is a *contingency* model. The best-known such model is SWOT analysis. An analyst using SWOT juxtaposes the *opportunities* and *threats* posed by the business environment, on the one hand, with the accumulated *strengths* and *weaknesses* of the business to determine the most appropriate strategic direction for the business.

This explicit linking of a business's environment to its strategy is the primary advantage of SWOT analysis. Unfortunately, this advantage is compromised by two disadvantages. First, SWOT analysis does not offer any insight into *exactly* what the strategic implications of any specific external factor or configuration of external factors might be for the choice of business direction. Rather, SWOT merely points out that the choice of business direction should be conditioned by environmental factors, specifically, the *opportunities* and *threats* posed by the environment. The model here, called 5^3, directly links *specific* environmental factors with specific organizational characteristics to identify the most appropriate strategic direction for a business.

The other disadvantage of SWOT analysis is that it is biased toward the selection of incremental shifts in business direction in an era in which radical shifts are increasingly demanded. Businesses' strategies and designs have, historically, been predicated upon the *efficient utilization of assets*, which is equivalent to the *efficient application of existing knowledge and skill*. Increasingly, businesses derive greater competitive advantage from the pursuit of *new, valuable, inimitable knowledge*. An implication of this ground shift in business strategy is that businesses increasingly compete by introducing *radical innovations that make obsolete competitors' existing capabilities—a form of *Schumpeterian competition*.[1]

Because SWOT analysis introduces the existing strengths and weaknesses of the business at the outset, it necessarily limits strategic choices to *incremental* improvements. Incrementalism may have been appropriate amidst the conservatism characterizing competition based on the efficient application of existing knowledge, but it is wholly inappropriate for competition predicated on radical change— competition predicated on the creation of new, valuable, inimitable knowledge. The 5^3 model is designed to recommend radical shifts in business direction where appropriate and incremental shifts when radical shifts are not most appropriate.

It particularly enables the user to focus on the key parameters of competition in the twenty-first century—the global reach of competitors and "e-time" speed of change.

Model Overview

The model relates five generic *constraints—Customers, Context, Change, Competition,* and *Capabilities*—to the *choices* every business must make (Figure 3.1). First, *constraints* are considered, and then the *choices* implied by the *constraints* are discussed. The *choices* implied by the five constraints divide into *five* broad areas, each of which is subdivided into *five* separate considerations, hence the label for the model—5³.

Customers

The definitive feature of business competition is that it is *judged* competition. The judges are the businesses' customers. The best

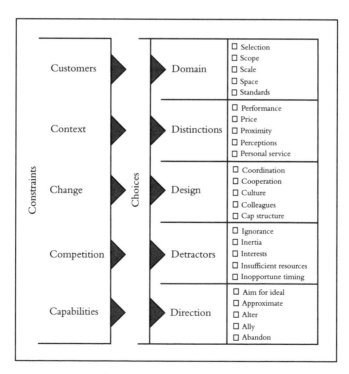

Figure 3.1   5³ model.

viewpoint from which to begin any analysis of business competition is the judges'—the customers'—viewpoint. Adopting this viewpoint poses three strategically critical questions:

- *Who are the judges?* While this may sound like a trivial question, the emerging "modular" and "virtual" corporations that predicate their competitive advantage on the creation of new, valuable, inimitable knowledge play a much smaller role in many more value chains. For such competitors, *who* the customer is has, or could, become a difficult question.
- *What are customers looking for?* By knowing what customers want, the business can know what combination of distinctions will best distinguish it from its rivals, in the eyes of judges.
- *Will customers be able to recognize what they are looking for prior to making their judgment (i.e., the purchase decision)?*

When distinguishing between product or service offering(s), customers must engage in a process called *causal attribution;* they must impute overall benefits from differences between the features of products or service offerings, so that they can choose that product or service which offers them the most benefit. A number of factors affect a customer's *ability* and *motivation* to complete this causal attribution process effectively.

Customers' ability to judge is affected by:

- *Frequency of purchase*—the more frequently the customer purchases a product or service, the more likely she is to be able to effectively judge between rivals' offerings.
- *Presence of actual differences*—the customer is unlikely to perceive differences across product or service offerings if few actual differences exist.
- *Opportunity to evaluate the various offerings* (and relatedly, the tangibility of the product class, that is, whether it is a product or a service)—if the customer has no opportunity to evaluate the various offerings prior to judgment (purchase), as is the case for the first-time purchaser of a service, an informed judgment cannot be made.

- *The availability of valid and reliable measures with which to differentiate between offerings*—if no measures exist which both reflect the underlying features and benefits being causally related and produce the same results whenever measurement of the same offering is being repeated, the customer will find effective judgment difficult.

- *The existence of confounding factors that obscure the link between product or service features and benefits to the customer*—often benefits to the customer are a function not only of the product's or service's features but of other causal agents as well (for example, the skill and motivation with which the customer uses the product or service).

- *The time lag between purchase of the product or service and the realization of benefits*—often a considerable time lag exists between the experience of the product's or service's features and the experience of benefits. Because other factors intervene, such lags complicate the attribution process, thus diminishing the effectiveness of customer judgment.

Customers' motivation to judge is affected by:

- *The monetary and emotional costs of making the wrong choice*—if the customer believes that the benefits derived differ dramatically across product or service offerings, they will be more motivated to detect those differences.

- *The monetary and emotional costs of failure of the product or service chosen*—if failure of the product or service to provide the benefits sought entails substantial cost, the customer will be highly motivated to ensure that failure of the offering chosen does not occur, that is, the customer will be highly motivated to become an effective judge.

These are particularly problematic issues for the multinational firm because customers may view the firm as being foreign and not really committed to the particular market. From an analysis of who the business' customers are, what benefits they want, and whether they will recognize those benefits when they are presented to them, can be derived the best set of distinctions that the business should strive to offer its customers.

Global Business Context: Technological, Social, and Legal

What customers demand of a business, along with their ability, or lack thereof, to distinguish between one product or service offering and another within a product or service class, acts to constrain the choices a business makes. But customers' judgments are not the only constraints upon these choices. While customers' characteristics constitute the primary determinant of what distinctions a business should adopt, other constraints impact the most appropriate design for the business. On one hand, the social and legal context within which the business operates conditions both customers' preferences and their performance as judges, as well as conditioning the regulatory environment in which the business operates. While decreasingly so, these factors still tend to be jurisdictionally specific, that is, they are homogeneous *within* national or regional boundaries and they are heterogeneous *across* national and regional boundaries. Social and legal constraints tend to oblige businesses to reflect in their organization design the jurisdictional boundaries they span.

What a business can offer to customers is also constrained *technologically*. Technology can be defined as that knowledge which permits people to manipulate their physical environment. As such, technology is grounded in physical laws which, unlike *social norms, laws,* and *regulations,* do not vary across national or regional boundaries. Overcoming physical limitations—inventing new technology—is perhaps the most important means by which businesses attempt to win in the eyes of judges. Because inventing new technology entails cost (often substantial cost), and costs must be incurred before the invented technology can impress judges and thus attract revenue, it makes sense for the inventor of value-producing new technologies to amortize these often substantial up-front costs of invention over the largest revenue base possible. Since national and regional boundaries are transparent to technology, one way that this imperative can be achieved is to expand geographically—to expand across national and regional boundaries.

Between the extremes of social and legal constraints, which direct the business toward the pursuit of local responsiveness, and technological constraints, which direct the business toward the pursuit of global leveraging of technology, lies the character of customers' needs. Often the benefits customers seek from a product or service class vary from one customer to another. When this is the case, different market segments are said to exist. Often market segments can be differentiated geographically, that is, the needs of customers are homogeneous within regions but heterogeneous across regions. This tends to occur most often for traditional consumer product and service classes. Product or service classes of more recent genesis and products and services sold into industrial and commercial markets tend to be associated with less geographic variation in customers' tastes. Geographic heterogeneity of customer needs directs the business toward the pursuit of greater local responsiveness; geographic homogeneity of customers' needs directs the business toward the pursuit of greater global leveraging or efficiency.

Increasingly, the design of business organizations reflects the tension between the social and legal context in which the business must operate, the overcoming of technological constraints that increasingly constitutes a key competitive advantage of the business, and the relationship between the heterogeneity of customers' needs and geographic dispersion. Social and legal constraints compel the business to be *locally responsive,* while overcoming technological constraints promotes the pursuit of global *efficiencies.* Whether customers' needs are heterogeneous or homogeneous and whether need heterogeneity correlates with geographic dispersion, determines whether the pursuit of distinctions will compel the business to favor local responsiveness or global leverage of efficiency.

Competition: Determines the Degree of "Strategic Freedom"

The pursuit of global efficiencies, which is driven by a need to amortize the fixed costs of creating new, valuable, inimitable knowledge over the largest revenue base possible, drives up competitive intensity in one relatively isolated domestic market after another as "foreign" rivals enter. Competitive intensity can be driven up in three ways in such situations: (1) the *number* of rivals is elevated, (2) productive *capacity* may be added, and (3) rivals realize that knowledge competition—competition predicated primarily on the creation of new, valuable, inimitable knowledge rather than on preferential access to raw materials or on the efficient utilization of assets (implying as it does infinite optimal scale) implies an inevitable "shake-out" among competitors.

The level of competition—competitive intensity—determines the degree of strategic flexibility a business enjoys. Absent competition, a monopoly can pursue almost any strategic option it wishes. As competition intensifies, however, the range of strategic options available contract, until sometimes no options remain. While competition affects all choices, it is related in this model primarily to direction.

In the past, many domestic markets were dominated by relatively few rivals who, if not overtly collusive, were sufficiently familiar with each others' strategic propensities that a de facto collusion occurred. Such situations did not demand of businesses very much strategic savvy. However, because business rivalry was primarily domestic in scope, governments were able to be highly economically intrusive. Thus, while in the past businesses did not worry as much about strategy, they did have to possess strong ties with governments, good lobbyists, and excellent tax accountants.

As one business after another "globalizes," the ability of governments to pursue policies predicated upon economic intrusiveness diminishes. As this happens, businesses are able to worry less about governments' arbitrary interventions into their affairs. Instead, they must worry more about the systemic factors that determine their likelihood of competitive success. Again, the 5^3 model is an attempt to articulate the strategic implications of such systemic factors for strategists facing the new, heightened form of business competition—knowledge competition.

Change: Volatility, Cyclicality, Trends, Discontinuities

When businesses predicated strategy upon the efficient utilization of assets, which is equivalent to the efficient application of existing knowledge, most businesses had a vested interest in maintaining the status quo, in not changing. *Change* would have necessitated the creation or acquisition of new knowledge which, due to the learning curve phenomenon, would not have been able to be applied as efficiently, thus violating the imperative that traditionally drove business strategy—the *efficient* application of *existing* knowledge.

Now that business advantage is increasingly predicated on the creation of new knowledge, the pace of change, like competitive intensity, is likewise increasing. In turn, this increased pace of change necessitates a dramatic shift in the practice of management. In the past, when most businesses had a vested interest in suppressing change, strategists could afford to expend considerable time and resources to reach the "right" policy decisions. They enjoyed this luxury because the costs of achieving the "right" policy decision could be amortized over many subsequent applications of the policy. The duration of application was long because the environment was slow to change; thus a "right" policy would tend to remain "right" for a considerable period.

With the rate of change now dramatically heightened, the period over which the costs of creating new policies can be amortized contracts, thus removing the luxury of expending considerable time and resources determining the "right" policy. Strategists, today, are in the unenviable position of being under far more pressure, due to the heightened competitive intensity associated with the globalization of business competition, to achieve the "right" policy while simultaneously being no longer able to expend the same time and resources to achieve these "right" decisions.

To resolve this dilemma, an entirely new model of strategy formation is being adopted. Strategists are moving from the traditional approach, which was characterized by relatively long cycles in which thought proceeded action, to relatively short cycles in which action precedes thought. Under this new approach, strategists act first, then reflect on the results of their actions. If the results seem positive, they should persist with the action; if the net results seem negative, the manager should try something else.

Adoption of this model, however, necessitates a change in the relationship between strategy formation and strategy implementation within a business. Under the traditional model, strategists, usually occupying a separate staff position, would determine policy, then disseminate the derived policies to those line managers responsible for policy implementation. Under the short-cycle act-think model, those forming strategy and those implementing strategy must be one and the same. One implication is that all actors in the business need to be able to determine for themselves what the overall strategic direction of the business should be. In the absence of such knowledge, actors would not be able to discriminate positive actions from negative ones. An objective of the 5^3 model is to provide every member of a business organization with a framework that allows them to discover, for themselves, what the overall direction of the business should be.

Strategists also need to be able to determine when the strategic direction needs to be altered. To reach such a determination, they need to achieve a better understanding of the nature of the changes that can affect a business.

Change assumes a variety of forms: volatility, cyclicality, trends, and discontinuity. The first two types of *change* mask an underlying equilibrium and thus necessitate no change in the business' overall direction. All that is required is sufficient slack to ride out the fluctuations or cycles. The challenge every business faces, however, is discriminating, ex ante, between mere volatility and underlying trends or discontinuities. Like frogs that fail to leap out of gradually heated water due to an inability to detect subtle temperature shifts, many businesses tend to interpret underlying structural change as mere volatility (and thus assume that it will soon pass). As a result, such businesses suffer the ultimate fate of a gradually heated frog.

It is debatable which is worse, gradually evolving trends or discontinuities. The former threatens a slow death, due to denial or simply an inability to perceive the underlying change. The latter is certainly more noticeable, but leaves little time for response.

Increasingly, discontinuity is being used as a *competitive weapon* by smaller rivals who lack the customer confidence, access to raw materials, capital, and distribution channels that their larger rivals enjoy, but who also lack the bureaucratic inertia of their larger rivals. These smaller, more nimble competitors consciously instigate discontinuities to reverse their larger rivals' competitive edge. In a sort of corporate *Aikido,* these smaller, nimbler businesses use their larger rivals' inertia to defeat them.

That *change* is used increasingly as a competitive weapon and implies that businesses must be responsive to the imperative to change. The increased use of *change* as a competitive weapon, then, means, first, moving to the short cycle act-think model of strategy formation described earlier (and all that that entails) and, second, eliminating those factors that detract from the business' ability to embrace *change—detractors.*

Capabilities: The Internal Constraint

Customers, context, competitors, and change all affect the strategic choices every business must make. Each of these constraints is external to the business. There is, however, one other constraint that conditions the choices every business must make: the capabilities the business has been able to assemble in the past. Because they are an historical fact and are massively inertial (an idea that will be explored more fully below), capabilities, unlike the other constraints considered thus far, although not external, are exogenous, as far as subsequent choices are concerned, and thus appropriately considered constraints.

Failure to include a consideration of the business's own capabilities leads the business toward a direction that may be strategically *necessary* but not be strategically *possible* for the business in question.

A capability can be defined as the combination of the knowledge, assets, and raw materials required to implement a chosen set of distinctions in a chosen domain. New knowledge creation is constrained by the twin imperatives: (1) it must produce *value* exceeding its cost of creation and, (2) by extension, it must be difficult to imitate—it must be *inimitable*. Knowledge, alone, however, cannot produce *valuable* goods and services. The *application* of knowledge, to produce valuable products and services, requires the addition of *assets* and *raw* materials. A capability, then, can be defined as a unique knowledge domain[2] plus the assets and access to raw materials necessary to add value to a value chain.[3]

Since it is easier to know more about a narrower subject than a broader one, and since competitive advantage under knowledge competition depends on the creation of new knowledge, the knowledge competitor, in order to know *more* and *more,* prefers to focus on *less* and *less.* This convergent pressure is offset, however, by the demand that the business must not only add value to a value chain, but that its output also be *efficiently priceable.* Since a business is a profit center, and profit is a function of revenue and cost, and revenue and cost are both functions of price, flows across the boundaries of any business must be efficiently priceable.

The efficiency with which a flow can be priced will depend on the ease with which the flow can be *measured.* This, in turn, will depend in part on whether flows are pooled, sequential, or reciprocal.

Pooling implies a one-way flow of goods and services and a high degree of independence between flows—one activity has little effect on another, sequential flows introduce a time dependence in which some steps necessarily precede others, and reciprocal flows permit bidirectionality in the sense that goods and services may move back and forth between steps. Pricing is significantly more efficient for pooled and sequential flows than for reciprocal flows.

The knowledge competitor's portfolio of knowledge domains may contract, then, to no fewer than that set which permits the business to produce efficiently priceable products and services. This typically implies that the boundaries of the business will be characterized by pooled or sequential flows, whereas the flows within the business will be characterized by reciprocity.

However bounded, any knowledge competitor's portfolio will always comprise two types of knowledge domain:

1. *Distinctive knowledge* possessed exclusively by the business that allows it to produce products and services whose combination of *Distinctions* is inimitable and therefore sustainably profitable.
2. *Universal knowledge* necessary to any activity that adds value. This is the knowledge that permits an organization to implement and sustain the types of organization described on pages 70–80.

Berkeley philosophy of language professor Donald Davidson and science historian Thomas Kuhn have introduced us to the idea that any knowledge domain is born as a metaphor.[4] Useful metaphors attract adherents who by enacting the metaphor "literalize" it. Once the metaphor becomes literal, a process of elaboration occurs that Kuhn refers to as "normal science." This distinction between the early or radical phase of knowledge formation and the subsequent incremental phase is useful to consider in a business context. Kuhn notes that new paradigm shifts (to use his term) or new metaphors (to use Davidson's) tend to come from outside the discipline or, in the case of interest here, outside the industry. As the metaphor becomes literal, however, through the process of imitation, the initial advantage conferred by the paradigm shift or new metaphor is lost. The knowledge competitor, then, must migrate from the initial competitive advantage that introduction of a new metaphor confers to other sources of competitive advantage. This means, again using Kuhn's term, doing *normal science*.

How quickly the innovator must move to new sources or competitive advantage is a function of how easily imitated or adopted the new metaphor is. Product innovations are easier to adopt than process innovations, for the simple reason that process innovations can be kept literally, behind closed doors, while product innovations must necessarily be out in the marketplace for customers and curious competitors alike, to examine and purchase. Innovations grounded in a knowledge domain that is shared across competitors is easier to imitate than one grounded in a knowledge domain that is idiosyncratic to the innovator. Shared knowledge domains tend to be embedded in *professorial* cultures (medicine, engineering, accounting, law, etc.), while idiosyncratic knowledge domains tend to be embedded in *organizational* cultures. Combining these two dimensions, professionally grounded product innovations are easiest to imitate (which is why they have to be artificially protected from innovation, via the patent process), whereas organizationally based process innovations pose barriers for potential imitators.

Sooner or later, all useful innovations will be imitated. By the time they are, the innovator must have migrated to other sources of competitive advantage or must be prepared to accept normal returns. In searching for new sources of competitive advantage, the innovator should look to those sources of advantage that, unlike the creation of new metaphors, tend to result from participation in the new value chain. Such advantages can be exhausted by the following:

- *Learning.* Since the innovator is, by definition, the first to participate in the new value chain he or she has created, he or she has the potential to sustain learning curve advantages over imitative rivals. To migrate to such a source of competitive advantage, however, the innovator must be an astute learner able to perform "normal science." Normal science can be conducted in either of two ways: deductively or inductively. Deduction refers to the process by which new knowledge is logically derived from the existing knowledge domain. Induction refers to the process by which observations lead to the creation of new knowledge. In practice, both methods are interrelated—new metaphors are elaborated (deduction), leading to new behaviors and new types of observations, which, in turn create novel data that must then be interpreted (induction). Realizing the new learning curve effects innovation creates, then, is analogous to "doing" normal science.

- *Leverage.* By being the first to participate in a new value chain, the innovator has the opportunity to achieve and sustain the highest volume of activity. If economies of scale are pronounced throughout the value chain, or in any important part of it, the innovator, enjoying the highest production volume, will enjoy cost advantages. This is an especially important concern in multinational firms, in which the opportunity to leverage knowledge is spread over a vast geographical range, but the ability to realize the gains is potentially limited by cross-cultural barriers (e.g., languages, but also other cultural differences).

- *Loyalty and lock-in.* By being first to enter the new value chain, the innovator has the first "crack" at new suppliers and customers. If the potential exists to create either significant loyalty or switching costs for either customers or suppliers, subsequent entrants to the value chain will be forced to "pry" customers and suppliers away from the innovator in what can be a costly process.

- *Locations.* In the downstream, distribution end of the value chain, being first to choose locations will provide a competitive advantage as long as the following conditions apply: (1) some locations must be preferable to others; (2) better locations must be relatively scarce; and, (3) preferred locations must be able to be retained without incurring increased costs. Given the global competitor's choice of a much larger set of locations than a single-country competitor, the multinational firm has a major advantage in this area.

- *Laws.* The innovators may be able to sponsor the introduction of laws which prevent imitation (patent and copyright laws); oblige others to adopt proprietary standards owned by the innovator; simply raise barriers to entry by restricting access to raw materials, labor, capital, or distribution channels (and hence to customers).

The creation and maintenance of *capabilities* lies at the heart of sustaining competitive advantage. Capabilities are founded in unique knowledge domains, which, it has been argued, start as novel metaphors and then through process or literalization and elaboration grow into mature knowledge domains. Both of these processes require massive commitments on the part of the organization—investments the organization should only walk away from with great reluctance. Further, to realize value from a novel knowledge domain, organizations must have access to raw materials and possession of the assets necessary to transform the raw materials using the unique knowledge. Often, such assets are highly specialized and cannot be abandoned without cost. Finally, the creation of a certain *capability* comes at the opportunity cost of not creating other *capabilities*. For these reasons, *capabilities* must be considered as a *constraint* on the subsequent strategic *choices* any business makes.

This is why strategic analysis using the 5^3 model must begin with a characterization of the business's *current capabilities*. However, subsequent analysis using the 5^3 model will inevitably indicate that the portfolio of *capabilities* either should be enlarged through internal development or acquisition, or reduced through outsourcing or divestiture, or both.

Under knowledge competition, the starting point for strategy-formation and organization design must be the current "portfolio of knowledge domains" (as opposed to the practice in traditional businesses, of seeking competitive advantage through the efficient use of assets: which implies organized primarily around the assets it owns). To begin analysis, the strategist must understand the current composition of his or her business' "knowledge portfolio." To determine this starting point, the strategist could follow these steps:

- Map the sequence of processes that collectively institute the value chains to which the business contributes.
- Identify those events, processes, or actions that the business itself completes (those conducted by others will be considered below).
- From the events identified in the previous step, isolate those which the business executes *better* than any rival (or, failing this *strong* test, those which constitute the best candidates for promotion to such status).
- Now, imagine writing a training manual for the steps identified in the previous section. The contents of such a manual and the

knowledge required to understand the manual constitute the knowledge domain(s) upon which the strategic *Direction* of the business would be built using the 5^3 model.

Choices: Key Questions Every Business Must Answer

Having now characterized the *constraints* that condition the *choice* of *direction* for a business, it is possible to consider *choice* itself. The *direction* that a business should choose is that which offers the most attractive *domain* in which the business can achieve *distinction* subject to all the *constraints* described above (see Figure 3.2).

Accomplishing this is equivalent to answering the following questions:

- Which goods or services should we participate in the creation of?
- Which processes in the value chain(s) in which we participate should we undertake ourselves and which would be best left to others?
- How big should we be (in size and in geographic scope)?
- Where should we sell the goods and services we produce?

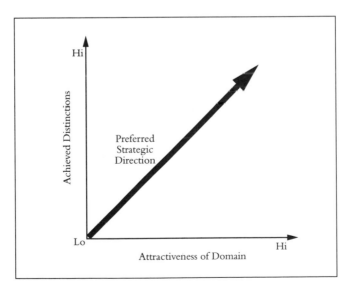

Figure 3.2   Strategic direction.

- What will we *not* do in order to win and maintain competitive advantage?
- How important is performance/quality to our customers?
- What price should we charge to our customers?
- How important is convenience to our customers?
- How important is "image" to our customers?
- How important is personal service to our customers?
- What do we need to know, and what assets and raw materials will we need in order to convert that knowledge into valuable goods and services?
- How should we coordinate all the components of the value creation process?
- How can we get all the participants in the value creation process to cooperate?
- What do all the participants in the value creation process need to "know" to communicate effectively with one another?
- How can we select and socialize participants so that they will come to "know" the same things?
- What should our capital structure be?
- What internal and external forces might prevent us from implementing the answers to all these questions?
- How can we best go about implementing the answers to these questions?

This list of questions constitutes the organizing principle for the remainder of the model. There is no intent to imply that strategists should work through the model in a linear fashion, nor is there any implication that this model constitutes the "right" prescription for the strategy formation process. Rather, think of this model as a check list, the intent of which is to ensure that all critical considerations are covered before a strategic *direction is* chosen.

The first of the five secondary elements in the model—*domain*—identifies the optimal competitive *arena* for a given business. The second step—*distinctions*—determines how to maximize competitive advantage within the *domain* chosen. The third step—*design*—identifies the organizational configuration that allows the business to achieve the distinctions identified as important within the chosen domain.

These first three steps of the model are *idealistic*—they ignore the *actual* strategies of the competitors who collectively comprise the industry being analyzed. Any normative model of strategy *must* accommodate the current competitive *status quo* of the business being analyzed. The last two steps of the model do this. The fourth step—*detractors*—considers the *internal* realities the business currently faces. The focus, here, is on those internal factors that can frustrate or even prevent implementation of the changes identified as most appropriate in the previous steps. While the fourth step addresses the internal realities of the strategy-maker's business, the fifth step considers the *external* realities. This fifth and final step—*direction*—selects the best strategic option for a specific business, given its actual strategic disposition as well as those of its competitors.

Each of these five elements are in turn subdivided into five distinct dimensions, described in more detail below.

Domain: What Is Our Business?

Increasingly, businesses seek competitive advantage by creating new, valuable, inimitable knowledge. Once this starting point has been identified, the analysis proceeds with a consideration of the five aspects or dimensions of domain. These five dimensions are described in more detail next.

Selection

The optimal range of goods or services in whose creation the business should participate is the *selection*. This range is discovered by considering the homogeneity or heterogeneity of identified customer needs and the actual as well as the perceived (by customers) commonalities across the *capabilities* required to produce each of the goods or services satisfying the identified needs. Every different customer need demands a different (sometimes only slightly different) value chain. The business should participate in every value chain for which it is best qualified, with the *caveat* that it may conceal its participation (as an original equipment maker, for example) if customers do not perceive that it is qualified, even though it is. Conversely, a business should appear to participate in value chains for which they may not be qualified (by licensing their brand name, for example) if customers perceive that they *are* qualified.

By participating in every value chain that can utilize its unique capabilities, the business amortizes the costs of creating, sustaining, and growing the knowledge required to implement those capabilities over the largest revenue base possible. Likewise, by participating in every market (country) where the firm can apply these capabilities, it will amortize the costs even faster.

Selection answers the question: What goods or services should we participate in the creation of?

Scope

Scope is the optimal range of the activities that must be performed to produce a good or service that the business itself should undertake—that is, those activities over which the business should exert direct control. This is determined by considering the *power* and *correspondence* of the other businesses contributing to the value chain.

If a step cannot be, or is not being, executed competently by others, the business must execute the step itself so that the overall value of the chain is not compromised by a weak link.

Partly because incompetence is often related to poor profitability and partly because a knowledge competitor should avoid broadening its knowledge focus, activities in which a business engaged due to the incompetence of others should be divested as soon as competence is established. Alternatively, means exist whereby the business can improve the competence of contiguous members of the value chain without directly engaging in vertical integration—a business can often help to smooth the cash flow of other members of the value chain to enhance other members' survival probability, thus enhancing the other members' ability to accumulate competence.

A business should also vertically integrate if other steps in the value chain, by their nature[5] confer sufficient power as either to undermine the profitability of other contributors to the value chain or to permit them to consciously ignore the demands of the business. Since such power often derived from significant barriers to entry, vertical integration in such cases may be impracticable, in which case the best strategies are either to develop countervailing power, derived from proprietary access to a value-producing knowledge domain or to form alliances with weaker participants in the powerful activity in order to undermine the attractiveness (in Michael Porter's sense) of the activity, and hence undermine the power that threatens the business.

Every new activity or process in which the business engages enlarges the knowledge domains over which it must achieve mastery. For this reason, the imperatives for vertical integration described earlier must be complemented by pressures to outsource or de-integrate activities that confer little power but for which competent performance has been established. De-integration has four important advantages:

1. It avoids the possibility that efficiency-sapping internal monopolies will develop (and relatedly, it keeps the business small enough that every participant can clearly perceive her own contribution—thus avoiding a "free rider" problem).
2. By reducing the number of links in any value chain over which the business exerts direct control, the number of value chains to which the business could add value is increased.
3. It permits each activity to achieve its own optimal scale.
4. It permits the business to remain focused on a minimal portfolio of knowledge domains, thus maximizing the probability that they will master those that remain.

De-integration should be pursued up to the point at which further de-integration would create flows across the organization's boundaries that could no longer be efficiently priced (a critical constraint since every business is necessarily a profit center).

Scope answers the question: Which steps in the value creation processes in which the business participates should we undertake ourselves and which would be best left to others? (This choice is otherwise known as the make-or-buy decision.)

Scale

The optimal level of output of the business is determined by considering the most economic scale of each of the activities over which the business must exert direct control (as determined in the previous step) as well as scale's overall importance to the success of the business.

The ideal scale of the business should equal the efficient scale of the largest efficiently scaled process in which the business engages.

Under knowledge competition, the most important processes are those leading to the development of new, valuable, inimitable knowledge. But, since the costs of such a process are incurred *prior* to and are thus necessarily independent of the subsequent value they generate, the optimal scale for this process is *infinite*. No business can achieve infinite scale, however, knowledge competition does exaggerate the potential advantages of scale.

Because of the heightened competitive intensity associated with knowledge competition, the knowledge competitor is compelled to amortize its knowledge development costs over the largest base of subsequent sales possible. This imperative clashes, however, with the need to reduce the size of the business to avoid "free riders." This dilemma is best addressed by ruthlessly and continuously de-integrating the business within the constraints outlined earlier.

Scale answers the question: How big should we be?

Space

The optimal geographic coverage of the business, space was determined in the past by national boundaries and was chosen to provide sufficient capacity to supply the domestic market. Now, under the heightened competitive intensity of knowledge competition, there is far greater pressure to achieve the optimal scale, which under knowledge competition approaches infinity. While infinite scale is not achievable, the business that is able to amortize its knowledge development costs over the largest base of subsequent sales derives a considerable competitive advantage. Thus, knowledge competition is a prime cause of *globalization*—to gain maximum scale economies, the knowledge competitor expands sales to *every* geographic market. *Achieving* a global presence requires sophisticated organizational and cultural knowledge, and is increasingly a strategic necessity. The ability to *achieve* globalization can constitute an additional source of competitive advantage in its own right.

Space answers the question: Where should we sell the goods and services we produce?

Standards

What are the *external* standards (laws and regulations) and *internal* standards (norms and values) by which the business will be bound?

External standards are determined once the geographic scope of the business has been chosen. Since external standards are imposed by nation states, the greater the geographic scope of the business, the more diverse becomes the set of external standards the business must accommodate, necessitating greater flexibility on the part of the business.

Internal standards are one of the few strategic elements not externally constrained. Still, the more stringent the internal standards, the less strategic freedom the business enjoys; so while not originating beyond the locus of control of the business, internal standards have the same constraining effect on strategy.

This would suggest that, to be competitive, businesses should adopt a *minimal* set of standards. The flaw in this argument is that while a minimal set of standards may confer greater strategic freedom upon a business, it also undermines the cultural "glue" (see *culture,* p. 74) that facilitates the internal integration of the business. Empirically, researchers have found that the most successful businesses tend to adopt *sincerely* and to abide by highly *restrictive* ethical standards.

Standards answers the question: What will we not *do to win competitive advantage?*

Distinctions: How Should We Out-Compete Our Rivals?

Given the business' particular set of starting capabilities has been determined, the next broad consideration has to be: How can we differentiate or distinguish ourselves from our rivals? Since the definitive feature of business competition is that it is a *judged* competition, the appropriate position from which to answer this question is the judges'—the customers'—viewpoint. Customers employ some combination of five generic criteria when judging any business.

Performance

To what extent can the product(s)/services, itself (themselves), produced by the business achieve distinction? This is determined by how well customers can, or could be taught to, distinguish between the various product or service offerings (see *customers,* p. 48) within the goods/service class(es) and whether the costs of achieving this distinction can be recovered.

Performance can be categorized into four moments:

1. The *presence or absence* of attributes valued by customers.
2. The *level* of the attribute most valued by customers.
3. The degree of variance around the "ideal" attribute level at the time of production. (This moment of performance is traditionally identified as "quality;" hence, "performance" is a superset encompassing but also exceeding "quality.")
4. The *rate of change over time* of the variance around the "ideal" level of the attribute. (This moment only applies to durable products.)

Whether *performance distinctions* should be sought depends not only on *customers'* propensity to recognize and value *performance* differentials between product or service offerings (and, hence, pay a sufficiently high premium to offset the costs of creating the *performance* differential), but depends, as well, on how long these *performance distinctions* can be sustained in the marketplace.

The *duration* of a *performance distinction* is determined by the following two factors (see Figure 3.3):

1. The time taken from the conception of an innovation until the market introduction of goods or services incorporating the distinction known as *time to market*. This factor is in turn determined by whether new ideas are parallel processed by all functional areas simultaneously, or whether series processing occurs, whereby each functional area develops aspects of a new idea sequentially. Parallel processing is more difficult to accomplish but implies a substantially shorter time to market.
2. The *time to imitation* of the innovation by rivals. This factor can often be externally regulated through either patent or copyright protection, but is otherwise *naturally* fixed by the *imitability* of the distinction which is, in turn, determined by the *uniqueness of* the knowledge domain that must be known in order to understand the innovative idea. The most difficult innovations to imitate are culture-based *process* innovations (as opposed to product innovations) because process innovations can be, literally, kept

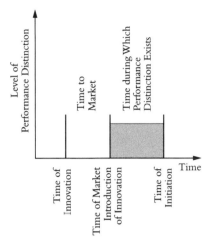

Figure 3.3 Duration of performance distinction.

behind closed doors (and away from rivals' prying eyes) and because cultural knowledge that is idiosyncratic to the business (as opposed to being based in technical or professional knowledge domains shared across business boundaries).

Performance answers the question: How important is quality (more broadly defined here as "performance")?

Price

Can price be used advantageously to distinguish a given business' product/service offering(s) from rivals' offerings? The answer to this question will depend on whether the business is (or could become) the beneficiary of cost differentials arising either from economies of scale, or economies independent of scale.

The latter includes:

- Learning or experience curve effects.
- Lower costing raw materials.
- Proprietary process technologies.
- Lower labor costs (costs, not rates).

- Lower cost of capital.
- Lower cost to access distribution and marketing channels.

Price answers the question: What price should we charge?

Proximity

Can closer proximity to customers—both in time and space—become a distinguishing feature of the business' goods/service offering(s)? This will depend on the ratio of customers' transaction costs to the total purchase costs and on the cost of *achieving* greater proximity to customers.

Proximity answers the question: How important is convenience?

Perceptions

Can the image[6] of the product(s)/service(s) constitute a distinction for competitive purposes? This will depend on the extent to which the product(s)/service(s) is (are) distinguished on other dimensions and their actual (or potential) symbolic uses—as well as serving a utilitarian function, most consumer products also signal to ourselves and to others who we are. A business can utilize this fact to further distinguish their product from rivals' offerings.

Perceptions answers the question: How important is image?

Personal Service

Can personal service[7] be used to augment other distinctions? This will depend on the complexity of the purchase, the customer's cost of time, and their price sensitivity (which, in turn, depends on whose money they are spending and, if they are spending their own money, on their wealth).

Personal service answers the question: How important is customer service?

Design: What Design Will Allow Us to Distinguish Ourselves within Our Chosen Domain?

Having identified the optimal competitive arena or *domain* given current *capabilities,* and the best way to *distinguish* ourselves from our rivals within the chosen *domain,* the next step in the model is to determine what organizational configuration would best permit us to realize the *distinctions* previously identified as most appropriate, within the *domain* previously identified. Obviously, the *domain* identified as optimal will vary depending upon the *capabilities* with which the analysis began. Similarly, the particular profile of distinctions will depend upon the *domain* chosen.

Design can be subdivided into five distinct categories.

Coordination

In the traditional business organization, the imperatives of coordination were subordinated to those of control. Control compelled the creation of a supervisory hierarchy to ensure that subordinates' actions conformed with their employment contracts (be they implicit or explicit). Over time, businesses discovered that hierarchies were most efficient if subordinates pursuing similar tasks were grouped under a single supervisor. This *functional* approach to structuring tended, however, to separate those whose tasks were most interdependent and were thus in most need of coordination.

The potential problem that this separation created was overcome through the elaboration of standard operating procedures (SOPs). Now, this functional model is being torn down through the process of re-engineering, which reverses the traditional privileging of control over coordination by reorganizing the business around chains of process interdependence, thus privileging coordination over control. Re-engineering is a stepping stone to knowledge competition.

Knowledge competition, depending as it does on the creation of valuable *new* knowledge, rather than on the efficient application of *existing* knowledge, is characterized by change too rapid to permit the effective development and enforcement of SOP. Rather, coordination in the knowledge competitor will be achieved by "marketizing" the organization. Each participant becomes an "intrapreneur"—an internal supplier to internal and external customers. Intrapreneurs' rewards will be tied to the satisfaction of "their" customers.

Effective "intrapreneurs" will possess the following skills:

- Undue competencies valuable within the internal market that constitutes the "marketized" organization.

- The ability to describe their unique competencies effectively yet accurately (since internal markets have effective communication systems and "memories").
- The ability to differentiate their competencies from those of alternative service providers, which implies a well-developed and current knowledge of *all of their* competencies available through the internal market (since every intrapreneur is also a customer, such knowledge has a double benefit).

The market mechanism alone is insufficient to ensure the most efficient coordination between participants in a business; some form of hierarchical overlay still will inevitably emerge. This hierarchy will definitely not be a management hierarchy, however. Management is an organizational feature unique to asset-centered businesses and is wholly inappropriate in the knowledge-centered competitor. Status within the knowledge competitor will probably be based on two abilities: the ability to teach and the ability to judge or arbitrate.

Since the knowledge competitor competes by creating new, valuable, inimitable knowledge, and since the process of creating new knowledge is called *learning,* it makes sense that the knowledge competitor will contain teachers—not transmitters of that which is already known, but those able to show others how to pursue new knowledge effectively. A typical career path in the knowledge competitor could well be: learn how to learn → learn → learn how to teach → teach → teach how to learn → teach how to teach. According to this career path, the most senior members of the business would be those who teach how to teach, which in this context means those who create new leaders.

It is argued that unlike entrepreneurs, intrapreneurs will be paid not in freely tradeable money, but in "scrip." This will increase the interdependence of intrapreneurs beyond the level typical of the traditional market (which is the whole point of the issuance of scrip in place of money). This heightened level of interdependence will necessitate that judges or arbitrators resolve the disputes that will inevitably arise among participants.

To sum up, the knowledge competitor will break down hierarchical structures and abandon standard operating procedures and will "marketize" the interior of the organization and appoint teachers and judges to ensure that the market works efficiently. The global nature of the knowledge competitor makes this process very challenging, with the need to pass the knowledge across geographic and cultural boundaries.

Coordination answers the question: How should we coordinate all the participants in the value creation process?

Cooperation

In the past, such market-mediated models of coordination have encountered two problems:

1. Equitable transfer prices could not be devised efficiently due to the absence of the independent benchmarks that external sales provide.
2. Intrapreneurs acquired informational advantages over alternative sources for their services that provided them with a negotiation advantage in subsequent rounds of contracting, rendering market mediation inefficient.

These two problems compromised cooperation to such an extent that many market-mediated exchanges were superceded by exchanges mediated by an employment contract—markets were replaced by business *organizations*.

There is a third alternative, however, that differs from both the traditional market-mediating spot, recurrent spot, or contingent claims contracts and from the traditional employment contract permitting the "marketizing" of the knowledge competitor. This third contractual form is distinguished by the issuance of *scrip* (whose value is tied to the overall value or performance of the business) in place of cash. The purpose of issuing scrip instead of money is that uncooperative acts, such as capitalizing on first-mover advantages in subsequent contract negotiations, become somewhat self-defeating since they undermine the value of the scrip in which noncooperative participants are paid.

One remaining problem with this means of achieving cooperation is that as the organization increases in size, a potential "free rider" problem can still arise—participants perceive that the performance of the organization will not be significantly impacted by their own uncooperative behaviors. The obvious solution to this problem is to minimize the size of the organization. This obvious solution is complicated, however, by the unique economics of knowledge competition that oblige the successful competitor to amortize his or her "up-front" knowledge development costs over the largest revenue base possible. The solution lies in the aggressive de-integration of all activities that can be excluded from the direct control of the business (the conditions for exclusion can be derived from *scope*)—or, outsourcing.

Just as the centrally planned economies of the Communist bloc have surrendered to market-based economies, so, too, are centrally planned corporate bureaucracies being obsolesced by coordinating mechanisms resembling markets which have been made possible by new means for achieving cooperation (i.e., measuring the value added by each participant and paying participants, at least partially, with scrip).

Cooperation answers the question: How can we get all the participants in the value creation process to cooperate?

Culture

Coordination and cooperation depend on communication, but communication is ineffective unless participants share a *system of meaning* so that the actions each undertakes in response to discussions with others closely resembles the expectations of *all* the discussants—without such shared understanding, both coordination and cooperation become impossible. When understandings are widely shared, we speak of a *strong culture*. Since knowledge is always culturally embedded, under knowledge competition an organization's culture becomes the basis of its competitive advantage. This corporate culture can, at least in principle, be passed across ethnic and national cultures, and thus can be extended and realized throughout a multinational firm.

MIT organization theorist, Edgar Schein, drawing on work done by anthropologists F.R. Kluckhohn and F.L. Stoedtbeck, argued that every culture was founded on a shared set of *basic assumptions* concerning what most of us would consider philosophical issues—a group or organization's relationship with its environment(s), the nature of human activity, the nature of reality and truth, the nature of time, the nature of human nature, the nature of human relationships, and group homogeneity and conformity versus heterogeneity and diversity.[8]

These factors and a number of others can be consolidated into the following list:

- *Them/us.* What are the criteria for membership; by what criteria are "we" distinguished from "them"? How permeable are the boundaries of the organization—how easy is it to become a "we" and to return to being a "them"? What is the relationship between "them" and "us"—do "we" dominate "them" or do "they" dominate "us"? Or are we mutually interdependent? Are we stuck with a given "them" or can we prospect for different "them"? Is "them" heterogeneous or homogeneous, smooth, or clumpy?

- *Titles.* How great is the differential between the highest and lowest level in the organization; how "tall" is the hierarchy? Do we have many finely graduated status levels within the hierarchy, a few levels, or none at all? How explicit are the boundaries between levels that do exist? What is the criteria for migration between levels? Is status ascribed or achieved? Is mobility high or next to impossible?

- *Truth.* Is truth relative or absolute? Do we subscribe to a coherence model of truth or to a correspondence model? How is truth discovered: is truth whatever the most powerful members of the culture say it is—"might makes right"? Is truth what the "experts" say it is? Is truth what we all agree it is? Is truth the result of scientific experimentation? Is truth is the result of logical deduction; or, finally, does truth result from the "force of the better argument"?

- *Teleology.* Is there a reason for our existence? If so, what is it? Do we all agree on this reason; what is the degree of consensus? How compelling is the reason?

- *Time.* When is it appropriate to focus on the part? When should we be future oriented? When should we anchor ourselves in the present? Is time linear, curved, or cyclical? Is time continuous or discontinuous? Do we segment time? If so, how finely? What is our time "horizon"; what do we define as long-term and short-term?

The contribution of Schein's assertion that all cultures either explicitly or implicitly make assumptions along each of the dimensions just described is that it justifies the claim made by many that culture is massively inertial. Since many of the questions just posed would be identified by most of us as philosophical in nature, and since most of us are not practicing philosophers, once a set of assumptions is adopted it is difficult to change because we are either oblivious to the choices we have made or we feel we lack the competence to change them. It is the philosophical nature of the basic assumptions that underpin any culture that causes culture to be so massively inertial, a characteristic of culture whose implications will be addressed at length under *Detractors*.

We know from anthropologists that a loose isomorphism exists between *capabilities* and *culture* such that many cultural elements will depend on the unique or distinctive *capabilities* a business develops and vice versa. Other cultural assumptions, however, may become common to all knowledge competitors because they facilitate the creation of new knowledge and because they are consistent with the values of the larger societies by which the participants in knowledge competition are primarily socialized.

Culture answers the question: What do all the participants in the value creation process need to "know" to communicate effectively with one another?

Colleagues

To recap the argument so far: the objective of strategy is to leverage a business' accumulated capabilities; capabilities are predicated upon the master of specific knowledge domains, both distinctive and universal: knowledge domains must be supported by a shared set or web of beliefs—a culture; and in order to realize value from a set of capabilities, congruence between the actions of one individual and another must be achieved, and congruence between individual participants' actions and the business' aspirations must also be achieved. These are the problems of coordination and cooperation, both of which depend on a strong web of shared meanings—a strong culture. To achieve a strong culture, participants must be shared into the culture; they must be transformed from participants into *colleagues*.

To create *colleagues,* follow these steps:

- *Interrogation.* Successful businesses have strong cultures due to the logic articulated above. In order to achieve a strong culture, the business must socialize new entrants into the culture. Socialization can be a costly and time-consuming process. These costs can be reduced, however, by selecting those who are already either partially socialized into the particular culture or who would be easy to socialize into the culture. Such individuals can be identified through an intensive interview process prior to hiring—an *interrogation.* However, this begs the question: Why would an applicant submit to the necessary *interrogation?* The answer is that most potential participants in a business would prefer to participate in a successful business than an unsuccessful business, and a successful business depends upon a successful culture that can be partially achieved through the selection process. Thus, potential participants should understand the necessity of a thorough interview prior to the offer of employment.

- *Indoctrination, instruction, and inspiration.* Even those open to and possibly even already partially socialized into the culture of the organization will require further socialization—*indoctrination.* With the stress in selection placed on fit between the potential participant and the organizational culture, a trade-off must necessarily occur—the business cannot simultaneously select for technical skills with the same determination that they may have in the past. This implies that they will then have to *Instruct* recruits, selected on the basis of cultural fit, in the necessary technical skills required by the business. *Indoctrination* and *Instruction* will ensure that the participant possess the ability to perform in the manner hoped for; they will not, however, ensure that the participant possesses the motivation to perform. And, since performance is a multiplicative function of ability and motivation, an enormous investment in enhancing ability will be negated if motivation is ignored. Studies of motivation demonstrate that money is a "hygiene"—its presence is not an effective cause of participant satisfaction; its absence, however, is an effective cause of dissatisfaction. High levels of satisfaction, levels that ensure consummate levels of task performance rather than merely perfunctory performance, depend on other motivators. Thus, to achieve consummate performance from participants, participants must be *inspired*. They must be provided with reasons for performance that enrich the meaning they attach to their own lives.

- *Information.* Once participants have been socialized into the culture, provided with the necessary technical skills, and motivated to convert their ability into performance, they need to be told how they are doing-they need to be *informed*. The feedback provided to participants needs to be timely, so that the actions and the feedback are strongly cognitively associated—the faster the feedback, the better. The feedback also needs to be unambiguous so that the participant can easily deduce the implications for subsequent behavior; be focused on the few most important performance dimensions; and be related to variables over which the participant feels he or she exerts control; otherwise, the situation will be perceived as inequitable.

- *Inspection.* Once participants have been given the ability and motivation to perform and the information about how they are performing, they must be *inspected* to ensure they are using the *information* to further enhance performance. The *inspection* must also be perceived as fair and unbiased if the rewards tied to the *inspection* are to produce increased or at least sustained performance levels. If the *inspection* is perceived by participants to be unfair, he or she will channel his or her energies into revising the inspection procedures rather than into obtaining better results.

- *Involvement and inclusion.* As the participant accrues experience in the business, it is appropriate to capitalize on that experience by involving him or her in increasingly important decisions that have payoffs that are broader in their organizational scope and extend over longer time periods. Long tenure in a successful organization should ensure that the participant has the ability to contribute to such decisions but it may not necessarily ensure participants' motivation to get the decision right. To motivate participants to get a decision with such broad and far-reaching ramifications requires that the rewards the participant receives also be broad and far-reaching. The only rewards that meet such criteria are vested stock options. Vesting stock ownership in long-tenured participants—*inclusion*—ensures congruence between those participants' decisions and the business' primary goal of maximizing stockholder wealth.

If each of these steps is completed successfully, the business will comprise a group of colleagues rather than an atomized assembly of individual contributors.

Colleagues answers the question: How can we select and socialize participants so that they will come to "know" the same things?

Capital Structure

The ideal capital structure of the knowledge competitor would achieve the following:

- Motivate participants to pursue new knowledge that enhances the long-term competitiveness and hence the value of the overall business.
- Encourage other contributors to the value chain(s) in which the business participates to share valuable knowledge that they have acquired.
- Permit the business to access outside capital without compromising the long-term perspective that necessarily characterizes competition based on learning.
- Realize the profits, which currently accrue to investment banks, that result from periodic revisions in the capital structure made in response to changes both in the risk/return/liquidity preferences of investors and in the projected risk and anticipated returns of the business.

A capital structure satisfying each of these conditions would:

- Convert participants' scrip into stock placed in pension plans, thus tying the value of scrip to the long-term (i.e., when the participant retires) value of the overall business.
- Achieve a level of cross-ownership of stock with other important members of the value chains) sufficient to create the perception of common interest but low enough to prevent the alienation of alternative suppliers or customers.

- Extract from institutional investors (whose actuarial calculations of future cash needs now obviate the need for the elevated levels of liquidity demanded when capital markets were instituted) long-term commitments not to trade stock unless prespecified performance criteria fail to be met, offering in return open access to internal decision making and, due to the absence of pressure for short-term returns, on average, higher long-term performance.
- Such a capital structure would sufficiently concentrate owner-ship so that cooperation with owners would be essential to any debt restructuring, a condition currently absent, thus permitting the unilateral restructuring of businesses by external investors, principally investment banks.

Capital structure answers the question: What should our capital structure be?

Detractors: What *Internal* Forces Could Prevent Us from Realizing Our Ideal Design?

By working through the 15 considerations just described, anyone familiar with the model can determine the ideal strategy and design for the environmental niche their business occupies. This is only half of the strategy formation challenge. Businesses compete in the world of *reality,* not in some *ideal* competitive space similar to that outlined earlier. Acknowledging this, the next two concerns address the business' *actual propensity* to change and the strategic options available to it given both its *ideal configuration* and the *current position* of the business, as well as the *positions* of its *relevant rivals.*

Businesses often fail to converge toward the ideal strategy for the competitive niche they occupy. Such failure to achieve strategic convergence is usually due to factors both *internal* and external to the organization. Once the strategically appropriate ideal has been chosen, the next steps are to analyze and overcome those internal and external factors that often sabotage strategic change initiatives.

The fourth step—*detractors*—considers the internal factors which include the following elements:

Ignorance

The external circumstances upon which strategies are predicated change, and even when they do not, they are often ambiguous. This ambiguity can be exploited by different interest groups to justify and legitimate alternative courses of action (including, especially, preservation of the status quo).

Overcoming ignorance of the strategic realities governing the strategic options open to a business undermines internal opposition and accelerates convergence toward the most appropriate strategic direction. Ignorance is avoided when all important decision makers are able to determine for themselves, or at least able to appreciate when told by others, the best strategic direction for the business and, relatedly, likely future environmental developments. To achieve this, participants require an all-encompassing model of strategic decision making such as has been attempted here.

Inertia

Implemented strategy produces capabilities. Capabilities shape culture. Cultures converge, over time, into logically coherent "paradigms." Because they are logically interlocked, because they determine *what* is perceived and *how* it is interpreted, because they are not only unquestioned but often *unquestionable,* and because they have *succeeded in the past,* paradigms *resist change.* Shifting paradigms, arguably, constitute the toughest challenge facing leaders of change. To deal with shifting paradigms is, therefore, a key source of competitive advantage. A business suffering from cultural inertia becomes predictable to its rivals, who, using a sort of cultural Aikido can turn its rival's cultural inertia against it and thus gain advantage in the marketplace at the rival's expense.

To avoid becoming a victim of cultural Aikido, participants in a business must become ironic in the sense in which philosopher Richard Rorty uses the term—at the same time they must stand up for their basic assumptions and, privately, continually question and modify those beliefs. Only through constant questioning and by a willingness to abandon beliefs that are no longer appropriate (in a moral and aesthetic sense as well as in a technical sense) will the business avoid cultural inertia.

Interests

It is a long way from the conundrum of inertia to the calculus of interests. Still, divergent interests within a business can block change as effectively as inertia. Changes that are good for a business may not be good for all its members. Often, the members most resistant to change are senior managers who:

- Have the most to lose.
- Possess the greatest emotional investment in past courses of action.
- Have enjoyed the greatest success under the old "regime."
- Can muster the most resources to fight change.

Conflicting interests can be overcome, but before they can be dealt with, they must first be identified.

The ideal design outlined in the previous section minimizes the threat from divergent interests in a variety of ways.

- Those who survive as participants in a knowledge competitor are predisposed to learning and are thus, by definition, less likely to be committed to fixed positions and outlooks.
- By marketizing the organization, a static concentration of power is avoided. Instead, power migrates continuously toward the most effective intrapreneurs—those most capable of satisfying important internal and external customers. Marketizing also eliminates the possibility that individuals will identify with parochial functional specialties or other subdivisions within the organization.
- By exchanging scrip for stock that is placed in participants' pension plans, the long-term interests of the entire organization are welded to the personal interests of participants, ameliorating the tendency to pursue self-interest at the expense of the long-term interests of the business as a whole.

Insufficient Resources

Inertia addresses the difficulty of arresting the articulation of past capabilities. It requires prodigious energy to arrest organized action, and similar energy to initiate action. Developing new capabilities often requires enormous capital investments, but of far greater importance is the investment of time and energy demanded of senior managers.

The ideal design presented in the previous section addresses the problem of insufficient resources in two ways.

1. It facilitates the long-term, informed involvement of highly capitalized institutional investors, thus ensuring access to large
   amounts of capital.
2. It promotes the autonomy of all participants, thus freeing those
   leaders who emerge to focus their attention on the implementation of new initiatives rather than on continuing to concentrate
   on the day-today running of existing operations.

Inopportune Timing

A well-known finance professor once said that there are no bad *decisions,* just bad *timing.* This may be an overstatement; still, inoppor-
tune timing is a major predictor of strategic failure. Ignorance and
ambiguity lead to a herd instinct—competitors all make the same
strategic moves at the same time. This is contrary to the pursuit of
distinction, which, it has been argued in a previous section, is fundamental to any contest whose outcome rests, as a business' does, on the
determinations of external judges.

This model is intended to give strategic decision makers the confidence they need to "zig" even as their rivals "zag." Boom times are
the wrong times to implement strategy because:

- Managers and workers, alike, are too busy.
- Labor markets are tight.
- Assets are overpriced.

Implement strategy during a bust when:

- Assets are cheap.
- Competitors lay off good people.
- Participants can spare the time to relax, recharge, retrain, relearn,
  repair, rebuild, reflect, and reassess their situation—in other
  words, when they have time to "do" strategy.

By considering all the detractors, ranging from the emotional to
the monetary, participants can muster the courage required to pursue
the kind of strategic contrarianism advocated here as the basis of sustainable distinction.

Direction: What External Forces Could Prevent Us from Realizing Our Ideal Design?

Internal factors are not the only impediments to convergence upon an ideal strategy; competitors also exert considerable influence over the strategic *Direction* a business is able to pursue. *Direction,* then, is predicated primarily on the strategic position of a business *relative to its competitors*—an *external* factor.

Once the "ideal" organizational configuration has been identified, a business in a given competitive arena can see how it measures up, before determining the best strategic direction. The options include:

Aim for the Ideal

The preferred strategic option for business is usually to aim straight for the ideal strategy as determined by the preceding steps. Choice of strategic direction, however, must moderate the *desirability* of the destination with the *probability* of its attainment. A variety of factors will determine this probability, prime among them being the positions and strategic trajectories of each competitor relative to the identified ideal. If rivals are currently closer to the ideal or are converging toward it faster, the attractiveness of that ideal may collapse as converging rivals battle for the same position.

Approximate

Each competitor has an interest in preventing others from achieving the ideal strategic position. Thus, it may simply not be possible for some competitors to assemble all the capabilities necessary to achieve their ideal. In this instance, a business may choose to settle for an approximation to the ideal. How satisfactory this choice is will depend on the extent of the industry's munificence.[9]

By being more mobile, the design presented earlier may permit a business to settle for an approximation to the ideal while it searches for ways either to converge closer to the absolute ideal or to establish a new one through a process of alteration.

Alter

If the business cannot move to the ideal strategic position, perhaps the ideal can be moved "closer" to the business. This is a powerful strategic option since it simultaneously improves a business's competitive position while undermining its rivals' positions. The danger here is that by altering the ideal, a business may sabotage overall industry attractiveness, thus exchanging a short-term gain in competitive advantage for a long-term diminution in performance. Even if it does entail undermining the attractiveness of the industry, this strategy may still be sensible for an individual business so long as it understands that it is profiting at the expense of the industry. This knowledge is critical since without it the business may erode its past profits by remaining in that area of the business too long.

Ally

Knowledge-centered competition and the globalization it engenders, increases competitive intensity by increasing the number of competitors in each domestic market. A silver lining of this development is the enlarged selection of potential strategic alliance partners created. If it is not possible to achieve the ideal alone, it may be possible to do so using strategic alliances, but it is necessary to know when, how, and what kind of strategic alliances to use.

The ideal design described above facilitates alliances in the following ways:

- The design encourages the self-definition of a business on the basis of capabilities instead of assets. Using the language of capabilities facilitates partner selection, which is predicated on the need for *complementary capabilities*. However, complementary capabilities implies *incongruent cultures.*
- The ideal design ameliorates the problems cultural incongruence may otherwise cause, because a knowledge competitor's culture (at least as prescribed above) is founded on the concept of utility rather than truth and on an ironic and reflective posture toward its own cultural assumptions. This perspective prevents a "we're right; therefore, you must be wrong" posture toward partners.

Abandon

Most emerging "global champions" were once "domestic champions." Success in their former, very different, competitive arena was largely dependent on preferential access to government and domestic capital markets. Since each of these advantages was coterminous with national boundaries, domestic champions tended to have truncated geographic *scope,* for which they compensated with inordinately diversified *selection.* Divestiture is endemic to the global transition—businesses are sloughing off ventures in which they can no longer compete in order that they may concentrate upon those in which they can. Divestiture seems simple, but, it is not. Still, success demands that the business abandon those endeavors in which the business deems a defensible competitive position impossible to sustain.

This model should aid abandonment by providing theoretical justification for focusing the business around as few knowledges, and hence processes, as possible. The model attempts to reinforce the view that the successful business should be in a continual state of flux, integrating new products or services, activities, or geographic regions and abandoning those which no longer fit with the evolving portfolio of capabilities.

Taking Up the Challenge

Now the challenge rests with the reader. This chapter has laid out a detailed framework for identifying strategic limitations and opportunities. Every business in the new economy has to operate in a state of rapid, if not constant change, adapting to the shifts in market, supplier, and competitor conditions all the time. The knowledge-based global competitor has to be able to identify the key drivers of competitiveness and then to act on them—always remembering that the terms of reference are likely to change before the previous strategy has fully played out. This is a tough environment, but one which the 5^3 model provides the guidance for the company to tackle.

Notes

1. The nature of Schumpeterian competition is succinctly captured by the following quote: "The fundamental impulse that acts and keeps the capitalist engine in motion comes from the new consumers' goods, the new methods of production or transportation, the new markets, the new forms of industrial organization that capitalist enterprise creates." (Joseph Schumpeter, *Capitalism, Socialism, and Democracy,* London: Unwin Paperbacks, 1987, p. 83. First published 1943.)

2. A knowledge domain can, in turn, be defined as a mutually reinforcing set, or web, of beliefs. The idea that it is not possible to hold one belief without holding many others is attributable to the great twentieth-century philosopher Ludwig Wittgenstein. His ideas are best captured in his last writings published under the title, *On Certainty,* and have been usefully

clarified by Harvard professor emeritus W.V. Quine (see W.V. Quine and J.S. Ullian, *The Web of Belief*). Wittgenstein's idea may be captured by the following example: We cannot "know" or believe that set of beliefs that constitute "Rocket Science" unless we "know" physics, we cannot "know" physics unless we "know" the calculus, we cannot "know" the calculus unless we know algebra, we cannot know algebra unless we know arithmetic, and we cannot know arithmetic unless we know how to count (this may explain why so few people know "Rocket Science"). The knowledge domain "Rocket Science," then, must include the belief that two succeeds one and is succeeded by three.

3. A value chain can be defined as a sequence of activities for whose combined successful performance a customer is willing to pay.

4. Davidson notes that metaphors do not have "truth values," that is, they are neither true nor false. In fact, Davidson notes that is why we use them—to break out of our current logically interrelated "webs of belief" (see Donald Davidson, "What Metaphors Mean," *Inquiries into Truth and Interpretation,* Oxford: Clarendon Press, 1984, p. 247).

5. See Michael Porter's article, "How Competitive Forces Shape Strategy," for methods of determining the power and hence attractiveness of a productive process or sequence of processes, *Harvard Business Review,* March/April 1979, pp. 137–145.

6. While in marketing, perception may be reality, for analytical reasons performance is separated from perceptions. Included under performance are only those product/service features which determine the classification of the product/service to a given product/service class.

7. Again, a distinction is drawn between this dimension and performance. Included under personal service are only those interpersonal relationships surrounding the "hand-off" of the product/service to the customer. Where the product/service being handed off is a service, the service itself would be considered in the first category.

8. See Edgar Schein, "Organizational Culture," *American Psychologist,* vols. 4–5, no. 2, pp. 109–119. This typology was developed by anthropologists F.R. Kluckhohn and F.L. Stoedtbeck (see *Variations in Value Orientations,* New York: Harper & Row, 1961).

9. Michael Porter's five forces model is an excellent diagnostic tool with which to estimate an industry's attractiveness and hence fiscal munificence. For more information, see Porter's article "How Competitive Forces Shape Strategy," *Harvard Business Review,* March/April 1979, pp. 137–145.

4

Managing Global Strategic Alliances

ANDREW C. INKPEN

Ten to fifteen years ago, international strategic alliances were a new organizational form for many firms. Most managers preferred to enter foreign markets either by exporting or establishing wholly owned subsidiaries. Alliances and joint ventures, with their inherent potential for conflict and ambiguity about the role of the parents, were generally seen as a poor third choice. But, penetrating foreign markets solely via exports proved difficult for many firms, and wholly owned subsidiaries were often slow to gain local market acceptance, and sometimes were not permitted by governments in emerging markets. Thus, reluctantly, managers began to get serious about using international alliances.

Today, strategic alliances have become a reality for most firms. The days when firms could do everything themselves are over, particularly in international business. Strategic alliances are collaborative organizational arrangements that use resources and/or governance structures from more than one existing organization. This definition includes a broad range of organizational forms, including equity joint ventures, licensing arrangements, and shared product development projects, among others. Thus, global strategic alliances are the relatively enduring interfirm cooperative arrangements that utilize resources from autonomous organizations based in two or more countries.[1]

A variety of strategic objectives have been suggested to explain firms' motives for the formation of international alliances, including risk reduction, economies of scale, the reduction of competitive uncertainty, and a search for legitimacy.[2] A firm that enters a foreign market for the first time is likely to use a joint venture, as is the foreign firm that seeks to obtain access to resources controlled by local firms. In both situations, alliances are often chosen because the alternatives of replicating a complete operation via full acquisition or greenfield investment are too costly and because the local partner controls resources that are deemed useful to the foreign partner. An alliance may be designed to market a product in a local market or it may involve the sourcing of materials, components, or technology, possibly for use in the foreign partner's home market.

Alliances also provide firms with a unique opportunity to leverage their strengths with the help of partners. In essence, alliances provide firms with a window on their partners' capabilities. Through this window, alliances create the potential for firms to acquire knowledge associated with partner skills and capabilities.[3]

Despite the rapid increase in the number of alliances being formed, many firms are plagued by underperforming alliances. The objective of this chapter is to show that although there is no single best way to manage an alliance, there are common principles that should contribute to alliance success. Overall, the purpose is to demystify the alliance management process and help managers make their alliances work better.

The Age of Alliance Capitalism

If this is the age of "alliance capitalism," as some writers have argued, alliances will undoubtedly become more important as a tool of competitive strategy. A driving force behind this trend is the realization by many firms that self-sufficiency is becoming increasingly difficult in a business environment that demands strategic focus, flexibility, and innovation. Nevertheless, many strategic alliances fail to achieve their potential and alliance failure rates remain high, frustrating the efforts of many firms to capitalize on cooperative strategies. Consider the following examples of recent unsuccessful partnerships, each of which was announced with a great deal of promise:

- In an effort to strengthen its telephony software skills, Motorola forms a joint venture with Northern Telecom. The joint venture is terminated 18 months later amid reports of internal conflicts and shouting matches over the lack of cooperation between the partners.
- Bell Atlantic and Olivetti form a joint venture to compete with Italy's state-owned telecom firm. Less than two years later, the venture is ended after months of disagreements between the partners, with Olivetti buying the Italian telecom firm.

In contrast to the many examples of poorly performing alliances, strategic alliances are manageable and should not be viewed as high risk, last resort options. In this chapter, various key factors that support successful alliance formation and management are examined.

The Objective of Successful Alliances: Mutual Value Creation

Underlying every alliance formation is an expectation of value creation. Thus, a question facing prospective alliance partners is: Will the partners adopt a mutual value creation perspective in which both sides respect and support their counterpart's collaborative objectives? Or, will the partners view collaboration as a means to achieving independent objectives in a zero-sum game atmosphere? Because alliance partners rarely have the same strategic objectives, their views of value creation will likely be asymmetric. However, this need not be a significant issue as long as the partners both understand their partner's objectives. One study found that partner strategic similarity was not related to alliance performance.[4] It is also important to emphasize that alliance longevity should not be equated with alliance value creation. Many firms view alliances as intentionally temporary, recognizing that these ventures will not last indefinitely. If alliance termination is an orderly and mutually planned event, the alliance may well be evaluated as extremely successful. An alliance that is prematurely terminated may also be evaluated as successful, depending on the criteria used to evaluate performance. Most firms, however, form alliances with expectations of a long-term relationship and do not have specific timetables for termination.

Given that partner interdependence is required to make alliances function, firms should seek to create mutual value with their potential partners, rather than trying only to enlarge individual benefits. This means that alliance negotiators must walk a fine line between strong negotiating tactics and the reality that if the negotiation is successful, the party across the table becomes a partner, possibly for many years. In the negotiation process, a firm must seek to maximize its own benefits. But, over the life of the alliance, how a partner firm benefits depends on the alliance value jointly created. Thus, alliance negotiations will not only be a process of value exchange for the two sides, but a process of value creation. The partners may have nothing to share if they do not create value jointly.

Moreover, the individual negotiators sitting across the table could find themselves working side-by-side in a new alliance organization. It is not unusual for managers on the negotiating teams to find themselves in positions such as joint venture president or general manager. In the absence of a mutual value creation perspective during the negotiation, there is a much higher probability that openness and trust will be lacking in the negotiation. Consider the following example where one firm was unwilling to reveal its true intent, leading to questions about hidden agendas and ulterior motives:

> We formed an alliance with Firm X. They told us that their evaluation of the alliance would be 30% based on the financial results of the alliance and 70% from elsewhere. The problem was that they did not want to talk about the 70%. We assumed that they were interested in getting into the telecommunications industry and that this was critical in linking up with us. We also assumed that they wanted to sell us their products. However, we never knew for sure.

For an alliance to be successful, it cannot be one-sided. All parties need an incentive to form, and remain in, the alliance. Although some argue that mutual value creation is an inappropriate focus given the often transitional nature of alliances, many alliance managers indicate that a focus solely on "what's in it for me" will not lead to successful collaboration. It may lead to unstable relationships that are value-creating for one partner and not the other. Thus, assuming that collaboration is viewed as more than a short-term means of filling gaps in competencies, mutual value creation should be the objective from all parties.

This is the perspective adopted by Warner-Lambert Company in its many strategic alliances. A major alliance with Pfizer Pharmaceuticals, formed in 1996 to jointly market a new drug developed by Warner-Lambert, is a good example. The director of strategic alliances for Warner-Lambert's pharmaceutical business described the Pfizer alliance:

> We live by the concept of co-destiny. We believe that our destinies are intertwined, so what is good for our business ally is good for us.

Note that this perspective also means ensuring that concessions in negotiating do not tilt the balance in favor of the partner. At the outset of the alliance, levels of bargaining power commensurate with ownership and resource contribution should be the objective. Over time, as partners' strategic missions, expectations, loyalties, and resource mixes change, the balance of bargaining power in the alliance will inevitably shift. Learning by one partner can lead to a shift in bargaining power and eventual alliance instability.[5] In the case of international joint ventures, as the foreign partner's local knowledge increases, the foreign partner's dependence on the local partner decreases, leading to a shift in bargaining power and greater likelihood of venture instability. When the foreign partner's alliance need dissipates because local knowledge has been acquired, the foreign partner may view a JV as unnecessary. In effect, over time the unique domain of the local partner shifts from being complementary to the foreign partner to being undistinguished.[6]

The Importance of Fit between the Partners

A strong fit between the partners is critical for alliance success. However, there is a tendency to view fit as primarily a strategic issue and to focus analysis on strategic questions. Clearly, strategic fit is driving the alliance formation. But, *strategic* fit in the absence of *organizational* fit is a recipe for failure. Many, if not most, alliances fail in the implementation where people make or break a deal. Unfortunately, many organizations wait until after the deal is struck to address organizational issues.

What does organizational fit mean? Three questions shape the nature of the required fit:

1. How extensively will the partners need to cooperate?
2. How effectively will firms be able to cooperate?
3. Can the partner systems and cultures be integrated?

Answering these questions requires an understanding of the partner firm(s), its culture, and the initial interfirm relationship that exists at the time of the alliance formation. When two firms decide to initiate alliance discussions, negotiations will be shaped by the initial relationship that exists between the firms. Potential partners will often be uncertain about working together, particularly if they have not previously worked together. On the other hand, new alliances that start with an existing stock of "relationship assets" may begin with a honeymoon period that effectively buffers the firm from early dissolution. Previous cooperative ties between alliance partners can generate an initial base of interpartner trust and also shape the form of subsequent alliances. If firms have worked together in the past, they should have basic understandings about each other's skills, capabilities, and willingness to follow through on promises.

It is possible that experienced partners can forgo the relationship building processes that will be necessary for partners working together for the first time. However, our research has shown that prior experience between partners is not necessarily a predictor of alliance success. Although a firm may have worked with its partner for many years in non-alliance relationships, the formation of an alliance often creates a new degree of intimacy between the partners. A prior partner relationship may influence the structure of the relationship (e.g., the equity split) and smooth the start-up period. New alliance managerial roles can be so different from those of prior relationships that the carryover of prior knowledge and its impact on the alliance management experience is limited. Thus, firms must ensure that the reality of initial partner relationships is clearly established and understood prior to negotiations.

Ideally, firms will be able to enter the negotiation process with substantive knowledge about their potential partners, including what the other party is seeking through negotiating an alliance, the party's strengths and weaknesses, the party's reputation and experience with alliances ventures, and so on. Detailed knowledge about the potential partner can help in planning the negotiation strategy and increase the probability of collaborative success. Knowledge about the partner can also be a source of bargaining power in the negotiation process.

A key reason for alliance failures is lack of understanding about partner objectives and motives. When firms think they understand their partners and do not, alliance failure will often be the result. This was the result in the following example, described by an alliance manager:

> Both partners were naive about the other partner's capabilities and about the nature of the joint venture. The American partner did not grasp the implications of the changing industry structure and how that would impact the joint venture performance. They did not appreciate the Japanese philosophy. The Japanese partner expected a much leaner partner, one who was prepared to work hard on the joint venture's behalf. They sensed that management in the American partner was not committed to the same things they were.

In the next section, critical issues associated with organizational fit are considered.

Determining Organizational Fit

Assess organizational climate similarity prior to alliance formation. Some possible steps firms can take to determine organizational climate similarity prior to alliance formation include:

- Build in "getting-to-know-you" time in the alliance development process. This may slow down the formation process but it will be worth it.
- To form an equity joint venture requires substantial commitment between the partners. Consider a less "intimate" alliance relationship before forming the joint venture.
- Ensure that personnel from different levels and functions in the partner organizations have an opportunity to interact during the negotiation phase.

■ Make organizational fit an explicit outcome of the alliance development process.

Ensure that there is organizational fit at multiple levels within the two (or more) companies that are partnering. Here is an example involving a Canadian firm and a U.S. Fortune 500 company. In this alliance, there was good strategic fit and good organizational fit at the CEO level only. In moving between the top management teams:

■ The executives from the U.S. company perceived the small-company Canadian managers to be "country-cousins" and relatively unsophisticated.
■ The small-company people felt the Fortune 500 company people were "specialized bureaucrats" who didn't really appreciate how to actually build and operate a business from the ground up. They felt they were spoiled by all the resources available.

When the two CEOs (who were both ready to walk down the aisle) were pushed to talk candidly with their respective senior management teams, both came to realize that there was mutual disrespect for their counterparts. Since these were the people who would be responsible for implementing any alliance, it was evident that this lack of organizational fit would be an insurmountable barrier.

Determine whether a geocentric attitude has been adopted by both partners. The key point here is that both partners enter the alliance discussions on organizational design with open minds. Neither should be slavishly fixated on a my-way-or-the-highway mentality about how the alliance should be organized. Both should be willing to acknowledge and act upon the idea that the alliance should potentially be organized in certain ways (i.e., a hybrid) that are not identical to how either parent currently operates.

Assess senior management commitment up front. In looking at key reasons for the success of Toppan Moore (a $1 billion, 27-year, Canadian-Japanese joint venture in Japan) and other long-lasting alliances, one constant is the commitment by senior executives.[7] Jim Saunders, a senior executive of Moore Business Forms, was willing to commit to a one-week trip, two times a year, for 15 consecutive years to make sure things stayed on track. Significantly, his Japanese partner was willing to do the same thing. Neither delegated this task away, even when their other responsibilities grew. The Japanese president of Toppan Moore described the evolution of Toppan Moore:

> So far, Toppan Moore has enjoyed immense success. This is not the norm for many joint ventures in Japan. One of the reasons is that Moore provided good circumstances for the development of the company. Moore is a very caring parent. They made a sincere effort to launch the company. They gave us a lot of autonomy. They didn't interfere. We were able to adopt certain managerial methods and arrange them to fit with Japanese business customs. Moore looks at Toppan Moore as a young company, and they have a long-term view of its growth. For instance, Moore has never asked us to have a detailed strategic plan. We make decisions on personnel, investment, and fund raising without detailed consultation. We are able to manage freely, and we have adopted many Japanese principles, such as a long-term focus, interdependence among companies, business diversification, and a management style based on loyalty and human feeling. Toppan Moore is very much a traditional Japanese company.[8]

Can we even roughly assess the "propensity to commit" by senior management prior to alliance formation? It is possible. Several simple scenario-like questions at the negotiations stage can give a fairly good idea whether an executive feels commitment is necessary and possible. A related measure is the need to assess whether the people negotiating the alliance are job-hoppers. Will they likely be around to provide constancy? Constancy in the partner managers assigned to oversee the alliance is a key factor in building organizational fit.

Overcoming a Bad Fit

The best strategic fit is unlikely to compensate for a poor organizational fit because there is a causal linkage from organizational fit to alliance performance. Poor fit will lead to poor performance because when the partners cannot work together, it is unlikely that a successful entity can be created. Nevertheless, there are cases of financially successful alliances in which there is poor organizational fit. The alliance between Northwest and KLM is a case where the partners have publicly feuded but neither is willing to end the relationship because of the substantial profits it generates. This is an exception and one that rarely occurs.

Companies that have formed alliances and then find themselves in conflict with their partners can take various actions:

- Consider a change in alliance management. I have observed many alliances where managerial selection mistakes are a key cause of poor organizational fit.
- Reassess the objectives for the alliances and establish common expectations about financial performance (making money can help smooth a lot of problems).
- Increase the communication between the partners at senior levels. This can have an important signaling effect on alliance operating managers.
- Reassess the allocation of alliance managerial responsibilities; taking on more or less responsibility may help the partners achieve their objectives.

Understanding Alliance Risk

Beyond the obvious risk of time and energies wasted in the event of alliance failure, forming an alliance involves several different types of risk. One risk involves the investment in relation-specific assets. When an alliance is formed, the partners must invest in various assets to create the new business. The risk is that some of the assets, such as plant and equipment and human assets, may have limited alternative uses in the event of alliance termination. For example, the Japanese automakers Subaru and Isuzu have a plant in Indiana to jointly manufacture automobiles. The plant is unusual in that it is really two assembly lines under one roof with only a few shared facilities, such as the paint shop. In the event that one partner seeks to leave the relationship, it is unlikely that another automaker would be willing to invest in this arrangement. Thus, both partners have made relation-specific investments that have limited value outside the alliance.

A second, and perhaps much more critical type of risk is competitive risk associated with loss of technology and markets. The practice of partnering with competitors is becoming commonplace. GE partners with Pratt & Whitney to build aircraft engines; General Motors jointly builds cars with Toyota; and Warner Lambert and Pfizer jointly market pharmaceutical products. Alliances between direct competitors, those with significant operational overlaps, are less likely to endure.[9] The rationale is intuitive: just because rivals collaborate does not mean they cease to be rivals. When partners are also competitors, the potential for conflict is exacerbated and the partners must ensure that sensitive information is not passed on to competitors.

Firms that are not competitors when an alliance is formed may become competitors if it is terminated. In a study of more than 40 Japanese-American joint ventures in the automotive sector, most of the Japanese firms were entering the U.S. market for the first time.[10] About one-third of the joint ventures were terminated after 2 to 3 years, with the Japanese partner acquiring the business in all but one case. The result? The American firms' former partners were now competitors, the American firms had helped their competitors get established, and the Japanese firms were intent on establishing a long-term presence in the U.S. market.[11]

A third type of risk involves the intangible assets of firm reputation and image. To exploit the brand equity of the Virgin Brand, Richard Branson has formed numerous alliances in businesses such as cosmetics, soft drinks, railways, and retailing. His typical alliance strategy is to contribute the brand and public relations expertise and rely on other firms to put up the capital. If these or other businesses fail because of partner mismanagement, there is the risk that the brand may become associated with failure.

As another example, assume that a U.S. consumer goods firm is interested in entering the China market. A local Chinese partner is found and a joint venture is formed to manufacture and market the U.S. firm's brand in China. The U.S. firm has now risked its brand equity in forming a joint venture. Nonperformance by the Chinese partner could irreparably damage the firm's reputation in China and perhaps elsewhere. On the other hand, the Chinese firm also risks its reputation. In some cases, Chinese firms have abandoned their local brands to gain access to foreign technology and management, only to see the joint venture fail, local brand awareness eroded, and no rights to the partner's foreign brand. In this situation, a local Chinese firm must ensure that the foreign brand is viable and can be established in the local market. As well, the local firm must recognize and antici-pate that introducing a foreign brand may have a negative impact on the local brand.

There are two additional sources of risk. When a firm forms a close relationship with another firm, it may disrupt a pre-existing in-terfirm relationship. For example, Firm X may be a customer of Firm Y. Firm Z is a competitor to Firm X. If Firm Y forms an alliance with Firm Z, Firm X may decide that, for competitive reasons, it can no longer buy from Firm Y. Finally, there is the risk of joint liability that may be created when a firm enters into an alliance. For example, if Firm A forms an alliance with Firm B and Firm B contributes a plant site that subsequently is determined to have major environmental problems, Firm A may be jointly liable for the problems and ultimate solution.

The challenge for firms in advance of alliance negotiation and startup is to determine the level of investment and associated safe-guards necessary to create a viable operating entity. At this point, relation-specific assets represent a risky decision supported by expec-tations that the present value of discounted future payments from the alliance will exceed their costs. The more likely one partner is to be-have opportunistically, the greater will be the other partner's reluc-tance to make relation-specific investments. An unwillingness to determine risk prior to negotiating contributed to the following sit-uation described by an alliance manager:

> Every single issue with our partners involves a protracted negotiation. If we say ten, they will say five. It doesn't matter if the issue is significant or not. If we say let's do "x" because "x" makes sense, they will chal-lenge us. They will even sign off on an issue and then want to renegoti-ate. Or, they will keep delaying until it is too late to do what we want to do and we have to do it their way. Even minor decisions require senior management approval. There is a tremendous unwillingness for anybody in our partner to accept risk.

Choosing Alliance Managers

In a recent *Harvard Business Review* article, John Browne, CEO of British Petroleum, stated that "you never build a relationship be-tween your organization and a company. . . . You build it between individuals."[12] This is a critical point and one that often gets overlooked, particularly by large firms involved in forming, managing, and terminating multiple ventures. Managers often lose sight of the reality that partner trust and forbearance are directly linked to the strength of interpersonal relations. In any alliance, the strength of interfirm relationships is largely a function of the relationships between individual managers who are involved in the day-to-day management of the alliance. When partners have not collaborated in the past, the possibility of untrustworthiness is heightened because relations are in their nascent stages and managers are uncertain about the skills, knowledge, and objectives of their counterparts. Without strong relationships between individuals at this stage, trust will not develop. In a worst case scenario, if enemies are created in the negotiation process, it is unlikely any cooperative agreement that emerges will be successful.

Given the importance of interpersonal relationships, the individuals who will be involved in alliance negotiations should be chosen carefully. As indicated earlier, *commitment by senior executives is critical.* Firms need to involve operational managers in the alliance formation process, beginning with initiation of potential ventures right through to formation and startup. Operational managers are managers from the firm's operational units, not from headquarters staff. Involving operations managers in the negotiations means that dealmakers and business development specialists do not drive the process. One business development manager said that his bonus was based on the number of deals completed. Suffice it to say, he had little interest in the actual outcome of the alliances he negotiated.

Who will manage the alliance? Ideally, managers involved in the formation process will also become part of the alliance management team. The managers who will actually manage the alliance and the partner relationship are in the best position to ask the tough questions early in the process. People expected to produce results when the alliance is formed are most likely to ask relevant operational and strategic questions during a negotiation. To be successful alliance managers, however, these managers must also be capable of working in a collaborative relationship with multiple bosses, high levels of ambiguity, and often, non-aligned performance objectives of the partners.

After the alliance is formed, firms are often surprised when their partners object to their choice of managers. This occurs frequently in international alliances. Sometimes the problem is with a misunderstanding of job titles, and in other cases the partners resent their lack of involvement in managerial decisions. Whatever the reason, firms must ensure that their plan for the alliance top management team is discussed during the negotiations. It is better to face the issues early rather than assigning a manager to the joint venture and then find out that your partner objects to the choice, leaving the assigned manager to wait months to determine his or her fate.

Alliance Governance and Trust

There are a variety of potentially difficult governance issues that will have to be resolved before and after an alliance begins operations. The optimal governance structure will depend on various factors, such as alliance objectives, the level of investment, technological conditions, and partner time horizons. Although an in-depth analysis of these issues is beyond the scope of this chapter, firms must recognize that the nature and form of alliance governance structures will evolve over time as the alliance strategy emerges and partners interact. What seems critical in the early stages of a negotiation may seem irrelevant after a few years of closely working together.

Ultimately, what determines alliance governance structures is the level of trust between the partners. Noncontractual safeguards are more likely when there is a high level of trust between the partners. For example, in cases of high trust, the alliance agreement can be less detailed because of the low perceived opportunism. Governance costs under conditions of distrust will be greater and procedures will be more formal, such as more detailed contract documentation, more frequent board meetings, closer scrutiny by lawyers, and more communication between partner headquarters and the alliance.

As a high level of trust develops, safeguarding procedures and monitoring costs can be reduced. For example, in new alliances between firms without any common cultural background or prior interactions, the basis for trust may be absent when the alliance is formed. In this case, the partners may have no choice but to rely extensively on contracts and monitoring. As interactions increase and attachment develops, trust may increase, at which point monitoring may no longer be necessary. When negotiating and managing alliances, managers must recognize the important role that trust plays, and will continue to play, if the alliance is to be successful. They must also recognize that as trust increases, governance will become easier and less reliant on strict contractual details. Too strong an initial focus on formal control can lead to poor managerial selection, as the following quote indicates:

> Our objective was to maintain control over the joint venture. We put our toughest, most authoritative manager into the joint venture. He was not going to lose control. He lasted about 18 months.

Negotiating and forming an alliance initiates a dynamic relationship that to be successful, will go through a series of transitions. Over time, partners and partner managers will learn about each other as the alliance becomes a viable operating entity. Successful alliances are highly evolutionary and go through a series of interactive cycles of learning, reevaluation, and readjustment.[13] Failing projects are highly inertial, with little learning by the partners. The implication is clear: as new knowledge is obtained and levels of interpartner trust shift, alliance managers must be willing to make changes in their cooperative relationship. As alliances age, previous successes, failures, and partner interactions will influence the level of trust in the alliance. With the success of an alliance, trust usually increases. Trust may also decrease over the life of the relationship. For example, when an alliance is formed, there is a subjective probability that a partner will cooperate. Experience will lead to adjustment of the probability, which in turn may lead to a shift in the level of trust.

Flexibility in Management and Performance Evaluation

One of the keys to a successful collaborative relationship is that the benefits to the partners are more than the deal itself. In other words, the scope of the collaboration expands beyond the narrow confines of the alliance agreement. Firms that insist on highly restrictive and legalistic provisions in their alliance agreements may find it difficult to increase or change alliance scope as new opportunities arise. After alliances are formed, it is inevitable that the partners will learn more about each other, which may lead to new areas for collaboration. As a result, firms should plan on building into their agreements as much scope as possible for uncomplicated and nonlegalistic changes. Japanese firms are said to prefer their alliance agreements to be one page to allow partnerships to grow and evolve. While this may be an exaggeration, our research has found that Japanese firms tend to be less concerned with contractual detail than American firms. I have also heard American managers complain that their joint venture agreements were so detailed that it was impossible to change anything.

In addition to flexibility in the actual agreement, it is important to have flexibility in the negotiation process. If the process is not going as planned, don't get forced into a corner. As well, ensure that there is time for review before a final agreement is signed. The review is designed to revisit the alliance intent and ensure that objectives will be met given the nature of the proposed agreement. This may mean slowing down the process, but it is better to ask questions before the alliance is formed. All too often, managers say that the problems associated with their alliances are the result of poor preparation and pressures to close the deal quickly. As a result, issues that later became problems were not dealt with during the formation and negotiation stages.

Systematic Alliance Formation

To ensure a systematic approach to alliance formation, some firms involved in multiple alliances have developed alliance development processes. The objective is to establish consistency in alliance development and a common set of parameters with which to evaluate and monitor alliance formation and performance. An alliance development process should include a series of checkpoints that must be satisfied before the process moves forward. The process should be designed to ensure that key questions are surfaced and debated throughout the alliance formation process. The questions include:

- Are there clearly understood and agreed upon objectives before venture formation?
- How will the alliance be integrated with the parent firm's strategy?
- Will there be cultural compatibility and organizational fit between the partners?

- Does the alliance leverage the complementary strengths of the partners?
- Will an exit strategy be defined up-front?
- Is there a monitoring process for new alliances?

Properly implemented, a systematic alliance development process will ensure that:

- Projects are strategic to the partner.
- Projects meet financial objectives.
- Projects move quickly through required corporate approval processes.
- Project risks and challenges are identified and understood by all parties involved in the formation process.

Controlling Alliance Instability

Alliances have also been described as a "race to learn," with the partner learning the fastest dominating the relationship.[14] In this scenario of inevitable instability, there are clear winners and losers. Yet some international alliances survive and prosper for many years, with both sides becoming more competitive in a win-win relationship. This raises the issue of why some international alliances are more stable than others. Alliance instability is defined as a major change in relationship status that was *unplanned* and *premature* from one or both (all) partners' perspectives. In most alliances, the partners do not have a specific plan for the termination of their ventures. The premature termination of an alliance can be traumatic to the venture partners. However, it is important to repeat that alliance longevity should not be equated with alliance success.

This section considers how managers involved in alliances can develop greater control over instability. Of particular concern for international alliances is learning by one of the partners that shifts the balance of alliance power. When knowledge acquisition shifts the balance of bargaining power between the partners, the cooperative basis for the alliance may erode and venture instability may be the result. Stability *should not* be equated with high performance. In addition, stability should not always be the primary alliance objective. If learning from an alliance or alliance partner is an objective, the alliance may have to be transitional. Nonetheless, if managers are aware of the factors influencing alliance stability, they may be able to prevent or control for premature changes in partner relationships.

For a firm interested in maintaining a stable, long-term alliance relationship, the Toppan Moore case introduced earlier has several important lessons. One, Moore chose to focus its activities on strengthening the alliance itself and building a relationship with its partner, rather than accumulating local country knowledge. Explicit attempts to build local country knowledge by capitalizing on local partner experience are usually transparent and may be interpreted by local partners as competitive rather than collaborative in nature. Two, Moore was willing to play the role of student and not just teacher, something that many western firms find difficult. Moore learned from its joint venture and permitted the joint venture to develop its own culture and systems.

In my research on Japanese-American joint ventures, several American firms recognized the risks associated with the Japanese partner's acquisition of local knowledge and tried to slow their foreign partner's localization efforts. For example, in one case, the joint venture agreement specified that the venture would not be allowed to compete directly against the American parent in the domestic automotive business. In another case, the American partner was committed to playing a major role in most facets of joint venture management. A joint venture corporate office was established and physically located within the American partner's head office to facilitate an exchange of ideas between American partner and joint venture personnel.

A local firm may be able to increase the difficulty of learning by the foreign partner. In my study of Japanese-American joint ventures, the Japanese firms generally controlled the manufacturing technology, a common situation when market entry is the foreign partner's primary alliance objective. If a local partner can establish its technology as an important venture contribution, the foreign partner's learning task will involve more than just local knowledge. As well, the local partner will have a better opportunity of outlearning its foreign partner because its reliance on the foreign partner's technology will be reduced. In the Japanese-American sample, only three joint ventures were classified as having equal technology contributions from both partners. In the other ventures, the American firms left themselves unprotected because of a reliance on their partner's technology and management of the manufacturing process.

Efforts to limit a foreign partner's learning will not always be successful, especially in an open environment like the United States. For example, in one of the Japanese-American ventures, the American partner wanted to provide the plant manager but the Japanese partner exercised its majority ownership and would not allow it. The American partner provided only one manager to the joint venture and the Japanese partner explicitly tried to limit the American partner's role in the joint venture operation. When the joint venture was terminated prematurely, the Japanese partner established another American plant to develop business with domestic automakers. In another case, an American partner executive indicated that "the Japanese partner wanted a foothold in the United States that we could provide. They used us and then threw us away."

Cultural Diversity and Stability

Another aspect associated with the control of instability is the cultural diversity of the alliance partners. Many articles on alliances have emphasized the problems that occur when firms from different countries form alliances. The presence of societal cultural differences between the partners, it is often argued, contributes to alliance instability.[15] Certainly, cultural diversity adds to the difficulty of international alliance management. However, our research suggests that the relationship between cultural diversity and stability depends on whether one is viewing stability from the local or foreign partner's perspective.

As a foreign partner gains local experience and builds its local knowledge base, the cultural gap between the foreign and local partners decreases. When that happens, alliance instability becomes more likely because access to local knowledge was one of the key reasons for forming the alliance. Therefore, if the foreign partner does not adapt to the local environment, the diversity between the partners may foster stability.

From the perspective of the local partner adapting to the foreign partner, the situation is somewhat different. If the local partner increases its understanding of its foreign partner's culture, venture stability may increase because the partners have a greater understanding of each other's behavior. In the sample of Japanese-American joint ventures, an area that was particularly difficult for American managers to understand was pricing decisions for Japanese customers. Japanese customers expected annual price decreases and saw increases in prices as a last resort option for suppliers. Consequently, the pricing structure of joint venture products was a major source of conflict between the joint venture partners. Increased understanding by the American partner about its Japanese partner's approach to pricing would potentially eliminate a major source of conflict.

Conclusion

To achieve an alliance outcome of high performance, high partner trust, and high value creation, various key managerial issues must be resolved. The challenge for many managers is to recognize that a knowledge-gathering phase early in the planning process is essential and not an option. Too many firms jump into alliance negotiations without adequate planning. The failure to properly plan an alliance and more specifically, the failure to plan for the negotiation increases the probability of alliance failure. Consider the following scenario described by a manager in an alliance that eventually failed:

> The joint venture was started on blind faith. Each partner had some expectations about the other which have not been met. There is an unresolvable conflict between the partners. Morota [the disguised name of the Japanese partner] is willing to lose money in the joint venture for as long as it takes to build up market share and quality in North America. Wilson [the disguised name of the American partner] expected faster production and higher efficiency. The only thing certain at the outset was that Toyota would be a customer. When the joint venture was formed, the partners thought they were in sync about prices and profit margins. Clearly, that was an incorrect assumption. Wilson wanted to make a quick buck and were skeptical of making long-term investments. Wilson expected a profit in 2 to 3 years. Morota expected the joint venture to lose money for 5 to 6 years.

Although not all of the problems described in this example are the result of poor planning and negotiation, had both partners properly prepared for the negotiation and addressed the issues raised in this chapter, the alliance either would have been more successful or it would not have been formed. Instead, the venture was formed with unclear partner understandings of how value would be created, why the venture should be formed, and what risks were involved. In other words, neither partner properly prepared for its alliance. The firms muddled through a negotiation and formation process and ended up with a poorly performing alliance that had little chance for success.

Not all alliances need go the way of the previous example. If alliances are formed and managed in the spirit of joint strategic and economic outcomes and the partners carefully consider the issues identified in this chapter, many of the often intractable cooperative issues can be identified before they derail an alliance. In some cases, after carefully considering these issues, firms may decide that an alliance is not the right course. Perhaps the risk of partnering is too high or there is a lack of competent managers to run the venture. It is far better to discover these things before the alliance is formed than after spending large amounts of capital, only to end up with a nonperforming relationship that is costly and difficult to end.

Notes

1. Arvind Parkhe, "Interfirm Diversity, Organizational Learning, and Longevity in Global Strategic Alliances," *Journal of International Business Studies,* vol. 22 (1991), pp. 579–602.

2. Farok C. Contractor and Peter Lorange, eds., "Why Should Firms Cooperate: The Strategy and Economic Basis for Cooperative Ventures," *Cooperative Strategies in International Business,* (Toronto: Lexington Books, 1988), pp. 3–30; Maheshkumar Joshi and Andrew C. Inkpen, "Cooperation in a Competitive World: A Framework of Global Strategic Alliances," *Competitive Intelligence Review,* vol. 7, no. 2 (1996), pp. 46–55.

3. Andrew C. Inkpen, "Creating Knowledge through Collaboration," *California Management Review,* vol. 39, no. 1 (1996), pp. 123–140.

4. Todd Saxton, "The Effects of Partner and Relationship Characteristics on Alliance Outcomes," *Academy of Management Journal,* vol. 40 (1997), pp. 443–462.

5. Andrew C. Inkpen and Paul W. Beamish, "Knowledge, Bargaining Power and International Joint Venture Stability," *Academy of Management Review,* vol. 22 (1997), pp. 177–202.

6. Peter S. Ring and Andrew Van de Ven, "Developmental Processes of Cooperative Interorganizational Relationships," *Academy of Management Review,* vol. 19 (1994), pp. 90–118.

7. After 27 years of operation, the Toppan Moore joint venture was terminated amicably. Moore's stake in Toppan Moore was sold to Toppan

Printing. According to Moore, the company decided to withdraw from the exclusive arrangement with Toppan to expand its activities in the Japanese market.

8. For a more detailed analysis, see P. Beamish and S. Makino, *Toppan Moore* (1992), Western Business School Case No. 9-92-G001.

9. Seung Ho Park and Gerardo R. Ungson, "The Effect of National Culture, Organizational Complementarity, and Economic Motivation on Joint Venture Dissolution," *Academy of Management Journal,* vol. 40 (1997), pp. 279–307.

10. Andrew C. Inkpen, *The Management of International Joint Ventures: An Organizational Learning Perspective* (London: Routledge Press, 1995).

11. An excellent discussion of the competitive risks of collaboration can be found in Joel Bleeke and David Ernst, "Is Your Strategic Alliance Really a Sale?" *Harvard Business Review,* vol. 73, no. 1 (1995), pp. 97–105.

12. Steven E. Prokesch, "Unleashing the Power of Learning: An Interview with British Petroleum's John Browne," *Harvard Business Review,* vol. 75, no. 5 (1997), pp. 146–168.

13. Yves Doz, "The Evolution of Cooperation in Strategic Alliances: Initial Conditions or Learning Processes?" *Strategic Management Journal,* vol. 17 (special issue summer 1996), pp. 55–83.

14. G. Hamel, Y. Doz, and C.K. Prahalad, "Collaborate with Your Competitors—and Win," *Harvard Business Review,* vol. 67 (January/February 1989), pp. 133–139.

15. Parkhe, "Interfirm . . . ," proposes that societal cultural differences between partner firms will be negatively related to alliance longevity. In contrast, Park and Ungson, "The Effect . . . ," found that Japanese-American joint ventures lasted longer than American-American joint ventures.

5

Comparative Corporate Governance and Global Corporate Strategy

ANANT K. SUNDARAM

MICHAEL BRADLEY

CINDY A. SCHIPANI

JAMES P. WALSH

At the cusp of the new millennium, it has become quite evident that the epic battle between communism and capitalism has been resolved in favor of the latter, at least for the foreseeable future. However, the *type* of capitalism that can best serve the needs of both the society and the economy appears open to debate: For instance, will it resemble

---

This article draws on the paper that the authors co-wrote: "Purposes and Accountability of the Corporation: Corporate Governance at a Crossroads," in the special issue on "Challenges to Corporate Governance" in the *Journal of Law and Contemporary Problems,* Duke University, Fall 1999. From here on, it will be referred to as "BSSW." In the interests of minimizing clutter, this article will use a minimum of footnotes and specific cites. See BSSW for the detailed references, cites, and more elaborate articulation of some of the key arguments.

the free-for-all, survival-of-the-fittest, shareholder-focused variety that we observe in countries such as the United States, or will it resemble the more negotiated, compromised, stakeholder-focused variety that we observe in continental Europe and Asia?

The answer to this question depends on the type of *corporate governance* systems that emerge and propagate themselves in the major economies of the world. Most economic activity worldwide is carried out by corporations, and their goals and conduct (and hence, the nature of their strategy and operations) are determined by the systems and the processes of corporate governance. Equally important, corporate governance systems and processes also have a major impact on the types of strategies that corporations formulate and implement.

Starting with a definition of corporate governance and a brief assessment of its role and importance, we first review some of the key elements of governance systems and the main internal and external mechanisms of governance. We then examine the three most important types of corporate governance systems—the United States, German, and Japanese—and describe their characteristics along these internal and external governance mechanisms. These three systems of governance capture the variants and the broad elements of the types of governance systems that we find in the triad group of countries: Anglo-American (US), Continental Europe (Germany), and the Far East (Japan). We then review the differences among the three systems to draw inferences for both the formulation and implementation of corporate strategy.

Finally, we summarize some of the key transformations that are under way in the three competing systems of governance, and argue that the Anglo-American system of governance may be trumping the others. We conclude with an assessment of the implications of this inference for global competition and strategy.

The United States, Japan, and Germany are the three largest industrial economies in the world, whose gross national products (GNPs) collectively account for slightly over one-half of the gross world product. The universe of the largest corporations of the world is mostly populated by firms belonging to one of these three countries. For example, as of the end of 1996, nearly 70% of the world's largest 500 nonfinancial companies were based in the United States,

Germany, or Japan. Firms from these three economies are most often among each other's leading global competitors in a wide range of sectors such as automobiles, chemicals, semiconductors, electrical machinery, and electronics, banking and financial services. To the extent that the nature of corporate governance is closely linked to the nature of industrial organization and market structure, their styles of governance become critical in global competition. Moreover, these governance systems have had major spillover effects beyond their respective borders. Many European countries, such as Austria, Belgium, Hungary (and to a lesser extent, France and Switzerland), and much of northern Europe have evolved their corporate governance systems along Germanic, rather than Anglo-American, lines. The newly liberalizing economies of Eastern Europe appear to be patterning their governance systems along Germanic lines as well. The spillover effects of the Japanese governance system are increasingly evident in Asia, where Japanese firms have been the largest direct foreign investors during the past decade. Variants of the Anglo-American system of governance are evident in countries such as the United Kingdom, Canada, Australia, and New Zealand.

The Asian Crisis of 1997–1998 in economies such as Thailand, Indonesia, the Philippines, and Korea have brought into further sharp focus the role of the three governance systems. The evolution of these economies in the years following the Crisis, and the type of governance that will underpin this evolution raise immediate and important questions regarding which type of governance system will be adopted and which will prevail in the long run.

Corporate Governance: Definition, Role, Mechanisms

Corporate governance refers to the top management process that manages and mediates value creation for, and value transference among, various corporate claimants (including the society-at-large), in a context that simultaneously ensures accountability toward these claimants.

Note several key aspects of the definition. First, corporate governance is a *process* rather than an outcome. And, it is an evolutionary mechanism rather than static or one-shot. It is not possible to take a "snapshot" view of governance; understanding it requires us to focus beyond just efforts (input) and outcomes (output), to examine how the governance practices arose and where they are headed. Issues of path–dependency predominate. Second, corporate governance is explicitly in the *top management* realm. As such, corporate governance practices define the role of the board of directors (i.e., how boardrooms think and operate), and they account for a considerable portion of the job description of a chief executive officer (CEO). In the modern corporation, no major strategy can be formulated for implementation at the corporate level (and quite often, even at the divisional level) without it being vetted and approved by the board. Third, note the emphasis on both *value creation* and *value transference*. Value creation is presumably the basic purpose of all corporate activity. While the concept of value is left deliberately vague in this definition, it captures the idea of economic value and hence, *profits,* and, in turn, *efficiency.* Arguably, a necessary condition of good governance is to maintain a focus on profits and efficiency in the way that a corporation is managed. However, the existence of value, in turn, implies the existence of economic "rents," and such rents in the presence of multiple claimants raise issues associated with the distribution of rents (i.e., they bring up questions of the *fairness* and *equity* in the sharing of corporate value). Good governance therefore would also imply (or more precisely, require), rightly or wrongly, some form of "fair" and "equitable" value distribution. Thus, as with all large socioeconomic questions, the methods and avenues to deal with questions of both efficiency and equity are at the heart of "good" governance.[1]

Fourth, the definition emphasizes the role of both *claimants* and *accountability*. The claimants in the corporation are stakeholders who, through either their implicit or explicit economic relationships with the firm, can (or will) legitimately stake a claim on corporate revenues and cash flows. Such stakeholders include shareholders, employees, customers, creditors, suppliers, competitors, and even the society-at-large in which the corporate form exists. This context, in turn, consists of an external environment that includes the macroeconomy (product markets, capital markets, labor markets, and the market for real assets and technology), laws and regulation, the property rights (including enforcement) regime, politics, culture, and the social and economic norms (none of which is limited to the "home" nation-state of the corporation). The idea that governance involves accountability captures the notion that good governance is a two-way street. Just as the corporation is responsible for governance toward its stakeholders, governance practices also simultaneously determine the process by which the firm's stakeholders (including the society-at-large) monitor and control the firm.

Despite the fact that governance is explicitly in the top management domain, and despite it being a *sine qua non* of the strategy formulation and implementation process, surprisingly little attention has been paid to it by scholars in management, business policy, and corporate strategy.[2] Where sufficient attention has been paid, it has primarily been empirically oriented, and largely rooted in the rather narrow tradition of corporate governance viewed as an agency problem resulting from the separation of ownership and control between the firm and its capital providers. This rather narrow concern with just the firm and its capital providers has been imported from the literature in finance.[3] This limited view of the governance problem that focuses on just the relation between the firm and its capital providers has become so dominant in the literature that it is almost automatically accepted.[4]

However, corporate governance is much more than simply the relationship between the firm and its capital providers. CEOs and corporate boards surely concern themselves with a much larger menu of issues. Indeed, it is for precisely the reason why governance issues have a deep and broad impact on most aspects of strategy formulation and implementation. We can obtain a better understanding of why (and how) as we examine the main external and internal mechanisms of corporate governance.

External and Internal Mechanisms of Corporate Governance

There are five main elements of the *external* environment of corporate governance: capital markets, product markets, labor markets (including the managerial labor market), the market for corporate control, and the regulatory environment.

External capital markets—both equity and debt markets—exercise discipline over the firm both because of the fact that firms have to subject themselves to its scrutiny whenever they wish to raise external funds and because they determine the structure of ownership of the corporation (debt versus equity, intermediated versus non-intermediated debt, dispersed versus concentrated equity ownership, institutional versus individual equity ownership, patient versus impatient capital, etc).

The discipline imposed by product markets is obvious: In competitive economic systems, firms that cannot consistently produce (any or all of) cheaper, faster, better, and innovative products that the consumer demands will not survive in the long run. Competition will ensure that only the fit will survive. Similarly, labor markets, especially that for managerial labor, ensure that managers from better-performing firms will be rewarded and worse-performing firms penalized by their price in the marketplace.

Among the most widely known external mechanism of governance (and most widely discussed in both the finance and strategy literatures)—especially in Anglo-American settings—is the disciplining role played by the market for corporate control. This market ensures that underperformers (and their managers) will get weeded out through acquisitions, and that acquiring firms will extract higher value from these firms by putting them to more efficient uses (i.e., by reducing costs and increasing revenues). An active market for corporate control ensures that such a threat will always be present; the existence of such a threat is sufficient to ensure its disciplining governance role on top management.

The regulatory environment can be a strong source of external discipline. Quite apart from the plethora of laws at the state and the national levels that control or circumscribe a firm's behavior *directly* (e.g., employment laws, safety laws, nondiscrimination laws, pension laws, liability laws), regulators intervene in the activities of corporations through the passage and application of tax laws and trade laws. There are also important mechanisms of *indirect* intervention in the affairs of the corporation: These include accounting and disclosure rules, and antitrust or competition rules.

There are numerous *internal* mechanisms of corporate governance, but we will focus on five of the more immediate and important ones: They are (1) the structure and role of the board of directors, (2) the role of the CEO vis-à-vis the board, (3) the nature of the compensation systems (especially for top management), (4) the nature of employment practices in the firm, and (5) the nature of internal control systems and incentive systems in place to measure and reward the performance of employees of the firm.

The role of boards in the governance process is central, as we have already noted. In most corporate economies, it is the board of directors that is charged with the task of mediating and managing the trade-offs among stakeholders, the task of approving strategy and budgets, and the task of setting compensation. The board is also typically responsible for ensuring that the firm acts in a legal and socially responsible manner. *In principle* (although, as we will see, not necessarily in practice), in most corporate economies, managers technically report to boards and it is the board that is ultimately responsible for the relationship with the firm's external environment, including its shareholders. Key questions in understanding the role of boards include issues of board composition (e.g., internal versus external appointees), board size, whether nonshareholding constituencies are represented, whether the board is independent, how board members are compensated (e.g., fixed compensation versus company stock and options). CEOs, as the ultimate go-betweens for company management and boards play a crucial role. For example, are they just responsible for the executive functions in the firm (Chief Executive Officer) or are they also in control of the board, its appointment, and its actions ("Chairman of the Board")?

Compensation and control systems are important in that they are responsible for aligning the reward (and punishment) systems to the goals of the firm. For instance, are managers paid with fixed salaries and bonuses, or are they also compensated with stocks and stock options? The latter type of compensation would presumably better align managers' and shareholders' interests, if the stated goal of the firm is to create shareholder value. Similarly, what is the role of performance-related versus performance-unrelated compensation (such as golden parachutes for top management in the event of a change of control)?

The final internal governance issue, and perhaps the most important from the standpoint of the day-to-day operations of the firm, is the nature of employment practices. Typical questions here include:

How are employees hired and promoted? How is their human capital built and retained? How long do they stay with the firm? Does the firm have a relationship-based contract with its employees or provide a lifetime-employment guarantee, or does it hire and fire at will or deal with its employees on an arms-length, what-have-you-done-for-me-today basis?

Understanding the role that governance plays in strategy formulation and implementation in the United States, Germany, and Japan requires us to understand how each of these mechanisms works in these respective settings. There are some stark contrasts (and interesting similarities) among the three systems, with implications for the way corporations from these economies operate and compete. We examine next the role, emphasis, and characteristics of the external governance mechanisms in these three economies, then we discuss the same for their internal governance mechanisms.

External Governance Mechanisms

Corporate Goals, Role of External Capital Markets, and Ownership Structure

Compared to Germany and Japan, external capital markets play a larger role in the U.S. economy. While Germany has nearly half a million corporations and over 3,200 joint-stock companies (Aktiengesellschaften, or AGs), fewer than 700 are listed in equity markets. This compares to the more than 9,000 firms listed in the three major stock exchanges (New York Stock Exchange, American Stock Exchange, and NASDAQ) in the United States, and 1,800 in Japan. Listed firms account for only about 20% of the revenues of the corporate sector in Germany, and stock market capitalization as a percentage of GNP (end–1997) is low—less than 40%, compared to 57% in Japan and 136% in the United States. Nonlisted German firms tend to comprise mostly the smaller and medium-sized enterprises, typically incorporated as GmbHs (Gessellschaften mit beschränkter Haftung).

The goals of German corporations are clearly defined in German corporate law. Implemented originally in 1937 (and subsequently modified in 1965), German corporate law defines the role of the board and the objective of corporations as the following (actual German words in parentheses):

The managing board is, on its own responsibility, to manage the corporation for the good of the enterprise and its employees *(Gefolgschaft)*, the
common weal of the citizens *(Volk)* and the State *(Reich)*.

Nothing specific was mentioned about shareholders until the 1965
revision. The law also provides that if a company endangers public
welfare and does not take corrective action, it can be dissolved by an
act of state. Despite the relatively recent recognition that shareholders
are an important constituency, corporate law in Germany makes it
abundantly clear that shareholders are only one of the many stakeholders on whose behalf the managers must operate the firm.[5]

In the United States, there is no formally recognized corporate
law at the federal level; all corporate law is at the state level (indeed,
the 50 states compete with each other for the incorporation business,
the clear winner among them being the State of Delaware, with
nearly two-thirds of the Fortune 500 firms registered there). In the
absence of such federally mandated corporate law, the "Principles of
Corporate Governance" set forth by a group of lawyers, judges, and
academics called the American Law Institute (ALI) have taken on the
role of providing the *de facto* guidance on matters of corporate law.
According to ALI, the corporation's primary objective should be
"corporate profit and shareholder gain," and while it "may" be rea-
sonably philanthropic and ethical, it "[i]s obliged, to the same extent
as a natural person, to act within [legal] boundaries."[6] The courts
brought this point home way back in 1919 in the case of *Dodge v.
Ford Motor Co.* where it stated: "the corporation is organized and
carried on primarily for the profit of the stockholders."[7] Shareholder
primacy is thus at the forefront of American corporate law.

The hallmark of the Japanese industrial organization system is the
groups or networks of firms with stable, reciprocal, minority equity
interests in each other, known as a *keiretsu*.[8] *Keiretsu* translates to "a
series of things organized to perform a function." Although the firms
in a keiretsu are typically independent, separate, joint stock companies,
they tend to have relational and implicit contracts with each other on
matters such as ownership, governance, and commercial contacts.
When the network of firms consists of a loose collection of firms from
the supplier to the distributor chain, they are called vertical keiretsus;
when the network consists of a loose collection of businesses in similar

product markets, they are called horizontal keiretsus. The horizontal keiretsus also typically include a large main bank that does business with all of the member firms. The main bank also holds minority equity positions in each of the member firms. Although the actual number of keiretsu firms is small relative to the total number of joint stock companies in Japan, they collectively represent about 25% of the total sales in the Japanese corporate sector and about 50% of the value of all listed stock in Japan. It is generally recognized that managing for the good of the whole group of firms in a keiretsu, rather than for any individual firm, is the basic goal of corporate managers.

A major change in the U.S. capital market since the 1970s has been the rise of the institutional investor. Between 1977 and 1996 the number of U.S. registered, public mutual funds grew from 427 (representing $45 billion in 8.5 million shareholder accounts) to 5,305 ($2.6 trillion in almost 120 million shareholder accounts). Such investments account for almost half of all equity in U.S. corporations. Over 25% of all U.S. shares are held by pension funds. Households own just over half of all outstanding domestic shares, more than twice the percentage owned by households in either Germany or Japan.

The ownership structure of equity in Germany differs quite substantially from that observed in the United States. Approximately 14% of the shares are owned by banks, and about 40% by other German corporations (both constituencies hold virtually nothing in the United States). Intercorporate shareholdings are common and difficult to disentangle from publicly available data sources. Less than 17% of the equity is owned by households (approximately 50% in the United States), a proportion that has steadily declined since the 1950s. Ownership is concentrated: roughly 25% of the listed German firms have a single majority shareholder, and such majority holdings account for about 65% of the value of all listed stock.

Importantly, a substantial portion of equity in Germany is in the form of bearer stock (unlike registered stock in the United States). As a result, such equity is left on deposit with the hausbank of the corporation which handles matters such as dividend payments and record-keeping. German law allows banks to vote such equity on deposit by proxy, unless depositors explicitly instruct banks to do otherwise. Inertia appears to work in favor of banks having these proxy votes. As a result, banks directly or indirectly control a large portion of the equity in German companies.[9] The chairman of the supervisory board is typically a representative of the hausbank. Compounding the influence and the controlling role of banks is the provision, in many company charters, that nonbank shareholders may not exercise more than 5% to 10% of the total votes regardless of the proportion of shares they own. (Banks are, however, exempt from this requirement.) Further, even when the shares are listed on an exchange, it is common practice for German corporations to list only nonvoting shares.

Share ownership in Japan is concentrated and stable. Although Japanese banks are not allowed to hold more than 5% of a single firm's stock, a small group of four or five banks typically controls about 20% to 25% of a firm's equity. The largest bank shareholder also is usually the largest debtholder in the company.[10]

Individual share ownership in Japan, like in Germany, has steadily declined from about 50% in the 1950s to about 20% at present. Another 25% of the equity in Japanese companies is accounted for by intercorporate stockholding, and these cross-holdings are rarely, if ever, sold. The agreement not to sell intercorporate holdings is unwritten and implicit. Indeed, the 25% of equity as intercorporate holdings is a number that remained remarkably stable during the past two or three decades. It is remarkable because, during the period 1985–1989 (when the Japanese stock market rose by about 150% and when we may have expected an increase in such holdings) and during the period 1989 to 1994 (when the stock market declined by about 60% and a decrease in such holdings may have been expected), the proportion of intercorporate holdings barely budged. Insurance companies in Japan hold another 20% of the equity. (They may not own more than 10% of the equity in a single company.)

Thus, in a typical Japanese firm, approximately two-thirds of the equity is owned by banks, insurance companies, and other corporations. This proportion remains fairly stable, and the closely held stock rarely, if ever, makes it into the financial marketplace.

Financial Structure and Policies

Turning to financing patterns, German companies, taken as a whole, are somewhat more leveraged than their American counterparts. Gross debt to total book assets was 60% in 1992, (51% for U.S. firms). But leverage is inversely related to size: debt-to-asset ratios are much higher for the smaller and medium-sized enterprises. Gross debt as a percentage of total assets in German companies averaged 60%, but the breakdown was 75% for smaller companies, 69% for medium-sized companies, and 40% for large companies.

The one notable difference between the leverage of U.S. and German firms is, however, the reliance of German firms on bank or intermediated debt, and the relatively minor role played by market debt instruments. The relatively minor role of market debt is explained by the severe restrictions placed by the German government on the issuance of such debt. Issuance of commercial paper and domestic bonds was discouraged until 1992 by complicated authorization procedures and transfer taxes. The issuance of foreign currency bonds was prohibited until 1990, and the issuance of Eurobonds required prior notification and was subjected to maturity restrictions. Bank financing of long-term debt has averaged around 50%, and this percentage has remained fairly stable during the past two decades. The other notable difference is German firms' reliance on internal financing. During the period 1984–1992, German companies met over 70% of their gross funding needs through internal financing. The relatively low role of equity financing is partly explained by taxes and regulation. Until 1992, there was a 1% tax on the value of all new equity issues, and secondary trading in equities was subject to a transaction tax. Companies (stockholders) also pay a 1% tax on their net asset value, a tax that must be paid even if the firm is not profitable.

Dividend payout rules are designed to protect creditor interests. German law stipulates that dividends may not be paid out from paid-in capital, even if such paid-in capital includes a premium over the face value of equity. This provision makes it difficult for German firms to undertake share repurchases. Moreover, companies must retain a portion of their profits as reserves, serving as added security for creditors.

Although their leverage has been decreasing over time, Japanese companies tend to be, on average, more leveraged than their U.S. or German counterparts. Gross debt-to-total book assets was about 80% in 1992, and 57% of the debt was bank or financial institution-intermediated. During 1984–1992, Japanese firms funded over 50% of their gross funding needs through debt. Retained earnings play a smaller role than in Germany and the United States. About 40% of the gross funding needs during the period 1984–1992 were accounted for by internally generated funds. There were considerable restrictions during the 1970s and 1980s on firms' ability to raise market debt such as commercial paper, domestic bonds and Eurobonds. Moreover, until 1988, there was a heavy transactions tax on equity transfers. As these restrictions have been eased, however, Japanese firms have been undertaking more issuances of market debt, especially in the Euromarkets, driven, in part, by wanting to reduce their dependence on the main banks and their bank debt. In the early 1980s, only 250 Japanese firms had issued bonds outside Japan; by the late 1980s, the number had grown to over 1,200. Rules on dividend payouts and share repurchase are similar to those in Germany, although Japanese firms are able to overcome the rules on share repurchases with some ease.

Market for Corporate Control and Restructuring Activity

The United States has an extensive market for corporate control. During the past two decades, the United States alone (as either acquirer or target) alone accounted for more than half of the mergers and acquisitions (M&A) activity worldwide, measured in both value and volume terms. Since 1981, the United States has witnessed two major M&A waves, the first being the deconglomeration wave of the 1980s, and the second being the building-focus wave of the 1990s, with this two-decade period seeing nearly 82,000 M&A deals valued at about $6 trillion. The year 1998 alone witnessed nearly 12,500 deals, for nearly $1.7 trillion. As of the time of writing, the M&A activity shows no signs of abating. The 1980s also was characterized by a substantial amount of hostile takeover and leveraged buyout (LBO) activity, both of which have dropped off dramatically during the 1990s (in which period, M&A deals have been predominantly friendly, with stock rather than cash being used as the medium of exchange in much higher proportions).[11]

The market for corporate control is poorly developed in Germany. During the period 1985–1989, only 2.3% of the market value of listed stocks were involved in mergers and acquisitions, compared to over 40% in the United States. Even when corporate combinations take place, they tend to be friendly, arranged deals. Hostile takeovers and leveraged buyouts are virtually nonexistent. For instance, Franks and

Mayer (1993) report that there have been only four hostile takeovers in Germany since World War II. There is, as yet, no commonly accepted formal takeover law, but there are informal guidelines. Antitakeover provisions, poison pills, golden parachutes, and the like are unheard of in Germany.

As in Germany, the market for corporate control in Japan is relatively inactive. Mergers and acquisitions were slightly more than 3% of total market capitalization during the period 1985–1989, and all were friendly transactions. The first ever (post–World War II) hostile takeover of a Japanese company by a non-Japanese company occurred only in 1999.

Although there are, on average, about 450 mergers or acquisitions involving Japanese companies annually, about half of these consist of Japanese companies acquiring non-Japanese companies, and most of the remaining consist of small deals among Japanese companies. Antitakeover defenses, poison pills, golden parachutes, and so on, are rarely present in corporate charters or bylaws. The words used to describe takeovers in Japanese—*miurisuru* (to sell one's body), *baishu* (bribery), and *nottori* (hijack)—suggest a cultural aversion to takeovers. Part of the reason for this cultural aversion appears to stem from the fact that organized crime groups such as the *yakuza* are often involved in stock-cornering, greenmailing, and the occasional takeover attempt. The late 1980s saw successful greenmailings of a number of Japanese companies, including some well-known companies such as Toyota, Fujiya, and Mitsui Mining. Although the Japanese Commercial Code prohibits firms from repurchasing their own shares, the fact that greenmailings have not been uncommon suggests that many Japanese firms seem to have overcome this provision in the law quite successfully.

There is also extensive market-based restructuring activity—bankruptcies and reorganization, divestitures, spin-offs—in the United States, with active involvement by courts and lawyers (the latter especially in the bankruptcy and reorganization process). In Germany, corporate restructurings tend to be private affairs with banks playing the lead role, and most workouts in financial distress tend to be informal rather than court-based. The absence of court-based workouts is not surprising. Although there are both reorganization and liquidation provisions in German bankruptcy law, the law is skewed toward protecting creditor interests, and the absolute priority rule is strictly followed. Thus, there is a bias toward liquidations in bankruptcies that end up in courts or enter the formal workout process, a situation that stakeholders prefer to avoid unless absolutely necessary. In Japan too, corporate restructurings tend to be private and informal. Courts or lawyers are rarely used, with the main bank usually taking the lead role in these transactions. Restructurings also appear to be accompanied by considerable top management replacement. Bankruptcy law in Japan has both liquidation and rehabilitation provisions, but as in Germany, the law is skewed toward protecting creditors' interests. However, there is no evidence of a bias toward liquidation in restructurings that result in formal workouts.

Disclosure Practices and Regulation

U.S. corporate governance is distinguished from the German and Japanese systems in its emphasis on corporate disclosure for the benefit of capital providers. This may be in large part because U.S. corporations are highly dependent on the sale of stock for raising external financing. U.S. corporations' reliance on the sale of stock for financing their expenditures is at least six times as great as in either Germany or Japan. The Securities and Exchange Act of 1934 mandated greater transparency in, and disclosure of, corporate activity, aimed at ensuring efficiency and fairness in the corporation's dealings with capital providers. Section 14(a) of the 1934 Act delegated to the Securities Exchange Commission (SEC) the power to regulate proxy communications. The overall effect of this legislation was to require adequate disclosure of financial information to outside investors. Insider trading is actively monitored and pursued by the SEC.

In an OECD survey of corporations across the United States, Germany, and Japan, the companies were rated relative to OECD guidelines for "full," "partial," or "not implemented" disclosure. Two-thirds of the U.S. firms surveyed met the "full" disclosure standard and the other one-third of U.S. firms surveyed had "partial" disclosure. This is contrasted with Germany where none of the firms surveyed met the OECD's "full" disclosure requirement and Japan where only 1% of the firms met the "full" disclosure requirements.

The United States follows less conservative accounting rules than either Japan or Germany. For example, securities in the United States are evaluated at market prices rather than historical cost. Accounting rules in the United States emphasize providing accurate economic information to potential investors and shareholders in particular, but de-emphasize the protection of creditors, employees, and other stakeholders. Accounting rules in Germany and Japan emphasize conservatism. For example, unrealized losses that are likely to be realized must be provided for in Germany, but unrealized gains may not be recognized; similarly, tangible fixed assets are carried at cost, less depreciation, so that true asset values are understated; marketable securities are carried at historical cost. Net income figures reported by German firms are suspect because of the extensive use of reserve accounting to build up hidden reserves; income-smoothing considerations tend to predominate. Until recently, Germany had no insider trading laws; if insider trading was discovered, the penalty was to simply turn over the profits. Similarly, in Japan, although there are rules against insider trading and monopolistic practices, the application of these laws is, at best, uneven and inconsistent.

In terms of other regulation, in the United States, protection for noncapital provider constituencies before the 1960s tended to focus on consumers, as with the Sherman and Clayton Acts dealing with antitrust issues and fairness in competition. Starting in the 1960s, however, regulatory efforts became increasingly concerned with nonshareholder constituencies as well as adding consumer protections. The former gained protection under the Civil Rights Act, the Occupational Safety Act, and the Americans with Disabilities Act, to name a few. Meanwhile, consumers benefited from—again, to name a few—federal Truth-in-Lending legislation and, on the state level, warranty provisions in the 1962 Uniform Commercial Code. Along with such added mandates on corporate managers to deal with non-shareholders' concerns has come increased latitude in managerial control of corporations. For example, in 1986 Delaware adopted Section 102(b)(7) of the Delaware Code, allowing corporations to amend their charters to limit directors' liability for non-intentional breach of duty of care to the corporation and its shareholders. Over 40 states have since followed suit.

Notwithstanding the United States's generally (in comparison to Germany and Japan) market-based approach to corporate governance, American courts since 1970 have recognized corporations as legal persons for various reasons. For example, the Supreme Court in 1976 extended Fifth Amendment protection to corporations, and in 1978 added First Amendment protection to corporate speech. Similarly, a majority of states now statutorily permit directors to consider the interests of nonshareholder constituencies in making managerial decisions.

Other External Forces of Governance

Nonshareholder constituencies play a far more important role in Germany and Japan than they do in the United States. As we will see in some detail the next section, employees and unions play a direct role in the governance process in Germany through their substantial board representation. No major corporate decision can be made without their assent (at the least, without informing them and bringing them along). We will also see that suppliers play a direct governance role in Japan, through the supplier clubs (or *kyoryokukai*) that meet regularly to touch base on the companies that they deal with. In the United States, although over 40 states have introduced alternative constituency statutes, they are mostly designed to protect employees and communities from corporate raiders in hostile takeover situations. Outside of an occasional hostile takeover situation, these statutes have not been rigorously or consistently applied—this is, in part due to the demise of the hostile takeover during the 1990s in the United States.

The additional final external governance mechanism that is worth noting concerns the role of managerial labor markets. The United States has an active market for managerial labor, especially CEOs and other top managers. Indeed, executive placement is a large, diverse, and flourishing business in the United States. Relative to the United States, intercorporate mobility is limited in Japan and Germany. Employees generally tend to stay with their initially chosen firms for most of their careers, thanks to the practice of lifetime employment in the organized sector of the Japanese economy, and the extensive apprenticeship and training system in the German corporate sector that builds firm-specific human capital from the early shop-floor stages of a person's career with a firm.

Internal Governance Mechanisms

Board Composition and Structure, CEO Role

In Germany, large firms with more than 500 employees are required to have a two-tier board structure: a supervisory board *(Aufsichstrat)* that performs the strategic oversight role and a management board *(Vorstand)* that performs an operational and day-to-day management oversight role. Membership overlaps between the two boards are prohibited, and membership overlaps between boards of multiple corporations are restricted, and rare. The supervisory board has the task of performing the watchdog role and is responsible for appointment and oversight of the management board. In firms with more than 2,000 employees, half of the supervisory board is required to consist of employees of the firm; the other half consists of shareholder representatives. The chairperson of the supervisory board is, however, typically from the shareholder side and has the tie-breaking vote.

Supervisory boards may also consist of representatives of firms with whom the corporation has vertical relationships (e.g., suppliers and customers). The management board consists almost entirely of the senior management of the company. Thus, board members tend to possess technical skills related to the product, as well as considerable firm- and industry-specific knowledge. The essence of this board structure is the explicit representation of stakeholder interests other than that of shareholders and that no major strategic decisions can be made without the consent of employees and their representatives.

The boards in U.S. companies have a single-tier structure. With slight variance from state to state, directors are elected by the shareholders at their annual meetings and can likewise be removed by the shareholders. In the majority of American corporations, a number of directors are named from outside of the company. The board of directors in the United States serves primarily a monitoring and oversight role. The managing itself is done by a management team under the direction of an executive officer. There is some evidence that suggests that boards of directors in the United States are effective in removing managers who perform poorly relative to other firms in the same industry. Control of a publicly traded corporation in the United States is split among shareholders, board of directors, and corporate officers and agents. Although, in theory, the shareholders maintain control over the corporation via their voting power, in practice, the incumbent directors commonly take advantage of shareholder apathy to perpetuate their own strategies, candidates, and agendas. (For instance, about 80% of the CEOs of large companies in the United States are also chairman of the board). The American proxy system for shareholder voting has been argued to be susceptible to manipulation by incumbent corporate management.

The structure of boards in Japan is similar to that in the United States, with single-tier boards. However, a substantial majority of board members consist of company insiders, notably the current or former senior and middle management of the company.[12] Nearly 80% of board members are from within the management ranks of the company. Unlike the United States, outside directorships are rare, as are overlapping board memberships across companies. The one exception to outside directorships is the main banks. Their representatives usually sit on the boards of the *keiretsu* firms with whom they do business. In 1989, banks collectively sent about 2,065 directors and auditors to 2,131 Japanese companies, which had a total of nearly 38,000 directors and auditors.[13] Unlike the case of Germany where employees, and sometimes, suppliers, tend to have explicit board representation, the interests of stakeholders other than management or the banks are not directly represented on Japanese boards.

Concrete evidence on the effectiveness and role of Japanese boards in disciplining management is unavailable, but in addition to the boards, three other constituencies seem to perform important monitoring roles. Banks play an oversight role, being closely involved in matters of top management selection and replacement, advice, commercial contacts, and intervention in times of financial distress. Involuntary top management turnover is higher following poor financial and stock price performance in Japanese companies with extensive bank involvement.[14] The other common governance feature among vertical keiretsu companies with a supplier network is the *kyoryokukai,* or suppliers' clubs that meet regularly to exchange ideas and information on people and firms with whom they do business. These clubs act as a check on management. The third source of top management monitoring is the Presidents' Club which consists of the presidents of the member firms of a *keiretsu* who get together at regular intervals (and sometimes informally) to touch base on activities within their group. Shareholders can theoretically remove directors by a two-thirds majority vote, but this rarely happens.

CEO Compensation

There is a great deal of emphasis on stocks and stock-options based compensation for CEOs in U.S. firms. The logic behind such compensation structures is simple: It aligns the incentives of the CEO and the company's shareholders. For instance, median (constant) pay levels for manufacturing CEOs increased by 68%, from $1.9 million in 1992 to almost $3.3 million in 1996.[15] The increase in pay is largely attributable to the increases in the grant-date value of stock option grants. With the exception of firms in the utilities industry, stock options replaced basic salaries as the single largest component of compensation. Approximately 63% of CEOs of the largest 1,000 companies received stock option grants in 1992, and an additional 12% of the firms offered stock options to non-CEO executives. Since 1992, these proportions have, in all likelihood, gone up. While earlier empirical evidence in finance indicated that there was no pay-performance relationship, more recent evidence finds that this has changed during the 1990s—the relationship between pay and performance has become positive and strong during the decade of the 1990s.

In Japan and Germany, stocks and options as the basis for CEO compensation is almost unheard of (although, as we will see later, this is beginning to change). The salary structure is based on a basic salary plus a bonus. As a result, the average salaries for CEOs of large firms in Germany and Japan are about one-half to one-third of that for their U.S. counterparts.

Apart from its structure, the one commonly remarked difference between U.S. corporations and those in Germany and Japan is *size* of CEO compensation. Whereas German CEOs are limited by law to a "reasonable" compensation, averaging about 21 times that of an average German worker,[16] the average American CEO makes at least 120 times the salary of an average American worker.[17] A recent attempt to rein in U.S. CEO compensation by disallowing corporate tax deductions for performance-unrelated salaries (such as golden parachutes) in excess of $1 million, has generally failed to accomplish its goal, because many large companies will absorb the extra tax bill rather than become noncompetitive in attracting top CEO candidates.[18] A side effect of inflated CEO salaries is the tendency of U.S. CEOs to leave the firm for more lucrative deals elsewhere, as opposed to German managers who commonly start with a firm as an apprentice and remain with the same firm, contributing their specialized knowledge and experience, for most of their careers.

Human Capital and Internal Control Systems

Japanese firms in the larger, organized sector of the economy place an emphasis on lifetime employment and on building human capital through maximizing asset-specific and relation-specific skills. Lateral interfunctional transfers of managers and horizontal information flows among functions and departments, both within the firm and across firms within the network are common. Upward mobility within Japanese organizations is carried out through a process of moving up through a cross-functional spiral rather than a series of promotions within a particular functional area. As noted, management compensation, including that of top management, relies on salaries and bonuses. Stocks or stock options are rarely used as a basis for remuneration. Total compensation of top managers, including bonuses, is about six to eight times the compensation of the most highly paid blue-collar worker, and about seventeen times that of the average worker. A managerial labor market along the U.S. style, especially for mid-career workers, is thin.

Internal management styles and control systems in Japanese firms rely on building long-term, consensus-based relationships and are characterized by a great deal of informal interactions, personal relations, and information-sharing among relatively culturally homogeneous individuals. There is an apparent reliance on trust, reputation-building, and face-saving considerations as the basis for contracting. The corporation is seen by its employees as much as a social entity as it is an economic entity. Companies rely on basic agreements and face-to-face contacts to resolve issues, and legal contracts or stipulations with stakeholders are rare.

While Germany does not have the formal lifetime employment practice as in Japan, employees tend to stay with firms for much longer than in U.S. firms. Careers are often built up from the ground level and are focused on building asset-specific skills, through the extensive apprenticeship system that is used to train workers and managers in Germany.

While internal control systems in the United States tend to be, by-and-large, focused on quantitative metrics for project evaluation and internal performance measurement (with an emphasis especially on accounting and financial metrics), often focused on a quarter-to-quarter basis, those in Germany and Japan tend to rely on both quantitative and qualitative metrics, with much less emphasis on financial and accounting variables, and tend to focus on the longer horizon.[19]

An Assessment of the U.S., German, and Japanese Systems of Governance

A Summary of the Three Systems of Governance

Although there are some apparent differences, there is a surprising degree of similarity between the German and Japanese governance systems. Similarities include the relatively little reliance on external capital markets; the low role of individual share ownership; the high role of institutional and intercorporate ownership, which is often concentrated; relatively stable and permanent capital providers; boards comprising functional specialists and insiders with knowledge of the firm and the industry; the relatively important role of banks as financiers, advisors, managers and monitors of top management; the higher role of leverage with emphasis on bank financing; informal as opposed to formal workouts in financial distress; the emphasis on salary and bonuses rather than stocks and stock options as the basis for top management compensation; the relatively poor disclosure from the standpoint of outside investors; and conservatism in accounting policies. Moreover, both the German and Japanese governance systems emphasize the protection of employee and creditor interests at least as much as the interests of shareholders. (The one difference is that employees play more of a direct role in German governance, while suppliers similarly play a role in Japan.) The market for corporate control as a credible disciplining device is largely absent in both Japan and Germany, as is the need for takeover defenses. The governance system itself may be considered a de facto poison pill.

The focus of the governance problem in the United States and, more generally, the Anglo-American system, appears to implicitly address the agency problems that arise in the context of information asymmetries and self-interested behavior among managers, equity-holders, and debtholders. In Germany and Japan, the governance systems appear to be focused on addressing problems of transaction efficiency and the appropriate scope of the firm. In the U.S. governance system, the solution to problems of transaction efficiency and firm scope is approached through the lens of the choice between markets (arm's-length dealings) and hierarchies (vertical or horizontal integration), while in the German and Japanese governance systems, the solution to agency problems between management, debt, and equity appears to be addressed by attempts to bundle or commingle the three constituencies into one. The German and Japanese systems of governance can be characterized as insider systems of governance, while those in the Anglo-American tradition as typified by the United States can be characterized as an outsider system of governance.

Most fundamentally, the distinction can be distilled into the following assessment: The U.S. approach to governance is comparatively *contractarian* in its scope and intent, while German and Japanese approaches to governance are relatively *communitarian* in their scope and intent.

Contractarianism versus Communitarianism

The contractarian view of corporations derives Coase's entrepreneur-centered argument that firms exist to minimize trading costs in external markets.[20] In Coase's original model, the entrepreneur is party to all contracts, bargains separately with each stakeholder, and has free rein to operate or dispose of the organization as he or she wishes. In a public corporation, the entrepreneur's functions are performed by distinct stakeholder groups for maximum efficiency; and for the contractarian it is the bundle of these stakeholders' mutual agreements, rather than any corporate status as a legal entity, which constitutes a corporation. Priority in this rather Darwinist model is placed on reducing transaction costs and on facilitating market forces to maximize efficiency and profits. Government's role in the contractarian paradigm should be limited to protecting property rights and enforcing contracts.

Although the contractarian model leaves the firm free to operate for maximum flexibility in response to the marketplace, critics point out that real-life contracts can never be written or anticipated for all possible contingencies, and that externalities can and do create significant barriers to both corporate efficiency and social justice. Even more damaging to the contractarian theory, argue its critics, is its reliance, in an increasingly global economy, on predictable property rules and judicial enforcement of contracts—neither of which can be counted upon in cross-border transactions.

In sharp contrast to the contractarian philosophy, communitarians argue that maximum economic efficiency does not entail maximum social welfare, and that a healthy society demands a balancing of these mutually incompatible objectives. In the communitarian theory of the firm, a corporation is a legal entity with specific rights, with limited liability for its managers and stockholders. The quid pro quo for the privilege of corporate entity status, then, is "[a] sense of social responsibility toward employees, consumers, and the general public [as] the appropriate attitude to be adopted by those who engage in business."[21]

Perceived strengths of communitarianism are its encouragement of socially responsible business dealings as well as increased efficiency in human capital (for example, employees in labor-managed firms will arguably work harder for their employer when the corporate governance system ensures them a greater stake than their weekly paycheck). Yet, taken past a certain point, a communitarian approach may well burden the corporation with added labor, regulatory, and other costs to a situation where the firm can no longer compete across borders. Just where that point lies—where to place the fulcrum on which we are to balance corporate efficiency and competitiveness with corporate responsibility to the community—is an issue at the very heart of the contractarian-communitarian dispute.

Thus the difference between these two paradigms of corporate governance boils down, very broadly, to a decision as to whether noncapital-providing stakeholders (consumers, employees, and neighbors) are to be given legislative protections in a communitarian system, or whether they are to be presumed, under a contractarian regime, to have the knowledge and means to make Coasian bargains with those persons managing the corporation.

Implication of the Governance Systems for Corporate Strategy

Strategic Implications

The attributes of German and Japanese governance—emphasis on lifetime employment, a significant governance role for employees and suppliers, concentrated and stable equity ownership with relatively permanent providers of capital, bank involvement, insiders with experience on the board, and emphasis on informal and face-to-face (rather than formal, contractual, court-based) relationships— have not been created in an institutional and historical vacuum. The very fact that these attributes have evolved and survived over time in two relatively successful corporate economies suggests that they must have their efficiency aspects.

The emphasis on lifetime employment and the employee role in governance must surely give employees a greater incentive to develop and supply firm-specific human capital. It also encourages greater employee loyalty to corporations, and perhaps helps to create a more engaged labor force that is willing to contribute to a team effort as opposed to competitive relationships within firms. Employees may also have a greater incentive to provide value-saving advice and may be more willing to make concessions in times of economic or financial distress.[22] Analogous arguments such as the greater ability to deal with quality control issues and to develop firm-specific arrangements, could be logically made with respect to suppliers.

Stable, concentrated, relatively permanent, cross-owned equity capital providers play a positive role too. Large shareholders' ongoing involvement means that they do not need time to move up from the bottom of a learning curve and can intervene quickly when crises hit.[23] Block ownership of shares facilitates a great deal of mutual monitoring and deters opportunism with multiple blocks checking each other, impelling managerial action, and facilitating power sharing, not domination. Such an equity ownership structure could lower the cost of equity capital.[24] In addition, the preponderance of insiders on the board encourages a great deal of information sharing, and brings firm- and industry-specific knowledge to the governance process. Other implications of stable, permanent equity ownership are obvious. Managers do not need to be constantly looking over their shoulders worrying about corporate raiders. They can manage for the long run, and can more effectively withstand the pressures to manage on a quarter-to-quarter basis.

Quite apart from the lending and the direct intervention roles that they play, banks may also facilitate the governance process. They are likely to have a great deal of access to inside information and hence can perform a monitoring role very effectively; the bundling of debt and equity claims with the same capital providers eliminates (or at least mitigates) the potential agency problems that can arise between debtholders and equityholders; and restrictions on cash distributions (e.g., on share repurchases and dividend payments) can lower the cost of debt since creditors' positions are made safer. Finally, it is no surprise, given the governance role of the banks, that resolution of financial distress in both Germany and Japan is a much more informal process compared to a country such as the United States.

The cooperation among firms under the Japanese system permits a degree of integration that is not possible under U.S. antitrust laws. The coordination along the value chain as well as consultation with competitors must enhance economic efficiency, although the lack of competition may stifle the incentives to exploit these efficiencies.

The stakeholder orientation and the relatively communitarian features of German and Japanese corporate governance are not, however, without their costs. The bank-centered nature of governance in both Germany and Japan poses a number of risks. Unlike the case of equity investors who, in both theory and practice, are concerned with the *systematic* risk of a particular asset vis-à-vis a well-diversified portfolio, undiversified debtholders are concerned about their credit risk, which, is determined by an asset's *total* risk (i.e., systematic plus unsystematic risks). Focus on total risk creates a number of adverse incentive problems on both the asset side and the liability side of a firm's balance sheet. On the asset side, it can create the tendency to reduce total risk through corporate diversification, or by ex ante constraining share value-maximizing investment. It can also induce a bias against start-up kinds of businesses, because focus on total risk minimization can lead to entrepreneurial risk-aversion in investment choices. In a related vein, it is inherent in the nature of bank credit to focus on asset types that are collateralizable and tangible, thus biasing investment choices away from asset types that are intangible and, hence, noncollateralizable. The latter type of asset typically tends to be more research and development and human-capital intensive. The evidence suggests that comparative advantages in global product markets depend critically on such assets (for example, consider such sectors as software, biotechnology, the Internet, and so on). On the liability side of a firm's balance sheet, a focus on total risk reduction can lead to excessive hedging and excessive investment in insurance. It can also focus a firm's accounting policies toward income-smoothing, rather than value-creating, considerations.

The heightened roles of both employees (Germany) and suppliers (Japan) in corporate governance can lead to inflexibility in sourcing strategies, in labor markets, and in corporate restructurings (e.g., asset sales, downsizing, spin-offs, deconglomeration). In contrast to U.S. firms, therefore, firms in Germany and Japan are less likely to be able to move quickly to meet competitive challenges from the global product-market arena. Employees' role in governance may also have an adverse impact on labor costs, further eroding firms' competitive positions on a global economy. Suppliers' role in governance, as in the case of the vertical *keiretsu* in Japan, can lead to potential problems of implicit or explicit vertical restraints to competition and, hence, antitrust problems.

In addition, a firm's globalization strategy might be seriously hindered because an entire vertical chain of relationships is less portable across borders than within a stand-alone firm. Moreover, as fixed claimants to a firm's revenue stream, both employees and suppliers have the incentive to skew corporate decisions toward total risk minimization strategies. This exacerbates the similar incentives that follow from the bank's role in governance.

The nature of equity ownership—intercorporate holdings as permanent and stable providers of equity capital—may also pose problems. Given the differences in laws, especially in the Anglo-American system of governance, the ownership structures are likely to be illegal in some countries and therefore less likely to be portable across borders. They are also inconsistent with the inexorable trends toward the globalization of financial markets, and with the increasing role played by private pension and mutual funds. Because such structures may be biased against external capital market dependence and because current owners may not want to dilute their ownership, stable crossholdings can create artificial capital constraints. The perceived stability in capital provision also may lead managers to undertake excessive investments in capacity and may create the tendency for product and brand proliferation as well as uneconomical diversification.

These equity ownership structures militate against the development of a market for corporate control which arguably is an important source of managerial discipline in the Anglo-American system.

The emphasis on lifetime (or at least long-term) employment may induce its own biases. It obviates any role for the managerial labor market as a disciplining mechanism. Further, it biases the firm toward corporate strategies that emphasize survival and market share maximization, rather than share-value and profit maximization, because of the obvious benefits of job stability that such strategies entail. Lifetime/long-term employment strategies also hinder inter-corporate mobility and inter-corporate socialization, thereby potentially stunting the development of industries that rely on cross-fertilization of ideas and human capital (e.g., Silicon Valley-type industries).

The Empirical Evidence

Recent and growing empirical evidence suggests that many of these theoretical risks are in fact real. Labor costs in manufacturing both in Germany and Japan have seriously eroded the competitiveness of their firms in the global marketplace. For example, as of the end of 1996, the average German manufacturer paid about $32 per hour of employee work, the Japanese manufacturer paid about $21, while in the United States, the comparable figure was about $17.75. Inflexible labor markets have contributed to the historically high unemployment rates in Europe during the 1990s (averaging at about 11% across the EU), while the unemployment rate in the United States has been steadily declining. Indeed, in 1999, something remarkable happened: The unemployment rate in Japan exceeded that of the United States. The U.S. economy created 22.3 million jobs (20.5 million in the private sector and 1.8 million in the government sector) during the period 1984–1996, for an employment growth of nearly 25% (27% growth in the private sector and over 12% growth in the government sector) during this period. In comparison, for the roughly similar period 1984 to 1995, the European Union witnessed an employment growth of just 0.6% in the private sector and a decline of 4.2% in the government sector (thus increasing overall unemployment, given the growth in the labor force during this period). A recent report of the OECD states that labor productivity across-the-board in Germany is about 80% of that in the United States, while labor productivity in Japan is about 65% of that in the United States.

As previously noted, private mutual funds play an extremely small role in the equity markets of both Germany and Japan; but so do private pension funds. Pension funds in the United States had over $4 trillion in assets in 1995 (55% of GNP), and the UK $814 billion in assets (73% of GNP), compared to $70 billion in pension fund assets in Germany (3.2% of GNP) and $41 billion in France (3.4% of GNP). Over 80% of the UK pension fund investments were in equity, compared to 13% in France and 11% in Germany. The negligible roles that the market for corporate control and the managerial labor markets play in both Germany and Japan have already been noted.

A more serious, longer term competitive issue for Germany and Japan may be the bias in the governance system against start-ups and R&D and human capital intensive industries. The average age of a listed firm in the United Kingdom is about eight years. In the United States, the figure is 14 years for stocks listed on the New York Stock Exchange and 13 years for NASDAQ-listed stocks. These numbers are in stark contrast to the average 55 years for firms listed on the pan-German stock exchanges. The share of less-than-10-year-old companies listed in the stock exchange is about 40% in the United States, compared to 0.7% in Japan. Compared to the United States, both Germany and Japan have a comparative disadvantage in high-technology sectors. This empirical analysis is also borne out by casual observation. Germany and Japan have nowhere near the number and variety of firms that we see in the United States in high R&D and human capital-intensive sectors such as computer software, the Internet, information technology, media, and biotechnology. A U.S.-style venture capital industry is virtually non-existent in either country. California alone generated more venture capital funds in 1996 than the United Kingdom, Germany, France, and the Netherlands combined.

Many of these are predictable consequences of the communitarian styles of governance in economies such as Germany and Japan. Compared to the United States, neither the German and Japanese systems appear as focused on shareholder wealth. The responsibilities of managers of the German corporation include management for the good of the enterprise, its employees, the citizens and the state. Shareholders were not even mentioned in corporate law until 1965, and then the law made it clear that shareholders were only one of several constituencies that management needed to be concerned with. Similarly, Japanese corporate governance emphasizes the protection of employee and creditor interests at least as much, if not more than shareholder interests.

The past decade has witnessed evolutionary shifts in all three systems of governance. There are a number of changes under way in the U.S. system of corporate governance including, the increasing influence of the sentiments reflected in the ALI Project on Corporate Governance; the shifting roles of institutional shareholders and independent directors on boards; the attempts to delink the jobs of chairperson and CEO; the changes in proxy voting rules instituted by the SEC; the Delaware court rulings on the importance of incumbent firm strategy in takeover contests; the regulatory moves away from director liability; and the increasingly contractarian imperatives of the global financial markets. However, as discussed earlier, these changes do not appear to challenge in any fundamental way the United States's focus on shareholder value and financial returns. Indeed, many of the changes in the U.S. governance system may be in the direction of actually *strengthening* its underlying contractarian focus. Further, there do not appear to be any systematic or widespread moves either in boardrooms or in the realm of public policy to make U.S. firms more communitarian in their approach to governance.

On the other hand, the changes in Germany and Japan appear to be moving firms in a direction away from their traditional insider/communitarian focus toward a contractarian style of functioning. Given the generally weaker state of affairs in corporate Europe and Japan during the 1990s, the pressures for change have been mounting dramatically. Often, these changes are being adopted reluctantly, and despite considerable political and labor union against such change.

Consider some examples from Germany:[25] During the past decade, many of the regulations prohibiting or constraining the issuance of equity and market debt have been dismantled. Insider trading laws have been passed; consideration is being given to changes in corporate law so as to allow firms to repurchase shares; banks are being encouraged to divest their corporate shareholdings and to reduce their lending exposures to individual companies; efforts are under way to develop a new set of standards for financial disclosure; German investors are now required to reveal the details of share ownership of more than 5% in a company; a new supervisory authority for securities trading is in the process of being created; special tax incentives are being offered for start-up firms in high-risk industries. An increasing number of firms are listing their shares abroad, especially in the U.S. markets; some degree of corporate restructuring through sale of unprofitable units, spin-offs to increase shareholder value, downsizing, deconglomeration, and so on, appear to be under way; and a few major companies have introduced stock option schemes as part of top management compensation.[26]

Similar changes are occurring elsewhere in Europe. The OECD reports that the governance systems of France, Switzerland, the Netherlands, and Sweden are becoming closer to the U.S. model, whereas they had previously hewed more closely to the German model. There are significant corporate governance debates under way in France. Many of the changes in both the regulations and in the conduct of French corporations parallel those chronicled above in the German case. France is currently debating the introduction of private pension funding schemes along the lines of those in the United States. In both France and Italy, laws are being revised to allow boardroom representation of minority shareholders. Norms are also being developed to limit multiple board memberships among a small group of financial and corporate elites. Perhaps most telling, there have been five hostile acquisitions of French companies each with a market value in excess of $1 billion since 1988. Italy saw its first significant hostile takeover in 1999: Telecom Italia, one of the largest companies in Italy, was taken over by Olivetti, a company that was less than one-fifth the size of the target. According to data from the Securities Data Corporation, the 1990s have witnessed a nearly ten-fold increase in corporate control activity in Germany and France (compared to the 1980s).

At the pace of activity at the time of writing, the year 1999 will probably witness *over $500 billion* in mergers and acquisitions activity involving European companies, a number that is nothing short of remarkable. Competition laws and antitrust regulations are being increasingly forcefully applied in the European Union. There are significant moves toward the adoption of a common set of accounting and disclosure rules under the International Accounting Standards.

In Japan, financial markets were liberalized to a significant degree during the 1980s. The Japanese government also recently announced new plans for further deregulation of the banking, securities, foreign exchange, and insurance sectors to take effect by 2001, along the lines of the "Big Bang" in London. Other changes are similarly under way that challenge the status quo in Japanese corporate governance: some keiretsu firms are reportedly beginning to sell their stockholdings; the notion of lifetime employment is under serious debate; after a few years of slowdown, 1996 saw a resurgence in the market for mergers and acquisitions, with over 600 deals being completed; the year 1999 witnessed the *first* ever successful hostile takeover of a Japanese company by a non-Japanese company; a significant number of large corporations have moved toward arm's-length relations with their main banks as Japanese banks are losing their capacity to act as enforcers of financial discipline; Japanese firms have become far more dependent on international capital markets for their global funding needs for both debt and equity, and the proportion of bank financing to total capitalization has steadily declined during the past decade; and the number of firms listing their shares in the Anglo-American stock markets has risen substantially during the past decade, to the point where 34% of the largest (by market capitalization) 100 Japanese firms listed on the Tokyo stock exchange are also now listed on either the U.S. or the U.K. stock markets.

The Asian economic crisis that began in the latter half of 1997—with the attendant economic contraction, currency depreciation, plummeting stock markets, unemployment, and banking crises—affecting Japan, Thailand, Indonesia, Malaysia, the Philippines, and Korea have brought into sharper focus the nature of corporate governance practices in those economies. Numerous writers, policymakers, and commentators have alluded to the opacity and crony capitalism in the governance systems in these economies, arguing that these attributes have exacerbated the crises, if not actually engendered them. It is too early to forecast just how these events will transform these economies, their politics, laws, institutions, and corporate governance practices. But it is clear that these Asian economies, like the post-communist economies of Eastern Europe and the former Soviet Union, are in transition into new and uncharted governance territory. A reasonable prediction would be that these changes are most likely to be in the contractarian direction, rather than toward the systems of governance prevalent in countries such as Japan or Germany.

Conclusion

In a world in which international capital flows, globalization, flatter organizational forms, more nebulous organizational boundaries, and human-capital intensive technologies have become the norm, communitarianism is under severe strain. Legitimate questions are being raised worldwide about the efficacy and the efficiency of communitarian styles of governance, and their lack of ability to cope.

This lack of ability to cope has to do *inherently* with the nature of corporate strategies that the communitarian styles of governance engender. These strategies result in excessive risk avoidance, overinvestment in capacity, brand/product proliferation, excessive hedging, too much conglomeration and a lack of product focus, an absence of external control mechanisms (such as external financial markets and the market for corporate control), insufficient attention to shareholder wealth creation, creation of artificial capital constraints, creation of a comparative *dis*advantage in human-capital intensive high-technology, and so forth. There is now widespread acceptance of the fact that the adoption of some *functional* and *practical* form of contractarian governance mechanism along the U.S. lines—with its transparent, market-driven, shareholder-oriented styles—may be the long-term solution to overcoming these governance-induced strategic weaknesses of German and Japanese companies.

Evolutionary shifts under way in countries such as Germany and Japan are posing significant challenges to their traditionally insider-oriented, stakeholder-based, relatively communitarian systems of corporate governance. Moreover, the governance systems of the three major industrial economies of the world—the United States, Germany, and Japan seem to be inexorably moving toward some practical, functional form of convergence. The nature of this convergence is unarguably in the U.S. direction rather than the other way around.

The implications of these dramatic changes for global strategy are clear: As we enter a new era of global competition, corporate strategies that rely on focus, deconglomeration, shareholder value creation, financial metrics in performance evaluation, a strong market for corporate control, and the freedom to restructure the firm with asset sales, spin-offs, divestitures, and so forth have become the clear imperative for firms that have to stay competitive in the global arena. Contractarian governance structures of countries such as the United States—which alone appear to provide the necessary context for the pursuit of such strategies—will, therefore, determine the shape and structure of corporate capitalism in the years to come.

References

Abowd, J., & Bognanno, M. (1994). *International differences and changes in executive and managerial compensation in differences and changes in wage structures.* Chicago: University of Chicago Press.

American Law Institute. (1994). *Principles of corporate governance: analysis and recommendations.* Author.

Aoki, M. (1990). Toward an economic model of the Japanese firm. *Journal of Economic Literature, 28,* 1–27.

Bank for International Settlements. (1997, August). *International banking and financial market developments.* Switzerland: Basle.

Berglof, E., & Perotti, E. (1994). The governance structure of the Japanese financial keiretsu. *Journal of Financial Economics, 36,* 259–284.

Black, B. (1992). Agents watching agents: The promise of institutional investor voice. *UCLA Law Review, 39,* 811.

Black, B., & Gilson, R. (1998). Venture capital and the structure of capital markets: Banks versus stock markets. *Journal of Financial Economics, 47,* 243.

Borio, C.E.V. (1990). Leverage and financing of non-financial companies: An international perspective. *BIS Economic Papers, No. 27.* Switzerland: Basle.

Bradley, M., Schipani, C., Sundaram, A., & Walsh, J. (1999, June). *Corporate governance in a comparative setting: The United States, Japan, and Germany.* Paper presented at the Academy of Legal Studies in Business National Meetings, St. Louis.

Bradley, M., Schipani, C., Sundaram, A., & Walsh, J. (1999, Fall). "Purposes and accountability of the corporation corporate governance at a crossroads" [In special issue *Challenges to Corporate Governance*]. *Journal of Law and Contemporary Problems.*

Business in Europe: Fortress against change, survey. (1996, November 23). *The Economist,* 62.

Carney, W. (1997). Large bank stockholders in Germany: Saviors or substitutes? *Journal of Applied Corporate Finance, 9.*

Coase, R. (1937). The nature of the firm. *Economica, 4,* 386.

Comment, R., & Jarrell, G. (1995). Corporate focus and stock returns. *Journal of Financial Economics, 37,* 67.

Conrad, A. (1991). Corporate constituencies in Western Europe. *Stetson Law Review, 21,* 73–95.

Continental shift: Elf Aquitane's chief illustrates the changes in Europe's executives. (1996, April 9). *Wall Street Journal* p. A1.

Corporate Governance Forum of Japan. (1998, May). *Corporate governance principles—A Japanese view (Final Report).*

Corporate Japan hit by gangsters. (1997, April 26). *Financial Times,* 23.

Crystal, G. (1991). *In Search of Excess.*

De Jong, H.W. (1995). European capitalism: Between freedom and social justice. *Review of Industrial Organization, 10,* 399–419.

Deutsche Bundesbank. (1992, November). West German enterprises' profitability and financing. *Deutsche Bundesbank Monthly Report.* Frankfurt, Germany: Deutsche Bundesbank.

Deutsche Bundesbank. (1994, October). Comparisons of the provisions of business enterprises in selected EC countries with own funds. *Deutsche Bundesbank Monthly Report.* Frankfurt, Germany: Deutsche Bundesbank.

Dodd, E.M., Jr. (1932). For whom are corporate managers trustees. *Harvard Law Review, 45,* 1145.

Donaldson, T., & Preston, L. (1995). The stakeholder theory of the corporation: Concepts, evidence, and implications. *Academy of Management Review,* 65–91.

Easterbrook, A.H. (1997). International corporate differences: Markets or law? *Bank of America Journal of Applied Corporate Finance, 9,* 23–29.

European business: Le Defi Americain, again. (1996, July 13). *The Economist,* 22.

Family values. (1996, September 30). *The Economist,* 79.

A fifth of Japanese companies admit to bad behavior. (1997, April 11). *Financial Times,* 6.

Financial market trends No. 62. (1995). *Organization for economic cooperation and development.* Paris: Author.

Franks, J., & Mayer, C. (1993). *German capital markets, corporate control, and obstacles to hostile takeovers: Lessons from three case studies.* London: Business School Working Paper.

Franks, J., & Mayer, C. (1997). Corporate ownership and control in the UK, Germany, and France. *Journal of Applied Corporate Finance, 9.*

Friedman, M. (September 13). The social responsibility of business is to increase its profits. *New York Times Sunday Magazine*, p. 32.

Fukao, M. (1995). *Financial integration, corporate governance and the performance of multinational corporations*. Brookings Institute.

Genay, H. (1991). Japan's corporate groups (Federal Reserve Bank of Chicago). *Economic Perspectives, 15*, 20–30.

Gilson, R.J., & Kraakman, R. (1991). Reinventing the outside director: An agenda for the institutional investor. *Stanford Law Review, 43*, 863.

Gilson, R.J., & Roe, M.J. (1993). Understanding the Japanese Keiretsu: Overlaps between corporate governance and industrial organization. *Yale Law Journal, 102*, 871–906.

Global accounting's roadblock. (1996, April 27). *The Economist*, 79–80.

Glouchevitch, P. (1992). Juggernaut: The German way of doing business. New York: Simon & Schuster.

Hopt, K. (1994). Labor representation on corporate boards: Impacts and problems for corporate governance and economic integration in Europe. *International Review of Law and Economics, 14*, 203–214.

Hoshi, T. (1997, April). *Understanding Japanese corporate governance*. Osaka University Working Paper.

Hoshi, T., Kashyap, A., & Scharfstein, D. (1990). The role of banks in reducing costs of financial distress in Japan. *Journal of Financial Economics, 27*, 67–88.

IASC Insight. (1997, October). *International Accounting Standards Committee.*

Industrial competitiveness. (1996). *Organization for economic cooperation and development*. Paris: Author.

International capital markets: Developments, prospects, and key policy issues. (1998, September). Washington, DC: International Monetary Fund.

International comparisons of hourly compensation costs for production workers in manufacturing. (1997, June). (Bureau of Labor Statistics: Office of Productivity and Technology). Washington, DC: U.S. Department of Labor.

Japan catches merger fever, again. (1997, January 2). *International Herald Tribune*, p. 9.

Jensen, M.C., & Meckling, W.H. (1976). Theory of the firm: Managerial behavior, agency costs and ownership structure. *Journal of Financial Economics, 3*, 305.

John, K., Senbet, L., & Sundaram, A. (1991). Multinational enterprise liability, border taxes, and capital structure. *Financial Management, 20*, 54–67.

Kang, J. (1993). The international market for corporate control: Mergers and acquisitions of US firms by Japanese firms. *Journal of Financial Economics, 34*, 345–371.

Kang, J., & Shivdasani, A. (1995). Firm performance, corporate governance, and top executive turnover in Japan. *Journal of Financial Economics, 38*, 29–58.

Kaplan, S.N. (1994a). Top executive rewards and firm performance: A comparison of Japan and the United States. *Journal of Political Economy, 102,* 510–546.

Kaplan, S.N. (1994b). Top executives, turnover, and firm performance in Germany. *Journal of Law, Economics, and Organization, 10,* 142–159.

Kaplan, S.N., & Minton, B. (1994). Appointments of outsiders to Japanese boards: Determinants and implications for managers. *Journal of Financial Economics, 36,* 225–257.

Kester, C.W. (1991a). The hidden cost of Japanese success. *Bank of America Journal of Applied Corporate Finance, 5,* 90–97.

Kester, C.W. (1991b). *Japanese takeovers: The global contest for corporate control.* Boston, MA: Harvard Business School Press.

Kester, C.W. (1992). Industrial groups as systems of contractual governance. *Oxford Review of Economic Policy, 8,* 24–44.

La Porta, R., Lopez-de-Silanes, F., Shleifer, A., & Vishny, R. (1997). Legal determinants of external finance. *Journal of Finance, 52,* 1131–1150.

The LGT Guide to World Equity Markets 1997. (1997).

Lightfoot, R., & Kester, C.W. (1991). *Note on corporate governance systems: The United States, Japan, and Germany.* Boston: Harvard Business School Press.

Logue, D., & Seward, J. (1999, Fall). Anatomy of a governance transformation: The case of Daimler-Benz [In special issue *Challenges to Corporate Governance*]. *Journal of Law and Contemporary Problems.*

Lorsch, J.W., & MacIver, E. (1989). *Pawns of potentates: The reality of America's corporate boards.*

Macey, J., & Miller, G. (1995). Corporate governance and commercial banking: A comparative examination of Germany, Japan, and the United States. *Stanford Law Review, 48,* 73.

Macey, J., & Miller, G. (1997). Universal banks are not the answer to America's corporate governance "problem." *Journal of Applied Corporate Finance, 9.*

Mayer, C., & Alexander, I. (1990). Banks and securities markets: Corporate financing in Germany and the United Kingdom. *Journal of Japanese and International Economies, 4,* 450–475.

Mergers and Acquisitions Almanac. (Various issues from 1993 to 1998). Securities Data Corporation.

Millstein, I., & MacAvoy, P. (1998). The active board of directors and improved performance of the large publicly traded corporation. *Columbia Law Review, 98,* 1283.

Multinationals and the national interest: Playing by different rules. (1993, September). (OTA-ITE-569). Washington, DC: U.S. Congress, Office of Technology Assessment.

Mutual fund factbook (37th ed.). (1997). Investment Company Institute.

New hard line by big companies threatens German work benefits. (1996, October 1). *New York Times,* p. C1.

The new state of corporate Japan. (1991, April 27). In *Survey: International Finance, The Economist,* 32–36.

Nishiguchi, J. (1994). *Strategic industrial sourcing: The Japanese advantage.* New York: Oxford University Press.

OECD economic surveys: 1994—Germany. (1994). *Organization for economic cooperation and development.* Paris: Author.

OECD economic surveys: 1994–5 Germany. (1995). *Organization for economic cooperation and development.* Paris: Author.

The OECD jobs study: Evidence and explanations: Part 1: Labour market trends and underlying forces of change. (1994). *Organization for economic cooperation and development.* Paris: Author.

Olivetti's lesson. (1996, September 5). *Wall Street Journal* Editorial.

The outsider. (1995, June 23). *The Economist,* 66.

Porter, M. (1992a, Sept./Oct.). Capital disadvantage: America's failing capital investment system. *Harvard Business Review,* 65–83.

Porter, M. (1992b, September). Capital choices: Changing the way America invests in industry. *Journal of Applied Corporate Finance,* 4–16.

Prahalad, C.K. (1994, Winter). Corporate governance of corporate value added: Rethinking the primacy of shareholder value. *Journal of Applied Corporate Finance,* 40–50.

Profits and pride are at stake in shakeup at ailing Olivetti. (1996, September 20). *New York Times,* p. C3.

Prowse, S. (1992). The structure of corporate ownership in Japan. *Journal of Finance, 47,* 1121–1140.

Prowse, S. (1994, July). Corporate governance in an international perspective: A survey of corporate control mechanisms among large firms in the US, UK, Japan, and Germany. *BIS Economic Papers, No. 41.* Switzerland: Basle.

Prowse, S. (1996). Corporate finance in an international perspective: Legal and regulatory influences on financial system development. *Federal Reserve Bank of Dallas Economic Review.*

Roe, M.J. (1993). Some differences in the corporate structure in Germany, Japan, and the United States. *The Yale Law Review, 102,* 1927–2003.

Roe, M.J. (1994a). German "populism" and the large public corporation. *International Review of Law and Economics, 14,* 187–202.

Roe, M.J. (1994b). *Strong managers, weak owners: The political roots of American corporate finance.* Princeton, NJ: Princeton University Press.

Roe, M.J. (1997). The political roots of American corporate finance. *Journal of Applied Corporate Finance,* 9.

Romano, R. (1993). A cautionary note on drawing lessons from comparative corporate law. *The Yale Law Journal, 102,* 2021–2037.

Shareholder rights go global. (1998, April 7). *International Herald Tribune,* p. 11.

Sheard, P. (1989). The main bank system and corporate monitoring and control in Japan. *Journal of Economic Behavior and Organization, 11,* 399.

Shivdasani, A. (1993). Board composition, ownership structure and hostile takeovers. *Journal of Accounting and Economics, 16,* 167–198.

Shleifer, A., & Vishny, R. (1997). A survey of corporate governance. *Journal of Finance, 52,* 737–783.

A specter in Europe: Shareholders demand rights. (1998, April 28). *International Herald Tribune,* p. 11.

Stakeholder capitalism: Unhappy families. (1996, February 10). *The Economist,* 23–25.

Start-ups. (1997, December 6,). *The Economist,* 113.

Statistical Abstract of the United States, (1996, 1997, 1998). Washington, DC: U.S. Department of Commerce.

Sugarman, D., & Teubner, G. (1990). *Regulating corporate groups in Europe.* Baden-Baden, Germany: Nomos Verlagsgesellschaft.

Summers, C. (1980). Worker participation in the US and West Germany: A comparative study from an American perspective. *The American Journal of Comparative Law, 28,* 367–392.

Sundaram, A. (1994). International financial markets. In D.E. Logue (Ed.), *The Handbook of International Finance.* New York: Warren, Gorham & Lamont.

Sundaram, A., & Black, J.S. (1992). The environment and internal organization of multinational enterprises. *Academy of Management Review, 17,* 729–757.

Sundaram, A., & Venkatraman, N. (1999). Organizational forms. In N. Venkatraman & J. Henderson (Eds.), *Research in strategic management and information technology* (Vol. 2). Greenwich, CT: JAI Press.

Swanson, C.B. (1996). Corporate governance: Sliding seamlessly into the twenty-first century. *Journal of Corporate Law, 21,* 417.

Technology productivity and jobs creation. (1996). *Organization for economic cooperation and development.* Paris: Author.

US multinational corporations: Operations in 1993. (1995, June). *Survey of Current Business.* Washington, DC: U.S. Department of Commerce.

Vagts, D. (1966). Reforming the "modern" corporation: Perspectives from the German. *Harvard Law Review, 80,* 23–89.

Various monthly issues on foreign trade statistics, from 1991 to 1996. *Survey of current business.* Washington, DC: U.S. Department of Commerce.

World investment report 1996. (1996). *Investment, trade and international policy arrangements.* New York and Geneva: United Nations.

Notes

1. The tensions between value creation and value transference (and how to resolve such tensions) have been at the heart of many major historical governance debates. See BSSW for a summary of some key debates in the United States over time, and between the United States and other major economies.

2. There are some notable exceptions (but they are few and far between): see, for instance, Porter (1992a; 1992b), Prahalad (1994), and Donaldson and Preston (1995).

3. Perhaps the best example of this perspective is the paper by Jensen and Meckling (1976), which, building on the earlier works of Coase (1937), Williamson (1964), and Alchian and Demsetz (1972), posits that incentives of corporate managers to maximize shareholder value is proportional to the fraction of the firm's shares they hold in their personal portfolios.

4. For example, in a comprehensive and authoritative summary of the corporate governance literature in finance, Shleifer and Vishny (1997, p. 738) define corporate governance as the process "that deals with the ways in which suppliers of finance to corporations assure themselves of getting a return on their investment," and readily admit that their ". . . perspective on corporate governance is a straightforward agency perspective, sometimes referred to as the separation of ownership and control."

5. A report in the *Financial Times* notes that there is no equivalent in the German language for the phrase "shareholder value." See Stefan Wagstyl, "Crumbs from the Table," *Financial Times,* Sept. 25, 1996, p. 15.

6. American Law Institute, "Principles of Corporate Governance," Section 2.01.

7. *Dodge v. Ford Motor Company,* 170 N.W. 668, 664, (Michigan, 1919).

8. M. Fukao, *Financial Integration, Corporate Governance and the Performance of Multinational Corporations.* Brookings Institute (1995).

9. In a study reported by the Organization for Economic Cooperation and Development (OECD, 1995) of large, nonmajority-owned firms in Germany, Baums and Fraune found that nearly 85% of the voting shares in 1992 was controlled by banks and their associated investment funds.

10. In his sample of Japanese firms, Prowse (1994) reports that in 45% of the firms, the largest shareholding bank is also the largest debtholder, accounting for about 25% of the firm's debt, on average. The five largest debtholders in a firm had, on average, 50% of the firms' debt and about 20% of its equity.

11. The *Mergers and Acquisitions Almanac* published by the Securities Data Corporation reports that the number of contested tender offers has fallen from a high of 59 in 1988 to only one each in 1991 and 1992. In 1997, which was a record year for the number of tender offers (200), only eight were contested.

12. Fukao, *Financial. . . .*

13. Fukao, *Financial. . . .*

14. J. Kang and A. Shivdasani, "Firm Performance, Corporate Governance, and Top Executive Turnover in Japan," *Journal of Financial Economics* vol. 38 (1995), pp. 29–58.

15. Murphy, (1998).

16. Fukao, *Financial. . . .*

17. G. Crystal, *In Search of Excess,* (1991).

18. Narayanan and Sundaram, (1998).

19. M. Porter, "Capital Disadvantage: America's Failing Capital Investment System," *Harvard Business Review,* (September/October 1992a), pp. 65–83.

20. See R. Coase, "The Nature of the Firm," *Economica,* vol. 4 (1937), p. 386.

21. See E.M. Dodd, "For Whom Are Corporate Managers Trustees," *Harvard Law Review,* 45 (1932), p. 1145.

22. OECD (1995) reports that Germany has among the lowest levels of strike activity among the OECD group of countries, and that an extremely high proportion of new recruits (71%) receive formal training from employers through apprenticeship systems "representing a considerable investment by both firms and workers (through lower pay), partly related to the expected long tenure." The report also points out that, in Germany, employment adjustments to output fluctuations happens more through the *number of hours* worked, compared to the United States where the *number employed* bears a much larger part of the adjustment.

23. M.J. Roe, "German 'Populism' and the Large Public Corporation," *International Review of Law and Economics,* vol. 14 (1994a), pp. 187–202. M.J. Roe, *Strong Managers, Weak Owners: The Political Roots of American Corporate Finance* (Princeton, NJ: Princeton University Press, 1994b).

24. Fukao, *Financial.* . . .

25. M. Bradley, C. Schipani, A. Sundaram, & J. Walsh, *Corporate Governance in a Comparative Setting: The United States, Japan, and Germany* (June 1999). Paper presented at the Academy of Legal Studies in Business National Meetings, St. Louis. M. Bradley, C. Schipani, A. Sundaram, & J. Walsh, "Purposes and Accountability of the Corporation Corporate Governance at a Crossroads" [In special issue *Challenges to Corporate Governance*], *Journal of Law and Contemporary Problems,* (fall 1999).

26. For a detailed discussion of the case of Daimler-Benz and its governance transformation (including its subsequent merger with Chrysler of the United States to become "DaimlerChrysler"), see BSSW; also see Logue and Seward (1999), in the same issue.

Managing the Functional Areas at the Global Level

6

Global Product Development

SUNDARESAN RAM

Product innovations are critical for the survival and growth of any organization. Most successful companies obtain at least a third of their revenues and more than 40% of their profits (over a 3 to 5 year period) from new products. More than 80% of these innovations are incremental in nature and build on existing platforms (continuous innovations); less than 20% of innovations are new platforms (discontinuous innovations). The product development game is plagued with the risk of failure, and the odds of creating a commercially successful product are quite low. Compare this low success rate with the tremendous costs incurred by companies for product development in one or more of the functional areas: R&D (pharmaceuticals, biotechnology, microprocessors), manufacturing (automobiles), marketing (consumer packaged goods). Given the tremendous financial stakes, targeting several countries has become a strategy for improving the odds of success through market diversification. Thus, simultaneous product development for multiple markets is no longer an option—it has become a necessity for corporate survival. If the R&D cost of a software platform like Windows 95 exceeds $50M, and the installed user base is 100 million users in different countries, the average cost per user is 50 cents—not bad for a product that has an introductory price of $95!

Only after the mid-1990s has research in the area of global product development gained momentum. This is not surprising, because it was in this period that we witnessed the explosive growth in the emerging markets of Asia, Eastern Europe, and Latin America. Further, the advent of the Internet has rendered the marketplace truly borderless and allowed consumers to purchase and use products developed and commercialized in another country. However, most of the recent research compares two or more markets and focuses on how cross-cultural differences affect product development and product success/failure. The adaptation of products for foreign markets is but one aspect of what could be considered global product development. If we walked into five organizations today and asked them to describe their global product development process, we are likely to get five different descriptions—part of the problem is due to what the term global connotes for each organization. In this chapter, we try to resolve these inherent discrepancies and develop a framework for depicting and defining the parameters of global product development.

We address three specific issues: (1) the four major strategic choices for product development across international markets; (2) the key differences in the product development process as it shifts from a domestic perspective to an international perspective; and, (3) a framework to evaluate organizations on their effectiveness in product development across multiple markets.

Product Development for International Markets: Strategic Choices

The extent to which a company can "globalize" its product development activities depends on two factors: internal integration and market responsiveness.

The discussion in the literature on standardization versus adaptation primarily addresses the responsiveness dimension (i.e., to what degree the product must be adapted to suit market conditions).

Internal integration is the extent to which a company can leverage its activities in the value chain across several products and multiple markets, maximizing resource efficiency within the organization, by exploiting economies of scale and scope. Integration is based on the premise that the power of an organization's R&D centers, manufacturing plants, and marketing muscle can be effectively harnessed and directed toward product development in several markets. There are several reasons why integration would seem logical, including:

- Customers in different markets have the same universal need (e.g., Intel's microprocessors need little alteration for use in different countries).
- Global customers demand a coordinated product delivery system (customers such as Citibank or American Express who expect the same level of products/services in every market where they are present).
- Global competitors (who are present in several markets and could seize the initiative by integrating first).
- High fixed costs (in manufacturing, technology investments, R&D) that need to be amortized over a larger customer base.
- Pressures for cost reduction: to compete in emerging markets where price competition is intense, or the buying power is low, the ability to drive down prices through cost efficiency becomes critical.

Integration thus builds a common organizational bond of cost containment by focusing and coordinating all value-creating activities across multiple products and multiple markets. Since 80% of new products tend to be incremental innovations, which eventually commoditize due to competitive parity, cost efficiency becomes crucial for maintaining profitability. In markets where there is intense competition, the cost advantage obtained through integration enables participation on the basis of price; in markets where differentiation is possible, a higher price can be extracted using the same low cost base. Without the cost efficiency generated from integration, entry into certain markets may not be viable at all.

Market responsiveness is the extent to which a company customizes its products to different markets. Due to differentiation, the more "responsive" products generate higher prices (revenues) from customers; however, there are higher costs (money, people, time) associated with the customization. Responsiveness becomes necessary when:

- Customers in different markets have distinctly different needs.
- Country-specific regulations demand product adaptations.
- Customers in each market demand speedy delivery.

There are four broad strategies for product development based on the extent of integration and responsiveness (see Figure 6.1).

Multidomestic Strategy

This strategy is appropriate if the customers in each market require special adaptations of the product, due to major differences in the market environment. A high degree of responsiveness may be required in individual markets for product categories such as food and clothing, where cultural norms dictate usage differences. For example, research conducted in India revealed that cereals were consumed by children primarily as an afternoon snack and with *warm* milk. So, traditional positioning of a breakfast food consumed with cold milk would just not work here.

A multidomestic strategy literally allows each country manager to develop her own domestic product development strategy, when market conditions are so different. The national subsidiaries are vested with a high degree of autonomy, and operational efficiency is emphasized on a country-by-country basis. Integration of activities

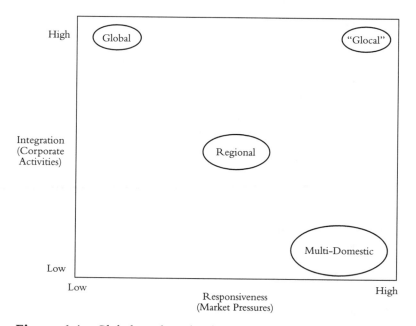

Figure 6.1   Global product development: Strategic choices.

across markets becomes problematic because of the high degree of responsiveness required. Each subsidiary conducts its own product/market research and decides on resource commitments for various products, while corporate headquarters primarily provides the financial controls and suggests the broad product portfolio. The net result is that, for the same new product, the amount of commitment varies from country to country, with some country managers choosing to provide zero support.

From a resource utilization perspective, the multidomestic strategy can be very expensive: the low level of integration precludes cost efficiency, and the high degree of responsiveness demanded by each market tends to escalate adaptation costs. Hence, the viability of the multidomestic strategy would depend on the profitability it can (and should) create due to the high degree of responsiveness. At the risk of generalizing, consumer products (such as food, clothing) tend to have strong cultural influences and require higher responsiveness; industrial products (such as castings, nuts, bolts) require little adaptation and provide for a higher scope of integration.

Regional Strategy

This strategy trades-off market responsiveness for a higher degree of integration in the functional areas. Product development is considered at the level of Southeast Asia, Eastern Europe, or Latin America, and country differences within each region are "smoothed out" for the sake of operational (and cost) efficiency. The regional chiefs or vice presidents have autonomy over product choices and resource commitments, operating under the broad product portfolio and financial guidelines provided by headquarters.

Global Strategy

When a company has an identical product development approach for all its markets, then it is said to have a global strategy. The operating philosophy is to look for and emphasize the similarities among the different markets, rather than the differences. The customers in each market obtain the same standardized product (low adaptation or responsiveness), while the value-creating activities of the company, such as manufacturing, R&D, procurement, and front-end marketing, are highly integrated *across* markets. In most cases, it is the sales and distribution activities alone that are relegated to the local market level. While industrial products (such as steel, castings, microprocessors) are more amenable to integration with minimal market adaptations, consumer product companies have embraced global product development to enjoy the immense cost efficiency it provides. Lego Toys and Gillette are examples of companies that demonstrate this approach for their modular toys and razors, respectively.

"Glocal" Strategy

"Glocal" strategy attempts to simultaneously reap the benefits of both integration and responsiveness, without giving up either. It could simply be stated as "Think Global, Act Local." The product mandate is at the global level; organizational roles become fluid, as there are multiple centers of excellence (rather than a single headquarters) that get involved in the development process. Since the company could pursue different approaches to the various markets, a high emphasis is placed on transfer of knowledge across countries. Organizational learning (i.e., transfer and assimilation of best practices across geographical and functional boundaries) becomes the critical element for successful product development.

When a company speaks of global product development, it typically uses any of the first three methods defined above (multidomestic, regional, global) or some hybrid thereof. None of these strategies per se is superior to another. However, it is important that the company makes a *conscious* choice of the appropriate development strategy, given its customers, competitors and the rest of the market environment in which it operates.

Anecdotal evidence suggests that few companies have adopted the "glocal" approach. While offering the best of both worlds (i.e., integration and responsiveness), it requires a tremendous shift in resources and mindset to move from global to glocal (radical increase in responsiveness), or from multidomestic to glocal (huge increase in integration). The most innovative companies of the future would strive for this "ideal" point on the product development approach. The critical issue is building a culture that focuses simultaneously on the cost efficiency provided by integration, and the cost management needed to create responsiveness.

The Product Development Cycle: Impact of Globalization

Next, we discuss how the traditional product development cycle (PDC), typically discussed in the context of one market, is impacted when multiple markets need to be simultaneously considered. The PDC, with its five major steps, is shown in Figure 6.2.

Idea Generation

Only one out of seven product concepts that enter the idea generation phase succeed in the marketplace. Hence, the success of the PDC depends on: (1) quality of ideas: maximizing the "good" ideas that enter this phase, (2) sources of ideas: maximizing the sources from which these good ideas are generated, and (3) ideas inventory: maintaining an "idea bank"—of the good ideas generated in the past.

Quality of Ideas

From where do organizations get their best ideas? Internally, the ideas flow from employees in key functional areas—such as R&D, marketing, sales, and production. Externally, the ideas could come from customers, suppliers, distributors, or just about any one involved in the value-adding activities provided by the company to its customers.

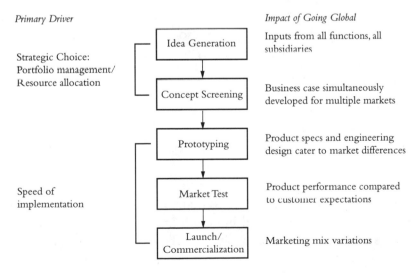

Figure 6.2   Global product development cycle.

How does an organization ensure that only best ideas enter this phase? It can do so by having a clearly defined *innovation charter.*

An innovation charter is a clear, concise statement of the company's philosophy regarding product development. (It is *not* the mission statement or any of the motherhood statements in the annual reports or elsewhere). The innovation charter should fit the company's strategic focus, state what the company does best, and identify what types of products/markets the company plans to pursue. More importantly, it should not be another of those documents that are created and shelved, and have no meaningful impact on the reality of product development. The innovation charter needs to be communicated by the top management to each employee at every opportunity—at lunch meetings, by e-mail, at the water fountain, at performance reviews. Similarly, the charter needs to be communicated to all stakeholders outside the company, who are potential sources of ideas.

As an example, let us consider the Scott Paper company (acquired a few years ago by Kimberly Clark), which manufactured paper products and soap dispensing systems for use in places such as office restrooms. The innovation charter of the company was to create products/processes that would allow the company to sell more soap and paper—since the highest margins were in these products: the soap dispensing systems were one way in which the company could sell more soap, just as Gillette gives away razors to sell more blades.

Once the innovation charter is clearly defined, communicated and assimilated by each and every "source," the quality of ideas that enter phase 1 of the PDC are likely to be higher.

Sources of Ideas

As the product development process becomes more international in scope, inputs from all subsidiaries as well as "partners" (suppliers, distributors, customers) in different geographies becomes critical.

Ideas Inventory

Finally, an organization needs to maintain a database of all the ideas generated, cross-referenced by source, time, and reasons for which it was proposed. Anyone involved in the product development process should be able to access this information, as and when needed. In short, good ideas proposed in the past will never be lost, and could be "borrowed" by anyone, anytime without having to "reinvent the wheel."

Concept Screening

In this stage, the product concepts with the most promising business cases are identified. The business case is developed on the basis of specific criteria for *internal fit* (e.g., does the concept fit with the company's strategic goals? Does it fit with the functional capabilities of the firm, such as manufacturing or marketing? Does it fit with the existing product line?) and specific criteria for *external fit* (e.g., What is the potential market—sales volume/profits? What is the likely penetration? How well will it compare to competitive offerings/substitutes?). Thus, IBM's failure in copying machines and Xerox's failure in computers can be attributed to the lack of internal fit, even though there was adequate external fit.

When a company simultaneously pursues multiple markets:

- The criteria for internal fit and external fit and the relative importance or weights of each need to be clearly specified.
- If the same criteria and weights are to be used across all countries, this needs to be stated clearly. Alternately, if the criteria are to be used differently for each country or each region, this needs to be clarified.
- The firm needs to identify which key markets (at a minimum) must show promising business cases for product development to proceed further.

Further, the screening is most effective if senior management from different geographies and different functions are involved—hence the need for cross-functional, cross-national teams that evaluate products for multiple markets.

Prototyping

In this phase, production and engineering need to design the prototype(s) catering to differences in customer needs across markets. Compared to the traditional process, where prototype development was typically sequential (first the key lead market, then followed by other lag markets), an early involvement of each country manager at this phase enhances the likelihood of a synchronized launch later.

Market Testing

When product performance expectations vary from country to country, and the product has been adapted to meet these varying expectations, extensive product testing may be required. If the performance expectations are more uniform, then market testing may be directed to the leading edge markets/customers who account for most of the potential. As always, the market testing phase could be skipped if the company has decided to commit to the product's success, faces time pressure, or does not want to tip off its competitors.

Launch/Commercialization

The launch is the most critical phase for successful implementation. It is the culmination of several months of intense effort, and in the global product development process, it is an effective way to shut out competitors in as many markets as possible. Any organization should, therefore, strive for a synchronized launch in all the major markets that account for the lion's share of the potential revenues. Accomplishing this ideal is, however, not an easy task due to the huge variations in marketing mix that may be required in each market. The more differences there are, from country to country, in the requirements for packaging, pricing, advertising, promoting and distributing the products, the greater the planning and coordination that is required for a global launch. If a company fails to attack all its major markets during the initial launch, it provides a window of opportunity for its competitors. Gillette, for example, attacks at least all its key markets on the first day of launch, as a pre-emptive measure against its competitors.

In today's intensely competitive environment, one of the major goals for corporations is to shrink the time to market. The time efficiency can be accomplished in two stages: (1) The product selection/resource allocation stage (consisting of idea generation and concept screening) is heavily influenced by senior management. Here time efficiency is achieved, if senior management clearly communicates its priorities for product selection and project funding. Thus, a clear *focus* on the right kinds of product ideas creates efficiency. Further, products that create excellent business cases for several key markets are more likely to get funded (than those that work in isolation). (2) The implementation stage (consisting of prototyping, market testing, and launch/commercialization) relies on the ability of the field troops to get the job done. It calls for *coordination* and *communication* among the different geographies, so that the launch can be synchronized across as many markets as feasible to have the maximum impact.

For the global product development to succeed, certain organizational factors need to be in place:

- An innovation council, comprising senior managers, who share and utilize their knowledge of the different markets to screen and fund the best development projects.
- Product development teams, which are cross-functional, cross-national, and not entirely virtual; the team members need to, on a frequent basis, debate the similarities and differences required from the same product for different markets.
- A product champion, who coordinates the efforts across the different markets, and is accountable for the deliverables of the project—without accountability, the development effort stagnates.
- An early buy-in from all the major markets for which the product is intended, and thereafter an ongoing involvement with the product development process.
- On-going communication between the different participating markets, in terms of trials, tribulations and minor victories along the way—this is the real "learning" that can engender future strength in the product development process.
- Incentives for innovative product ideas.
- Involvement of the top management in the product development process beyond the resource allocation stage into implementation. (This implies constant contact with the development team members wherever they are located.)

Today, most organizations are involved in the struggle of creating the right structure and right process to make global product development a reality.

Global Product Development:
A Self-Assessment Scale

Based on the most important facets of global product development, we have developed a scale that every organization can use to assess its effectiveness (see Figure 6.3). The scale is self-explanatory and addresses four critical areas: corporate philosophy, communications, management, and results. The first two areas, Corporate Philosophy and Communications, address the key role played by senior management: the development of a clearly defined innovation charter, and repeated propagation of this philosophy to all employees so that they assimilate it. The third area, Management, addresses the importance of the implementation process: maximizing speed from implementation to commercialization, creation of cross-functional, cross-national teams, and building accountability through a product champion. The fourth area, Results, identifies benchmarks that companies can use to evaluate the effectiveness of their product development process: the two measures suggested are the types of products developed (incremental innovations versus new platforms); and the sales generated by *global* products (i.e., products developed simultaneously for several international markets). A score below 70% in any of the areas would indicate a critical deficiency in the organization's product development process.

Conclusion

Successful global product development is ultimately based on the transfer of best practices within an organization. This implies high coordination of all value-creating activities from the outset without compromising on market responsiveness. Companies that succeed in global product development will have:

- A clearly defined innovation charter, that is assimilated by every employee.
- A large commitment (time, money, people) to new product development *across* multiple markets.
- Open communication of the nature and extent of this commitment to employees and other stakeholders (suppliers, distributors, customers; shareholders).

Corporate Philosophy

1. A clearly defined innovation charter?

0	10
Poorly Defined	Clearly Defined

2. Extent of pressure on everyone in your organization to innovate?

0	10
No Pressure	A lot of Pressure

Communications

3. Top management's communication of product development priorities

0	10
Very Effectively	Very Ineffectively

4. Frequency of contact between top management and product development teams in all global subsidiaries

0	3	10
Annual Basis	Monthly Basis	Daily Basis

Management

5. Mastery of the drudgery (speed of commercialization)

0	3	10
Below Industry Average	Industry Average	The Best in the Industry

6. Incentives for being innovative (effort, *not* just results)

0	10
Poor	Excellent

7. Composition of product development teams

(A)

0	10
Primarily Corporate HQ	Representatives of all Global Subsidiaries

(B)

0	10
Primarily Marketing and R&D	Cross-Functional

8. A project champion for every global product development effort?

No — 0   Yes — 10

Results

9. Number of new products developed in the last 3 years with a global focus (score 4 points for a platform; 2 points for a major adaptation; 1 for a minor adaptation

0	10
None	Six or More

10. Percentage of annual revenues from global products

0	10
Less Than 10%	50% or More

Figure 6.3   Global product development: A self-assessment.

- Incentives and career progress for entrepreneurial employees, who can create commercial product successes and leverage it across markets.

References

Chryssochidis, G.M., & Wong, V. (1998). Rolling out new products across country markets: An empirical study of causes of delays. *Journal of Product Innovations Management, 15*(1), 16–41.

Davidson, W.H., & Harrigan, R. (1977). Key decisions in international marketing: Introducing new products abroad. *Columbia Journal of World Business, 12,* 15–23.

Davidson, W.H., & Haspelagh, P. (1982). Shaping a global product organization. *Harvard Business Review, 60,* 125–132.

Duarte, D., & Snyder, N. (1997). Facilitating global organizational learning in product development at Whirlpool Corporation. *Journal of Product Innovation Management, 14*(1), 48–55.

Hill, J.S., & James, W.L. (1991). Product and promotion transfers in consumer goods multinationals. *International Marketing Review, 8,* 6–17.

Kumar, V., Ganesh, J., & Echambadi, R. (1998). Cross-national diffusion research: What we know and how certain we are. *Journal of Product Innovation Management, 15,* 225–268.

Mishra, S., Kim, D., & Lee, D.H. (1996). Factors affecting new product success: Cross-country comparisons. *Journal of Product Innovation Management, 13*(6), 530–550.

Sheth, J.N., & Ram, S. (1987). *Bringing innovation to market: How to break corporate and customer barriers.* New York: John Wiley & Sons.

Song, X.M., & Parry, M.E. (1997). A cross-national comparative study of new product development process: Japan and the United States. *Journal of Marketing, 64*(2), 1–14.

Souder, W.E., & Jenssen, S.A. (1999). Management practices influencing new product success and failure in the United States and Scandinavia: A cross-cultural comparative study. *Journal of Product Innovation Management, 16*(2), 183–203.

Souder, W.E., & Song, X.M. (1998). Analysis of US and Japanese management processes associated with new product success and failure in high and low familiarity markets. *Journal of Product Innovation Management, 15,* 208–223.

Walters, P.G.P., & Toyne, B. (1989). Product modification and standardization in international markets: Strategic options and facilitating policies. *Columbia Journal of World Business, 24,* 37–44.

7

Global Supply Chain Management

WILLIAM E. YOUNGDAHL

Western Digital, a major manufacturer of computer disk drives, in 1999, decided to turn over the logistics of its entire global supply chain to a single third-party logistics supplier, GeoLogistics.[1] Western Digital produces all of its disk drives in Singapore and Malaysia and must deliver these drives to a global customer base. Prior to this decision, the company had contracted with five freight forwarders. The decision to go with a single provider followed a process of developing a set of strategic objectives for the supply chain. These objectives included: (1) flexibility to respond to rapidly changing customer requirements, (2) predictable supply and reliable delivery to satisfy demand requirements, (3) Internet shipping tracking capabilities to permit proactive replanning and customer notification, (4) improved performance measurement, a difficult challenge when operating with five providers, and (5) a long-term relationship or alliance with the provider that would ensure that Western Digital would receive an appropriate degree of management focus and attention from the supply chain provider.

Western Digital executives had long since determined that the details of supply chain management were not part of the company's desired core competencies. The decision to contract with a single provider of supply chain management services underscores Western

Digital's strategic decision to separate its core competencies of disk drive design and manufacturing from the vital functions of managing flows of materials and related information. The company has achieved world-class supply chain management capabilities through an alliance rather than holistic growth of supply chain management competencies.

The purpose of this example is not to convince readers to outsource all supply chain functions to a single provider. In some cases, such as Dell Computer Corporation, the supply chain is and will continue to be a coveted distinctive competency—core to the competitive advantage of the organization. Globalization and rapid evolution of information systems capabilities, as well as current attempts to standardize supply chain information protocols, are some of the trends that are creating a new competitive arena in which supply chains will compete against one another. Static supply chains characterized by well-defined links will give way to virtual supply chains in which balances of power and contribution will shift within seemingly unlimited bounds. Finally, the trend is not limited to large corporations. Smaller companies have been greatly expanding their global presence in recent years.

Global supply chain management is about managing value creation on a global basis. A supply chain determines the cost structure and capabilities of an enterprise. In the case of Dell Computer Corporation, the supply chain defines the value of the company. Furthermore, globalization of markets and direct sales through the Internet call for new ways of linking chains of suppliers and customers globally. Companies that formulate and execute effective global supply chain strategies will prosper; those that do not will vanish. Never before have senior executives been more pressed to understand, formulate, and implement effective global supply chain strategies.

The next section discusses global operations strategy. Our strategy laying out how and where we perform value-adding production and design processes largely determines our options for global supply chain strategy. Later, four evolutionary stages of global supply chain management are described, followed by concluding remarks.

Global Operations Strategy

Most "global" companies have evolved from earlier stages of domestic, then multinational operations.[2] During the initial stage of globalization, executives begin to explore modes of preliminary foreign entry including exporting and licensing. The organizational learning acquired during this initial stage builds the confidence required to enter the multinational stage during which the company will develop operations in multiple countries while maintaining a headquarters operation in the home country. The domestic orientation yields to a multinational orientation of decentralized markets. During this stage, localization of products through decentralized product development stretches the reach of the company to multiple new markets around the globe. Finally, the alliances that made the multinational enterprise possible help propel the organization to the level of advanced global operations. At this stage, the focus shifts from how to manage disparate regional operations to one of integrating and exchanging knowledge and technologies within a global network of capabilities. It is this advanced stage of global operations that defines and creates progressive global supply chain management.

Decades ago, Goodyear established a tire factory in Oxo, Mexico, just outside Mexico City to serve primarily the Mexican market. When the Mexican economic crisis of 1994 hit, the bottom dropped out of the domestic tire market. Rather than build inventory to keep the plant running or face the even less desirable alternative of laying off unionized Mexican workers, the company changed the strategic role of the factory by shifting from a local market orientation to one of being a low-cost producer serving global markets. Leveraging its existing markets and supply chain capabilities, Goodyear shifted much of its excess output to markets in the United States. Additionally, engineers from the Oxo plant developed a tire for export to European markets. Shifting from a manufacturer that produced at 75% of capacity serving a closed Mexican market to a manufacturer that had to create global reach required extraordinary leadership. Hugh Pace, the managing director, was able to lead the transformation of the strategic role of the Oxo plant from a local market server to an exporter by reconfiguring its global supply chain.[3] Knowledge of the linkages between global operations strategy and global supply chain management facilitated establishing and implementing successful global supply chain strategies.

Formulating a sound global supply chain strategy begins with a solid understanding of global operations strategy. One way of conceptualizing the strategic role of operations is to think deeply about the very reason for having operations in various locations around the globe.[4] How do "foreign factories" contribute to objectives such as achieving low cost, providing market responsiveness, and providing knowledge to the global enterprise? Each of these roles, depicted in Figure 7.1, adds value to an enterprise's global supply chain in different ways.

The primary role of both offshore and source plants is low-cost production, supporting a physically efficient supply chain strategy. An

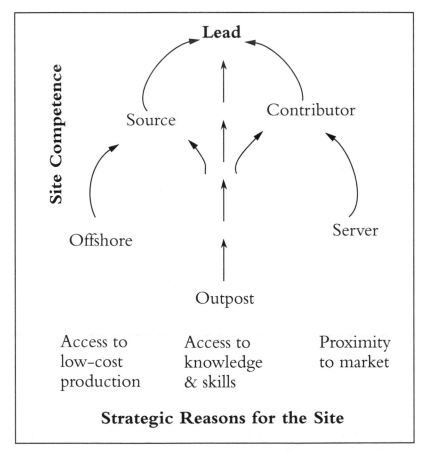

Adapted from Ferdows, K. (1997). "Making the Most of Foreign Factories," *Harvard Business Review,* March–April, pp. 73–88.

Figure 7.1   The strategic roles and evolution of foreign factories.

offshore plant is one that has been established to exploit access to low cost production of specific items that are exported for sale or further value added. The plant provides neither product nor process innovation. Rather it follows specific directions from process and product design centers elsewhere in the supply chain. Similar to the offshore plant, a *source* plant also exploits low-cost production inputs. Additionally, however, a source plant assumes some product, typically individual parts, and process development responsibilities.

Server and contributor plants are established to serve specific markets, supporting a market-responsive supply chain strategy. A *server* plant is established to supply specific national or regional markets. A *contributor* plant also serves local markets while assuming responsibility for product customization, process improvements, or product development.

Outpost plants are established primarily to gain access to knowledge and information. These plants are located in regions known for certain capabilities, such as the Silicon Valley. By feeding useful information to a global supply network, these outpost plants provide a vital knowledge management function.

Finally, *lead* factories possess a full range of product and process capabilities. They are centers of excellence for the global supply chain. The evolution from low-cost producer or simple market access to assuming full responsibility for design and manufacturing involves extensive technology transfer and learning that can take well over a decade, particularly in developing nations. For example, Hewlett-Packard's plant in Singapore evolved from offshore, producing low-cost components, to lead with full responsibility for the design and manufacture of portable printers over a period of about 20 years.

Sorting out roles of operations depends on product development strategies of an organization. There exist three basic structures for developing products for global markets: single product development, multidomestic product development, and global product development.[5] When developing its new Escort model (called Focus), Ford abandoned its multidomestic approach and designed a world car using global product development. Honda, when designing a recently launched Accord model, abandoned its single product development approach and used global engineering capacity to design regionally customized versions of the new Accord.

Single product development strategies aim to develop global products that will appeal to many markets. R&D activities and manufacturing are centralized at headquarters. Developing global products, those companies are able to reach greater economies of scale by concentrating activities at a single location (headquarters). Companies develop a one-size-fits-all product when global demand for the product is not diverse and cost savings from economies of scale are important. There are several potential disadvantages to the single product development approach. When manufacturing is concentrated in one location, the company is more sensitive to political risk, currency risk, and trade/tariff barriers. Additionally, it has limited access to worldwide resources including technological innovations, low-cost labor, and expertise. Last, lack of proximity to local markets makes it difficult to cater to local needs.

The *multidomestic product development* approach decentralizes development processes to regional levels for fully independent regional product development. This approach regards competition in one country as independent from competition in other countries. Close proximity to main regional markets allows each region to carry out its own R&D activities for products completely tailored to the region. Manufacturing is also carried out in each region. Companies use a multidomestic approach when it is important to fill niche segments of regional markets. But problems with this method are that the value chain is repeated in every country, thus not creating any synergies, and the company does not attain any economies of scale producing products on just a regional basis.

In contrast to the two methods previously described, *global product development* coordinates the use of worldwide resources to avoid redundancies, achieve economies of scale, and meet regional customer needs. Companies may either keep their main R&D facilities located at headquarters with regional subsidiaries responsible for customization, or they may establish centers of excellence, or lead organizations, around the globe. A global network of regional lead organizations provides robust global design capabilities while minimizing political and economic risks.

Organizations leverage global product development capabilities to achieve their corporate goals globally. A company may strive to achieve product diversity in each region, thus tending toward more regional customization of its products. Or a company may eliminate redundancies to achieve economies of scale that allows it to market a single cost-efficient global product. The more dispersed yet integrated global product development structure can also help to obtain better information about new markets and technologies. Last, this global product development approach with the regional centers of excellence lends itself to modular consortium manufacturing that will be described later.

As individual operations evolve in terms of increasing design capabilities or shift from a market to cost focus or vice versa, required supply chain capabilities will also evolve or change. Understanding how a global supply chain must change in response to changes of operations strategy begins with an understanding of the basic elements of supply chain management.

The Basics of Supply Chain Management

The number of senior executives with supply chain management in their job description has skyrocketed. Logistics, transportation, procurement, and other long neglected functions have recently gained respect under the umbrella of supply chain management. Senior executives are being pressed to formulate supply chain strategies—essentially pushing the envelope with respect to current definitions and limitations of how to create value through the orchestration of a network of stakeholders.

Supply chain management has been defined as an integrative end-to-end approach to dealing with the planning and control of materials and information from suppliers to end customers. Given the extent of cooperation required along the chain, effectiveness depends heavily on the management of upstream and downstream relationships with suppliers and customers. The following definition of supply chain management does a good job addressing these upstream and downstream relationships and the central focus on optimizing shared resources to achieve profitability and customer satisfaction:

> The manufacturer and its suppliers, vendors, and customers—that is, all links in the extended enterprise—working together to provide a common product and service to the marketplace that the customer desires and is willing to pay for throughout the life cycle of the product and

service. This multicompany group, functioning as one extended enterprise, makes optimum use of shared resources (people, processes, technology, and performance measurements) to achieve operating synergy. The result is a product or service that is high-quality, low-cost, delivered quickly to the marketplace, and achieves customer satisfaction.[6]

At a more basic level, supply chain processes include planning, sourcing, making, and delivering. These four elements of the Supply Chain Operations Reference (SCOR) Model were identified by the Supply Chain Council, a not-for-profit trade organization consisting of 73 founding member companies across the world, to provide a cross-industry standard for supply chain management. That is, the development of supply chain strategies and management of value chains must include these four elements no matter what industry we consider.

Planning involves processes to balance aggregate demand and supply to develop a course of action that best meets the established business rules or objectives. Supply chain executives must assess supply resources, aggregate and prioritize demand requirements, plan inventory, develop distribution requirements, develop material plans, and perform rough-cut capacity planning for all products and all channels. Additionally, this stage involves managing the planning infrastructure, including make/buy decisions, supply-chain configuration, long-term capacity and resource planning, business planning, product phase-in/phase-out, manufacturing ramp-up, end-of-life management, and product-line management.

Sourcing includes the processes to procure goods and services to meet actual or planned demand. This stage includes tactical steps such as obtaining, receiving, inspecting, storing, and issuing material. It also includes elements to aid in developing the sourcing infrastructure. Examples include vendor certification and feedback, sourcing quality, in-bound freight, component engineering, vendor contracts, and initiation of vendor payments.

Making includes processes to transform goods to a finished state to meet planned or actual demand. On a tactical level, making involves requesting and receiving material, manufacturing and testing products, packaging and holding—and/or releasing products. Managing the make infrastructure spans the development of capabilities including engineering changes, facilities and equipment, production quality, shop scheduling/sequencing, and short-term capacity management.

Delivering includes processes to provide finished goods and services to meet planned or actual demand. Order management, transportation and installation management, and warehouse management are the key elements of the delivery stage. In addition to the myriad tactical elements, this stage includes development of the infrastructure required for managing channel business rules, ordering rules, managing delivered inventories, and managing delivery quality.

Managing these planning, sourcing, making, and delivering activities on a global basis represent formidable challenges for supply chain executives. The supply chain concept extends the focus of operations beyond the firm. Globalization extends supply chains across borders. Finally, as organizations focus on core competencies activities are being redistributed among supply chain stakeholders according to defined competencies.

Globalization mandates the integration of product development, production, and distribution. This challenge occurs in an era characterized by the need to integrate on a global basis as well as pressure to segment the world market. Additionally, issues such as tariffs, exchange rates, culture including language, and differing tastes, to name a few, layer a new set of complexities onto an already complex supply chain management scenario.

Stages of Global Supply Chain Management Strategy

A global supply chain strategy represents an organizational commitment to deliver products to customers on a worldwide basis. As a concept, it is central to corporate operations, a potential source of competitive advantage through management of relationships and operational coordination from supplier to customer. The supply process is a core capability. The purpose of global supply chain strategy is to support the strategic goals of the global enterprise.

The objectives of global supply chain management are usually described by two opposing goals: *effectiveness* in satisfying customers' needs on a worldwide basis and *efficiency* from the perspective of achieving the lowest possible total supply chain cost. Effectiveness ultimately measures how well the output of global supply chain operations meets customers product *and* service needs and requirements in terms of delivery, responsiveness, flexibility, and an ability to offer a variety of products and services.

The evolution of global supply chain management, in most enterprises, consists of four phases: (1) achieving basic functional abilities within and integration among functional groups within operating units; (2) achieving global enterprise-wide integration of systems and procedures; (3) optimizing global supply chain resources by identifying and exploiting constraints within the supply chain; and (4) constructing virtual supply chains to leverage core competencies of supply chain suppliers on near real-time bases to satisfy changing needs of global customers. The fundamental foundations of planning, sourcing, making, and delivering mark the starting point of the journey to world-class global supply chain management. The transformation to an integrated or even virtual global supply chain begins with getting the basics right. These basic operational abilities, once mastered, enable an enterprise to progress to more advanced stages of supply chain management including global integration, supply chain optimization, and the creation of virtual supply chains.

Stage 1: Functional Supply Chain Competence

Imagine attempting to integrate a global supply chain of your own company's factories, suppliers' factories, transportation providers, distribution centers, warehouses, and customers. Now imagine the task if none of your own factories has effective planning and control systems in place. Delivery reliability is abysmal. Factory floors are choked with work in process inventory to the point that lead times for customer orders are completely unpredictable. Your suppliers do not differ significantly in terms of their own operational capabilities. Since great savings can be achieved by shipping full container loads of product versus partial loads, the time spent waiting to fill containers further delays deliveries to other operations within the supply chain and to customers. The message is clear: Strive for basic effectiveness and efficiency of operations before major integration efforts.

The basic thought processes used to achieve lean production provide a useful conceptual framework for achieving the basic effectiveness and efficiency required as a foundation for global supply chain management. While lean production may be more appropriate for discrete assembly operations than for process operations, the basic steps of identifying customer value and ensuring value-added processes by eliminating nonvalue-added activities apply to most if not all operational settings. These basic steps include (1) identifying value from the customer's perspective, (2) identifying value streams and eliminating waste, (3) removing barriers to effective flow, (4) producing to the pull of customers demand, and (5) continuing the cycle of pursuing perfection.[7]

If each entity (and activity) along the value chain does not focus on a shared definition of customer-defined value, different operating units within the company will be making and executing plans to satisfy multiple and often conflicting internally generated performance objectives. Customers' perceptions of value are determined by assessments of benefits to cost. Benefits include lasting results from product purchases such as product reliability and the extent to which the product satisfies desired needs. Customers also benefit from the standpoint of perceived service quality before, during, and after purchase transactions. Customers' costs include financial costs of purchase, maintenance and disposal of products as well as customer burden.[8] Burden relates to how difficult it is to do business with an organization from both consumer and business-to-business points of view as well as the uncompensated aspects of product and service failure.

Once a clear definition of customer value has been identified by customer category (e.g., consumers and intermediary business customers), process mapping should be employed to identify any steps along the extended supply chain processes of making, sourcing, and delivering. It is a good idea to use multifunction teams including involvement of suppliers and major customers. This involvement will ensure that customer value has been properly defined and nonvalue-added activities will be identified and eliminated from both internal operations as well as suppliers' operations.

Uninhibited flow material and information depends on the thoughtful identification of bottlenecks or constraints along the supply chain. From the standpoint of global supply chains, major bottlenecks include clearing of customs and loading of shipping containers. When Western Digital decided to turn over its entire

$50 million global supply chain to a single third-party logistics supplier, GeoLogistics, it did so after identifying these border-crossing and shipping components of its supply chain as significant material and information-flow bottlenecks. From a more local standpoint, right-sizing of production equipment and the use of cellular manufacturing can reduce the need to run large batches of production to justify machine utilization goals. By reducing lot sizes, flow of product through factories accelerates. Reduced lead times and increased responsiveness to customers' needs result.

The accelerated flow contributes to the ability to initiate production on a just-in-time basis when customer demand exists. This concept of demand-pull production underlies the philosophy and practice of just-in-time manufacturing. For example, Dell Computer Corporation does not begin production of a particular computer until it receives a customer order *and* payment. Having removed excess inventory and nonvalue-added steps from its supply chain, Dell generally ships product within a day or two after order receipt.

Finally, laying the basic foundations of an effective and efficient global supply chain requires continuous reexamination of customer value and relentless removal of waste from supply chain processes. Supply chain planning must include development of a course of action to deploy resources to satisfy customers' needs in a profitable manner and processes for reexamining assumptions about customer value, effectiveness, and efficiency on a continuous basis. This underlying foundation facilitates the level of integration required to achieve the next phase of global supply chain management.

Companies using the lean manufacturing approach need to be close to the customer. Having regional presence with manufacturing, or even product development, offers many benefits. Access to local talent, local market knowledge, local supply base, and learning about local values and culture are just some of the reasons why customer proximity is important when designing and manufacturing complex products on a global basis. For companies offering customized products while using a global product development structure, postponement (local customization) is a good option. While the basic design of a new product is done using the regional design and manufacturing centers, customization of this basic design could be done using local resources including the addition of localization kits added to the base product at local or regional distribution centers. For example, in its European and Asian markets, Hewlett-Packard delays final customization of DeskJet printers. Global base printers are sent to a local distribution center for installation of power supplier and packaging.

Stage 2: Global Supply Chain Rationalization and Integration

The challenge of responding to changing market requirements on a global basis requires extensive coordination of design, production, logistics, and transportation. The somewhat paradoxical result is that progressive organizations strive for common processes to achieve global flexibility. Additionally, design considerations including a reduced number of common product platforms and greatly strengthened relationships with top-tier suppliers who are taking on more design and sourcing responsibilities have helped to reduce the complexity of integration. Consider the message delivered two years ago by Kenneth R. Baker, GM's vice president for research and development:

> As you are no doubt aware, GM Chairman Jack Smith has outlined a broad program aimed at transforming General Motors into a truly global organization. As the world's number one vehicle manufacturer, we've always been international. In fact, about 40% of our sales are outside North America. But being global means more than selling to international markets. It means taking advantage of your global resources to do a better job of bringing customer-valued products to market, faster and for less money than your competitors can.[9]

GM and others have realized that achieving global efficiency and flexibility calls for striving for as much commonality as possible to better integrate the efforts of regional design and manufacturing centers. Simple examples include the use of common part numbers and common accounting procedures. Common information systems and processes for handling data and information represent much more complex challenges. GM has recently adopted R/3, an enterprise resource planning system developed by the German company SAP, to integrate its worldwide financial systems. Enterprise resource planning solutions such as SAP's R/3 system allow employees throughout a global enterprise to share common information. From GM's perspective, the R/3 software will allow an employee in Paris to share and work with the same information available to employees in Detroit, while having it translated into French in real time.[10]

Another example of GM's approach to common practices is the development of common product platforms that serve a diversity of markets and customers while simplifying and rationalizing design and manufacturing. The approach is not new; GM developed its first common platform in 1959. What is new is the pace at which the automaker is moving to reduce the number of common platforms across the company. Based on an initiative forwarded by Jack Smith in 1992, GM is reducing the number of basic platforms from 12 to 5. Even Saturn will not be exempt from sharing platforms with other divisions of the company.

In addition to rationalizing resources and developing common processes, this stage of supply chain evolution involves increased partnering with top-tier or tier-1 suppliers. From the standpoint of manufacturing strategy, original equipment manufacturers (OEMs) have traditionally maintained responsibility and control over the design and manufacturing of systems and modules, especially to the extent that these systems and modules contain the embodiment of knowledge they deem to represent core competencies. The current trend toward modularity involves shifting much of what was considered to be the roles and responsibilities of OEMs to tier-1 suppliers. Furthermore, traditional tier-1 roles and responsibilities, such as assembly and component design, are shifting to second- or even third-tier suppliers. In the process, OEMs assume a technology-transfer-facilitator role to ensure that appropriate engineering and manufacturing skills and knowledge transfer to and among the suppliers.

From the standpoint of planning, greater responsibility has also shifted to the tier-1 suppliers. The tier-1 suppliers must now manage a greater number of assembly and components suppliers that may be located throughout the globe. To some extent, the burden of supply chain planning has been shifted from OEMs to major suppliers. Planning in real time while accounting for myriad potential constraints has become a shared responsibility of both OEMs and suppliers. These capabilities characterize the next stage in the evolution of global supply chain management—global supply chain optimization.

Stage 3: Global Supply Chain Optimization

Supply chain optimization can be characterized as a level of supply chain collaboration that involves sharing of information not only for independent planning purposes but also for collaborative synchronized planning efforts. One of the greatest challenges facing operations managers is that of coordination. Joseph C. Andraski, a vice president at the Sales & Integrated Logistics Co. of Nabisco, Inc., suggests that collaborative planning initiatives designed to exchange information and marketing intelligence need to extend beyond the reaches of a particular company to the entire supply chain community. For example, forecasts must be created across supply chain partners including suppliers of raw materials and packaging supplies.[11]

Generally speaking, enterprise resource planning systems are transaction-based information management systems that provide an over-the-shoulder look at what has taken place. Ability to simulate what-if planning scenarios is limited at best with these types of systems. Achieving supply chain optimization calls for a new breed of software solutions. Many software solution vendors have stepped up to the plate to facilitate this new stage of global supply chain management.

Sara Lee Casualwear operates a supply chain with 20 plants and contractors in the United States, Mexico, and Central America. National Textiles is Casualwear's main supplier of cut parts. Sara Lee Casualwear must plan at an SKU, or individual product item, level that includes style, color, and size. Dealing with this complexity and the added wrinkle of seasonal demand, the company determined that its main business drivers are inventory obsolescence, customer service, and inventory turns. Consistent with these drivers, the company developed a value proposition consisting of the following elements: (1) improve visibility into operations, (2) improve production planning, and (3) improve customer service.[12]

Sara Lee Casualwear management decided they needed to model the many complex routings of each SKU. To achieve this goal, they installed a supply chain optimization software solution, RHYTHM, from i2 Technologies. What-if analyses that took a week and a half using conventional data analysis methods can now be done in a few hours. By identifying and exploiting constraints in the global supply chain, executives can rapidly and proactively allocate production across global resources to improve customer service. An added benefit is lower total supply chain cost.

These rapidly emerging advancements in supply chain optimization are enabling a new frontier in global supply chain management—virtual global supply chains. Fueled largely by the power of the Internet but also by effectiveness of relationships, this newly emerging stage of global supply chain management holds great promise for revolutionizing virtually all aspects of business.

Stage 4: Virtual Global Supply Chains

The current revolution in global supply chain management pushes the limits of the meaning of virtual—capturing the desired essence or effect without the burden of conventional notions of reality. That is, virtual supply chains deliver products and services to customers while breaking conventions of time and space. Although the Internet will eventually dominate both the front-end and business-to-business connections of the supply chain, other types of virtual supply chains exist in which conventional notions of supply chain management gave way to radical new ways of distributing responsibilities and power throughout the value chain.

Modular consortia factories provide a tangible departure from the conventional reality of the nature of relationships that manufacturers have with their suppliers. Essentially, modular consortium manufacturing moves what could have been a global supply chain with tremendous transportation challenges into a consortium of suppliers residing within a single factory. Consider the case of Volkswagen's modular consortium in Resende, Brazil, a joint investment between Volkswagen and seven major suppliers. The operations director in Resende has said that the building belongs to Volkswagen and the furniture belongs to the suppliers.[13]

The modular consortium concept revolutionizes approaches to manufacturing and outsourcing. This virtual global supply chain strategy involves dividing the overall product into modules as previously described. The key difference between modular consortium manufacturing and modularity in general is that with modular consortium manufacturing the key suppliers are responsible for assembling their modules directly on the automobile manufacturer's (OEM's) floor.

The modular consortium supply chain model depends on deep trusting relationships with a small number of first-tier suppliers. Suppliers assume responsibility for final assembly of the module in the vehicle, design of the assembly, and management of the entire supply chain for the module. The automobile manufacturer provides the overall physical plant and space on the assembly line. It also assumes responsibility for final testing and overall coordination of the plant.

The modular consortium manufacturing approach works well for establishing regional manufacturing capabilities. Collocation of suppliers facilitates fast response, lean manufacturing. Additionally, regional manufacturing capabilities hedge against global risks including currency and demand fluctuations. When a particular region becomes more expensive or a market diminishes, production can be reallocated to lower cost regions or regions with higher demand. Although the top-tier suppliers collocate with the major manufacturer, the role of these suppliers becomes much more global in that they are now responsible for global sourcing as well as integrating global design of their own modules. The fundamental capabilities developed in the previous supply chain stage, optimization, position suppliers well for this new role of integrator and supply chain manager. For executives finding themselves leapfrogging their supply chains from basic functional production to modular assembly, the transition will require significant transfer of technology including managerial systems, knowledge and skills, and even the values and culture consistent with new module development.

The modular consortium manufacturing approach works well for serving relatively stable regional markets, but what about rapidly changing global markets such as the fashion industry? This situation calls for a different type of virtual supply chain, one that can be constructed and deconstructed rapidly to meet changing market needs. Li & Fung, Hong Kong's largest trading company, exemplifies this emerging capability. With thousands of suppliers around the globe, Li & Fung has managed to "virtualize" the supply chain by ruling it without owning it.[14]

Victor Fung views his operation as a smokeless factory. He has his own factory managers who plan production and balance lines, but these managers do not directly manage employees and Fung does not own the factories. To Fung, the consequence of owning factories would be the management of over a million employees. By focusing on coordination of factories that have granted large contracts, typically 30% to 70% of capacity, Fung achieves significant control over its suppliers' operations while maximizing flexibility, the essence of virtual management. Essentially, the company focuses on the front and the back end of the supply chain. Front-end processes include design, engineering, and production planning. Back-end processes include quality control, inspection, and management of logistics. The lower value-added processes including raw materials sourcing and production are carried out by the trading company's 7,500 suppliers, of which about 2,500 are active at any given time.

Michael Dell's direct model provides the ultimate example of a virtual supply chain. By asking the simple question "If we want to earn higher returns shouldn't we be more selective and put our capital into activities where we can add value for our customers, not just into activities that need to get done?"[15] Michael Dell dispelled fundamental assumptions underlying supply chains. A decade ago, computer manufacturers firmly believed that making components constituted an integral capability that served as a source of competitive advantage; some still do. Like Victor Fung, Michael Dell enjoys all of the flexibility of ownership without the shackles of capital outlay.

Dell focuses on the velocity of inventory rather than the quantity. By working with reliable suppliers such as Sony, Dell can actually manage zero inventory in some cases. It does so by using UPS to match computers from Austin with monitors from Sony's factory in Mexico. The bundled packages are then shipped directly to the customer. Close coordination with suppliers and customers replaces inventory with information.

Using Internet technology, Dell installed extranet Web sites at its major suppliers. The sites provide real-time access to order and manufacturing information to synchronize production with customer demand. Dell is also using the Web to fully integrate its outsourced service providers who perform on-site repairs. Dell has also tailored extranets called Premier Pages to allow major business customers, about 65% of Dell's online sales, to configure and order computers and peripherals. Work is being done to integrate these extranets with the customers' enterprise resource planning systems.

Building virtual supply chains requires an extension of recently popularized ideas of knowledge management to supply chain management. Broadly defined, knowledge is information that can be put to business use. The challenge of global supply chain management in the next millennium will be to use knowledge rather than excess inventory to hedge against marketplace uncertainties. Additionally, the trend toward modularity and supplier alliances calls for a new level of trust that can only be attained through sharing of useful information. Finally, creating a virtual global supply chain can provide many of the benefits of vertical organizations without the burden of cost or loss of flexibility.

Virtual supply chains can be constructed using the Internet to connect globally dispersed suppliers, and customers, and other supply chain stakeholders such as freight forwarders. Alternatively, a virtual supply chain can reside largely under a single roof as a big case of regional modular consortium manufacturing. Ultimately, virtual global supply chain management relies on careful consideration of the balance between where value should be added and help to maximize customer value and flexibility while minimizing total supply chain costs.

Conclusion

The preceding section provided information that can guide executives in thinking about the state of supply chain management and their own companies based on typical evolutionary stages. The stages are summarized in Table 7.1.

Achieving excellence in global supply chain management requires a thoughtful integration of corporate strategy, marketing strategy, and supply chain strategy. The stages of global supply chain management are cumulative. That is, effective achievement of integration depends on reducing nonvalue-added steps from the basic processes of sourcing, manufacturing, and delivery of products. Additionally, effective planning systems or at least capabilities provide a foundation for leading efforts toward global supply chain integration. Similarly, attempting to optimize global supply chains before working out the basics of efficiency, effectiveness, and integration can be a very costly and time-consuming effort since it will by necessity involve developing these latter capabilities. Finally, implementing virtual global supply strategies depends on having already achieved the supply chain optimization goals of identifying and exploiting constraints.

Table 7.1 Stages of Supply Chain Strategy

Stage	Characteristics
Functional supply chain competence	• Basic soundness of planning and control systems. • Effective but not fully integrated communication with suppliers. • Learning of value-adding core processes for manufacturing, sourcing, and delivering.
Global supply chain rationalization and integration	• Adoption of common business processes, generally supported by some form of enterprise resource planning. • Consolidation of supply base. • Shifting of system level design and manufacture to top-tier suppliers.
Global supply chain optimization	• Identification and of constraints on a global basis. • Forward-planning "what-if" capabilities. • Use of supply chain optimization software.
Virtual global supply chain management	• Integration of e-Commerce into all aspects of supply chain management. • Regional modular consortium manufacturing. • Rapid construction and the deconstruction of temporary global supply chains to meet changing market needs. • Management of the highest value-added processes only. • Substitution of information for inventory.

The evolutionary path to revolutionary virtual global supply chains provides some evidence that the flexibility versus efficiency tradeoffs[16] that we generally no longer accept at a factory plant level can also be avoided on a global level. At the extreme ends of the spectrum, customers might be willing to trade cost for flexibility. However, trends suggest that such tradeoffs are becoming exceptions rather than rules in the minds of most customers in most industries. The regional modular consortium manufacturing approach being adopted by automakers provides both efficiency in terms of lean production and flexibility when combined with global product development capabilities, global platforms, and modularity. Likewise, the approach adopted by Li & Fung demonstrates that even diverse and changing global suppliers can be integrated rapidly into virtual global supply chains characterized by high levels of control, coordination, and knowledge management with minimum capital outlay.

Finally, the impact of the Internet on global supply chain management cannot be overstated. Use of the Internet increases Industry clock speeds, or evolutionary life cycles, and rates that could not have been imagined a decade ago. Changes such as modularity, empowering top-tier suppliers with major system design and manufacturing responsibilities, and the Internet will lead to significant opportunities and challenges. For those orchestrating virtual supply chains, the challenge of the holding the chain together will be immense. Consider what happened to IBM when it essentially lost control over its two major module suppliers, Microsoft and Intel. The increased power of mega-suppliers in many virtual supply chains will force executives to question not only the roles of their companies but also the very nature of industry dynamics. The Internet promises even greater attacks on our assumptions.

The extent to which companies will be able to connect with customers over the Internet has only begun to be realized. As the distinction between products continues to blur to the point of commoditization, convenience and service will dominate executives' agendas for supply chain strategy formulation. While a great deal of planning and thought is required to construct front-end e-commerce points of entry to virtual supply chains, speed is of the essence. Now is not the time to charter a two-year exploratory task force to examine how to connect customers and suppliers through the Internet to develop a virtual global supply chain. A useful executive-level exercise at this point is to reflect on the question, "What should we have been doing over the past three years to prepare for this global supply chain revolution?" After answering the question, move swiftly and decisively to close the would-have and should-have gaps.

The journey is not without risks. The computer industry provides an excellent example of the risks of letting go of much of the supply chain. When IBM partnered with Microsoft and Intel, the intent was to gain efficiencies by outsourcing two key non-core competencies, module design and production of the operating system and processor. The strategy propelled IBM to the leader in personal computers. Modularity spread quickly to storage and motherboards creating dozens of tier-1 suppliers producing interchangeable modules. Modularity, however, did lead to the unintended consequence of the development of an IBM-compatible industry. Executive must be aware of the potential impact of supply chain decisions—decisions that will ultimately revolutionize entire industries, as was the case in the computer industry. Consider, for example, the potential impact of global supply chain management on the auto industry:

Jane Morley arrived home on a summer evening, weary from a day of endless meetings. But she felt energized as she sat down in front of her computer. Her car, a trusty old Saturn, was on its last legs, and several friends had recommended autobuy.com as the best place to find that perfect set of wheels. Mitts, Jane's golden retriever, moseyed into the room and thumped down at her feet.

"Put the salesman in the back seat." Jane muttered autobuy's TV jingle as the cable modem quickly brought the multimedia site to life. Knowing she wanted something to show that she had moved up in the world, Jane clicked on the sporty two-seater zooming around the screen. A message came up asking which she wanted to choose first, the inside systems or the body. She knew that from a performance standpoint it was best to start from the inside and then choose a body that matched, but she wanted to make a fashion statement. So she clicked "Body."

Immediately, a second window popped up suggesting that she take a personality test that could help her pick the most appropriate style. A friend had warned her about this: Take the test and you'll get spammed by marketers for years. Getting rid of the distraction, she studied the dozens of different bodies that were available.

Jane could see how she would look inside each model, because the digital camera mounted on her computer display had taken two pictures that allowed the site to map a 3D rendering of her face onto the mock driver. Although a few of the newer styles were tempting, Jane loved the retro models from past decades. She was torn between the 1990s and the 1960s, so she spent several minutes comparing different models in various simulated environments. "How about this one?" Jane asked Mitts, who looked up in surprise. Finally, it was the 3D rendering of the 1964

Mustang gliding over a winding mountain road that grabbed her. "Perfect!" she said.

Having settled on the basic style, she needed to choose a color. The "InfiniColor" system let her see herself in the Mustang in a mind-boggling selection of colors, but she quickly went for the Classic Red.

Next, she moved on to the guts of the car—under the hood. Since the Mustang wasn't big enough for one of those bulky fuel cells, she had to stay with a traditional engine. But that was OK—she wanted the power anyway.

The car was made up of ten different modules, and several manufacturers had versions of each one. Prices were displayed next to every choice. Although autobuy.com offered detailed information on each system to allow an informed choice, Jane chose to zip over to ConsumerReports.org to get the low-down. The service cost ten dollars, but Jane was happy she did it. For example, she noticed that the cheaper transmission from Transco had some reliability problems, so she decided to shell out the extra hundred for the higher-rated Visteon model.

But she didn't need any advice when it came to the engine. Everybody knew that Lakemens was best. Although the Lakemens 450 MV6 was almost twice the price of the respectable Nissan 333, she consoled herself with the 5% discount she received for agreeing to put the "Lakemens at Work" logo on the driver-side door. "After today's budget meetings, I deserve it. Right, Mitts?" she muttered.

Ten minutes later, Jane had selected the remaining modules and secondary options, and she viewed a detailed picture of her handiwork with considerable satisfaction.

But she still had to think about the delivery option. Standard delivery? Or, could she wait an extra four weeks for the Brazilian assembled version, which was $500 cheaper? Or, did she want to pay a $600 surcharge and have it in 2 days? Feeling a bit guilty about that pricey Lakemens 450, she decided to forego the fast delivery and settle for the standard one-week delivery.

Jane accepted the offer for financing, and chose biweekly payments over three years. Thinking it would be nice to have the extra money for the holiday season, she seized the opportunity to skip the December payments by spreading the amounts over the remaining eleven months. The $29 fee seemed quite reasonable, anyway. With the click of a button she authorized autobuy to check her credit rating, and before she knew it she had Digi-signed the loan papers and closed the deal.

A message appeared advising Jane of an incoming call from autobuy.com. Jane accepted, and the welcoming face of a middle-aged woman appeared on the screen. "Hi! I'm Beth," said the lady in a friendly Australian accent. "Great choice, and thanks for using autobuy.com. You can pick up your new car next Wednesday at the Car Country Megalot on Central. If you have a trade-in, bring it down, or John can pick you up in our shuttle. And remember our famous guarantee: If you're not completely satisfied with your new car, just bring it back in the original condition within 5 days for a full refund."

"Thanks," Jane replied, and she ended the call.

She looked down at Mitts, and said, "How about that mountain road next Wednesday?"[17]

It's a future that will arrive sooner than we might think.

Notes

1. J.G. Parker, "The 3PL Plunge," *Traffic World,* (April 26, 1999), pp. 16–17.

2. S. Kadzban and J. Motwani, "How to Integrate and Refine Global Operations," *Review of Business,* vol 17, no. 1 (1995), pp. 26–34.

3. W.E. Youngdahl, D.A. Waldman, and G. Anders, "Leading the Total Quality Culture Transformation at Goodyear-Oxo, Mexico: An Interview with Hugh Pace," *Journal of Management Inquiry,* vol. 7, no. 1 (1998), pp. 59–65.

4. K. Ferdows, "Making the Most of Foreign Factories," *Harvard Business Review,* (March/April 1997), pp. 73–88.

5. V. Chiesa, "Strategies for Global R&D," *Research Technology Management,* (September/October 1996).

6. F.A. Kuglin, *Customer-Centered Supply Chain Management: A Link-By-Link Guide,* AMACOM (1998), p. 4.

7. J.P. Womak and D.T. Jones, *Lean Thinking: Banish Waste and Create Wealth in Your Corporation* (New York: Simon & Schuster, 1996).

8. J. Heskett, W.E. Sasser, and L. Schlesinger, *The Service Profit Chain* (Boston: Harvard Business School Press, 1997).

9. K. Baker, "Leading the Globalization of Product Development—Visions, Challenges, Call to Action," (1997). Available: www.gm.com/about/info/overview/RD_Center/websiter/intro/9707kbLeadGlob.html

10. Anonymous, "GM Picks SAP to Improve Information Technology," *Wall Street Journal,* (November 13, 1997), p. B7.

11. J.C. Andraski, "Leadership and the Realization of Supply Chain Collaboration," *Journal of Business Logistics,* vol. 19, no. 2 (1998), pp. 9–12.

12. M. Pereira, "Improving Customer Service at Sara Lee Casualwear," (1999), Available: i2.com.

13. S. Pires, "Managerial Implications of the Modular Consortium Model in a Brazilian Automotive Plant," *International Journal of Operations & Production Management,* vol. 18, no. 3 (1998), pp. 221–232.

14. J. Magretta, "Fast, Global, and Entrepreneurial: Supply Chain Management, Hong Kong Style—An Interview with Victor Fung," *Harvard Business Review,* (September/October 1998), pp. 101–114.

15. J. Magretta, "The Power of Virtual Integration: An Interview with Michael Dell," *Harvard Business Review,* (March/April 1998), p. 74.

16. M.L. Fisher, "What is the Right Supply Chain for Your Product?" *Harvard Business Review,* (March/April 1997), pp. 105–117.

17. This futurist example was developed by Ewan Gillespie, a graduate student at Thunderbird, The American Graduate School of International Management.

8

The Transnational Experience: Anticipating Legal Issues

SHOSHANA B. TANCER

The manager of a company in the process of establishing operations outside of its home market is confronted with a number of legal issues that are frequently overlooked in the strategic plan. In part, this is the result of the transparency of legal rules and regulations. They have become such an integral part of doing business in a single environment that it is assumed that they are universal. This assumption is erroneous and can lead to major difficulties. For the U.S. manager who has been working with a U.S.-based company, the apparent "Americanization" of legal systems worldwide creates a level of comfort; it appears that the norms and procedures to which he is accustomed are in fact operational. But this is not the case. These American-style laws have been superimposed on local legal systems that are very different from those with which the U.S. manager is familiar. The growing harmonization of laws through multilateral treaties and agreements may lull the manager into an even higher level of comfort. Nonetheless, he is acting at his peril, if he makes an assumption that he can proceed as he has in the United States with equal success.

As a practitioner as well as an academician, I have become only too aware of the fact that businessmen who are engaged in taking their businesses "overseas" will do thorough financial and marketing studies, but will ignore legal issues which are as important. This is true whether the company has the luxury of time in determining its growth or whether the company is responding to a merger or acquisition.

This chapter will review some areas in which legal norms are different from those in the United States and which require appropriate attention.

The Basic Legal System

As multinationals span the world and make demands on local governments and as governments respond to the demands of these companies promoting harmonization of law through bilateral and multilateral treaties and international conventions, the businessperson must still remain cautious when dealing cross-border. The very similarities between systems may make one complacent, but there are still and will remain for some time to come, three basic legal systems which must be understood: the common law, civil law and Islamic law.

Common law, adopted by the founding fathers of the United States as our basic legal system, relies upon customary law and the precedents of judicial systems. Civil law is a function of legislative codes that are interpreted by scholars and on which the decisions of courts have little importance. Islamic law is based on the teachings of the Koran. The United States, Great Britain, and most Commonwealth nations still use common law; most European nations and their former colonies, including Latin America and Quebec, use civil law and Islamic law is prevalent in Middle Eastern countries as well as Malaysia and Indonesia. Islamic law governs not only personal matters such as family relationships, but also may have a major impact on business transactions. Islamic law forbids the charging of interest on loans, for example, and refers to such assessments as usurious no matter how low the payments may be. It is therefore, necessary, to be careful in drafting contracts and loan documents to make sure that the intent of the parties does not conflict with the legal system's requirements.

In the United States, we have become very used to a functioning system in which legislatures pass laws, administrative agencies issue regulations and the courts interpret them and issue decisions that create precedents for other courts and litigants to follow. In the process of litigation, lawyers represent clients. It is their duty to present the facts of their case in a manner most likely to cause the judge or the jury to find in favor of their clients. The process is often an expensive and lengthy one. Prior to trial, there is a prolonged discovery period in which both sides are trying to obtain as much evidence as possible by interviewing the parties, the witnesses and any other relevant individuals, including experts so as to build their case. It is thus the lawyers who determine the direction the case will take. If there is a jury, which constitutional right may be waived by the defendant, the jury is to determine the facts, and the judge the law. In the U.S. system, the attorney, who advises the client as counselor, usually is the same person who drafts agreements, and other legal documents. In our age of increasing specialization, this attorney is less likely to also engage directly in the litigation, although he may well be advising the litigator as to the history and the substantive aspects of the matter. In Great Britain, the distinction between the solicitor, who acts as counselor, and the barrister, who tries the case has existed for centuries, and the British have become used to the possibility of having to pay two legal fees.

In the civil law system, the heir to the Napoleonic Code, the lawyer plays a very different role. Although the lawyer will act as a counsellor or advisor to the client, as is the case in the United States, the *abogado* or *avocat* does not draft documents, whether transactional, probate, or for domestic relations purposes. Those functions are carried out by a person who has also received extensive legal training, but has chosen to become a *notario*. The *notario* is the individual who not only drafts documents, but is the one who attests to the validity of the document, the identity of the parties and the witnesses. When dealing with land transfers, the *notario* also has conducted the title search and historically has acted as the title insurance company, guaranteeing good title. It is no wonder that this person is a very highly paid professional. The title *notario* is, however, easily confused with our notary, who merely needs to be an adult of good moral character who is authorized by the state to attest to the identity of the person signing a document. This confusion is particularly poignant when poor non-English speakers are enticed by the sign *notario* to believe that the person offering advice and preparing documents has the same background as in their homelands. American businessmen doing business in Latin America or France, for example, will frequently be surprised by the expense of the legal profession and yet there is no alternative. One must use the *notario* for only he has the authority to prepare most legal documents. In civil law countries, frequently it is the form rather than the substance that carries great weight, and documents that do not have the appropriate seals or stamps or authentications cannot be admitted for evidence in court or as proof of purchase or sale with the pertinent authorities.

Civil law countries are also generally less litigious. In part this may be the result of the role of the lawyer in the court. It is the judge in these countries who determines the direction of a case, the judge who decides which evidence to bring forward, the judge who makes a decision based on the more philosophical writings of jurisprudential scholars who have read and reread the relevant Code which covers the matters under consideration. The lawyer does not make impassioned pleas to a jury, because there is no jury; there also is no pretrial discovery conducted by the lawyer; and in general, the entire court proceeding is much more rapid than here in the United States, but delays in reaching decisions can be lengthy.

It is essential to have good local professional advisors. No matter how skilled your U.S. attorney or accountant may be it is almost impossible for that individual to keep up with all of the changes which occur in another nation as well as with what is occurring in the United States. In addition, however, to having such advisers, it is essential to keep the U.S. team in the loop, for there have been numerous times when the best solution from an offshore viewpoint could create tremendous problems in the United States. There have been occasions in my legal practice when suggestions from overseas professionals would have put clients at risk for additional taxes or undermined their very ability to work in the United States through noncompliance with immigration law requirements. As a result, U.S. advisers would be able to caution the foreign consultants, before action is taken, that maybe the second best alternative should be considered. If such practice is not followed, the likelihood of problems down the line is significantly greater. Naturally, all advisers should be kept apprised of plans on an on-going basis in a timely manner even if on their face they do not seem relevant to a particular professional's expertise. The wisdom of "a stitch in time saves nine" is certainly true in this arena.

Structure of the Overseas Operation and Its Impact on the Parent Company

Businessmen in the United States are aware of the variety of choices of business organization: sole proprietorship, partnership, limited partnership, limited liability company, s corporation, and c corporation. It should be remembered that the use of the word *company* may have a meaning to a businessperson, but legally it simply means that there is a business entity. Each form has its benefits and its drawbacks and in deciding which alternative to choose. The flexibility of the sole proprietorship is offset by its lack of protection. The corporate form requires a good deal more paperwork, but provides ease in adding equity members and does provide the shield to protect the owners' assets from attack.

When one is beginning operations in other countries, there are a number of questions that must be resolved and that will have significant impact on the future of the company. Do you want to have a separate establishment cross-border or maintain a branch? How will you assure that liabilities which accrue in one country cannot attack assets in another? What will be the impact on the company's total tax burden? Each of these should be dealt with as part of the strategic plan and should be reviewed in an on-going manner to make sure that the decisions previously made conform to present goals and policies.

The U.S. businessperson should be aware that in other nations, there are similar forms of business organization, but once again although similar not identical. It is interesting that both in Germany with the G.m. b.H *(Gesellschaft mit beschräkter Hauftung)* and in Latin America with the S. de R.L. *(sociedad de responsibildad limitada)* a form of organization has existed for decades which is just now being recognized by some of the United States: the limited liability company. This hybrid in the United States provides the limited liability of the corporation, while giving members the ability to pass through to their individual tax returns either the profits or the losses of the company.

Whereas sole proprietorships and partnerships are prevalent worldwide, as is the corporate form, it is necessary not to be lulled into a sense of complacency and simply approve the creation of a corporate form. In the United States, the same corporate structure exists for General Motors and for the small family-owned business. Under civil law, however, distinctions have been made between the legal structure and governance of the large publicly held company and the small business. As a result, in the United States, the small business must deal with many of the formal requirements of disclosure, accounting, and keeping corporate records of the large institution. At the same time, when the small company grows into a larger one, it may retain all of its existing structure and ownership. Under the civil law, however, it is very difficult and expensive to convert from the form used by a small business into that of a larger one.

One must also be aware that in civil law countries there are differences in the creation and organization of the corporation. In Mexico, for example, the company can be governed by either the Board *(junta directiva)* or, if the Articles so indicate, by a single administrator. Mexico also demands the appointment of a statutory auditor, a *comisario,* whose function is similar to that of the outside accounting firms in the United States. In Mexico, one also must choose between flexible capital and fixed capital. If the corporate structure creates a *sociedad anonima,* the initial stated capital can only be changed with the permission of the government. If, however, one establishes a *sociedad anonima de capital variable,* it is very easy to increase capital contributions as needed. Further, civil law requires a much greater initial capitalization than is typically demanded of U.S. companies and the capitalization must be fully paid within a given period. As in the United States, capital contributions may be in cash or in goods, but the value of goods must be appraised by an independent authority under civil law.

Just as in the United States, the choice of the form of organization is critical for tax and other purposes, so too in foreign jurisdictions one must carefully select the form of organization, if any. One must first determine whether it is necessary to establish a presence in a given country. For many years, Mexico, for example, allowed U.S. companies to engage in sales into Mexico without having a presence there, so long as the agent in Mexico had very limited duties and responsibilities. If they conducted other activities, the business had to have a "Mexican presence."

One of the advantages of the North American Free Trade Agreement for Canadians, Mexicans, and U.S. citizens, is that this agreement provided for national treatment for the citizens of the other nations and this includes the "right of establishment." One should be aware that under U.S. and Mexican law, a company incorporated within their territories is a national company regardless of ownership. In Canada, however, nationality is determined by the nationality of those who control the corporation which has been established in that nation. This must be considered when one is discussing the possibility of a corporation's obtaining national treatment within the NAFTA environment.

Right of Establishment in the Host Country

Until recently, there were extensive restrictions on foreign investment in many nations based on national security considerations or fear of competition. The rationale for many of these decrees was the need to control the economy, which had been penetrated by foreign investors. The decades of the 1960s and 1970s are replete with examples of nations that sought to regain what they believed would be their "economic destiny" by expropriating properties belonging to the multinationals. It was not just Chile which took back copper mines in the days of Eduardo Frei and Salvador Allende; but the province of Saskatchewan took potash mines during a period in which Canada was particularly sensitive to the degree of U.S. involvement in her economy. This was the period in which nations also believed that they had to have government control of high profile sectors of the economy.[1]

In the 1980s and 1990s, however, a number of factors led many nations to realize that government control of certain sectors of the economy was not viable and actually was hurting rather than helping national development. The Conservative government of Margaret Thatcher in Great Britain sought to make sure that the British society including the workers became owners of formerly government-owned businesses, such as the railroads and the telephone company, among others to try to overcome the heritage that had led to high unemployment and little incentive to work by the British public. The former Communist nations of eastern Europe and the newly independent states of the former-Soviet Union wanted to prove that they were throwing off the economic as well as the political heritage of their former regimes. The developing nations realized that they would be able to raise funds and thereby pay down the debt which was drowning them if they sold off the sectors and or industries which far from remaining the "commanding heights" had become white elephants. Thus the push for privatization. Even here in the United States, we have been affected by the rationale for downsizing government and privatizing the provision of services, whether in prisons or health care. The United States did not have companies owned by government, but during the same time period, actively began the process of deregulation of various sectors, including the airlines, trucking, banking, and telecommunications.

Privatization was usually accompanied by liberalizing the foreign investment restrictions. Although not all privatizations immediately relied on the infusion of capital from abroad, it was soon recognized that there was need for technology transfer and capital infusion. The Czech model that gave all citizens vouchers that would provide them an interest in a company, several companies, or a fund, quickly proved to be unsuccessful. There was no technology transfer, the ownership was too diffuse to provide direction and the company had lost its primary source of funding, the government. Each privatization effort learned from the experiences of those who had gone before it. In Mexico, there was a different goal entirely: the reduction of the external debt and infusion of capital to modernize such sectors as telecommunications and banking. In these privatizations, either strategic alliances were sought and/or auctions were held in which the government established the parameters of those who would be eligible to participate and further set minimum prices below which the company would not be sold. For Mexico to attract foreign investment such liberalization was necessary, but more was needed. Mexico had a history of devaluation and of expropriation. Foreigners needed assurance that under the Salinas administration Mexico had changed. Mexico tried to prove that it was ready to accept the responsibilities of a modern state. It had joined the GATT in 1986 and then proceeded to pass a series of legislative initiatives that provided some degree of comfort to those who would invest. A new intellectual property law came into effect in 1991; an environmental protection act, modeled after the U.S. Clean Air Act, in 1992. President Salinas then modified the existing foreign investment act under his authority to issue decree legislation, significantly changing the extent of foreign ownership which was possible in most sectors, reserving only the primary petroleum

industry to the Mexican government but permitting others to participate in the secondary petrochemical sector.[2]

Most important to U.S. and Canadian investors, however, was
the negotiation and adoption of the North American Free Trade
Agreement (NAFTA) which is a treaty under Mexican and Canadian law and therefore cannot be simply changed by subsequent administrations. NAFTA protects foreign investment from member
countries and requires that there be no performance requirements,
special export rules; or local content demands made, although each
of the three nations excepted certain sectors. For example, Mexico
kept petroleum out of NAFTA; the United States, nuclear energy
and air transportation and Canada, "cultural industries." These are
just a few of the exemptions at the national level, however, and the
U.S. businessman should be alerted to their existence at the outset.[3]
In the financial services sector, for example, there are limits as to the
percentage of total market which any individual foreign company
can attain, and also the aggregate which can be in foreign hands. In
the telecommunications industry, basic telephone service is limited
to nationals of the home country in most places in the world, even
though the markets have been opened to those who engage in enhanced services. Some of the early flyers in this sector, such as the
"call back" services, have subsequently been declared illegal in some
emerging markets. This is to protect the national industry which
makes significant revenues from international calls.

In the European Union, there have been even greater attempts at
harmonization of laws and limiting the restrictions that have historically been imposed among and between the member nations. At
present, this is accomplished through the issuance by the European
Commission of regulations and "directives" that direct the member
nations to comply by a given date with a given policy. One of the
most recent directives relates to opening the telecommunications industry to ownership by other companies, sometimes even by other
government-owned companies. These directives are the result of negotiation between the member governments and the bureaucrats at
the Commission. Once issued they are considered to have the force
of law. Remember, however, that the process is not yet complete
and there is therefore the need to look to national law as well as
the Commission-generated rules to determine what is and is not
permitted.

The World Trade Organization, the creator of the Uruguay Round in 1995, is the secretariat for the GATT. It acts as the administrative office to educate and cajole its member nations into compliance with their obligations, resolve disputes, and enforce decisions. The purpose of GATT since its creation in 1948 has been to liberalize trade. With the confluence of the fall of Communism, the decision by most emerging countries to become market-driven economies rather than state-controlled ones, and the continued pressure by the developed nations to have greater liberalization, many of the historic restrictions are being removed and liberalization is now the watchword. Although a government has paid lip-service to the notion of liberalization, the system frequently continues to create major problems for foreign businesses. The U.S. Trade Representative has for years complained that we do not have a level playing field with Japan, because our markets are open whereas theirs are not. The Japanese response is that their laws permit such investment. However, until recently, the distribution system in Japan has prevented such investment from becoming profitable, which is after all the goal of doing business internationally.[4]

The businessman who engages in international transactions must be cautious and make sure that those barriers to investment and/or trade that still exist in given nations are understood and respected. Rhetoric and practice do not yet go hand in hand.

Personnel Policies

Although the manager has become accustomed to dealing with the U.S. Department of Labor and the EEOC, he must also be aware of social legislation in other countries. Many U.S. managers are not aware of the need for their employees working abroad to meet restrictive immigration requirements. They assume that because Americans can travel almost everywhere without getting government permission, so may they work. This is an assumption that can lead to immediate and serious problems, as has happened when a U.S. company with new operations overseas, leased space, purchased equipment, had a dynamic advertising campaign and came to realize that their managers would not be able to work abroad to manage their business.[5]

Employers in overseas operations may find themselves operating in an environment that does not seem rational. The practices may be based on historical norms and requisites that may no longer be appropriate. Yet the foreign employer finds himself helpless and frequently caught between two conflicting mandates. Some nations have labor laws that purport to protect the worker, but which may in fact have the opposite effect. We, in the United States, not so long ago had laws which prevented women from working more than eight hours a day in banking. This was to protect the woman. Over the years it became apparent that women were not obtaining promotions in any way commensurate with their male colleagues. The explanation of the banks was clear and understandable from their perspective: the men were more productive and processed their work more quickly. They were, therefore, more deserving of raises and promotions. At that time in Arizona, the typical male executive reached officer rank within 2 years, the woman in 11. In the 1970s, the feminist movement brought this and similar protectionist measures to the attention of the state legislature which then ended them.

Mexico has similar legislation protecting pregnant women and provides them 12 weeks maternity leave. Unfortunately, the law has had an unanticipated effect. Indeed, a woman is entitled to this paid time off, but there is a problem as to who is responsible for paying the wages and attendant benefits. If she has been employed for the previous 30 weeks, the social security system will pay. If, however, she has not been employed for that length of time, her employer must bear the burden of paying for this leave. In Brazil, the law is very similar. Laws of this sort can lead to abuse by workers, who know they are pregnant when hired so that they can receive the benefit, which in Brazil is four months. Employers respond by attempting to assure that workers are not pregnant when first hired; and some continue with this practice for the duration of employment. This is a particularly severe problem in the twin-plant sector, the so-called *maquiladoras,* where there is high turnover, and workers do not usually accumulate the requisite 30 continuous work weeks. This has led to a complaint under NAFTA dispute resolution mechanisms whereby under the Labor Side Agreement, each nation must enforce its labor laws. The U.S. labor movement is charging that by allowing this practice to continue, Mexico is violating her own law which does not permit discrimination in the workplace.[6]

Historically, in the United States, it has been the prerogative of the states to mandate what benefits must be provided employees including maternity leave. As a result, some states have liberal policies, such as California, and others have no such requirement, as is the case in Arizona. Even the much heralded Family Medical Leave Act is severely limited. It permits workers who are employed by companies that have 50 or more employees to take time off for maternity leave, caring for sick spouses, parents, or children, only provides unpaid leave for three months with a guarantee of a return to an equivalent or similar position. And these workers must have worked for that employer for at least 12 months and worked for at least 1,250 hours in 12 months immediately prior to requesting the leave.[7]

The U.S. businessperson must recognize that in other parts of the world, the employer is providing many benefits that are not available to our workers. In many transitional and developing countries, employers are required to provide health care (either directly or through contributions to a government program); housing allowances; and day care centers for the workers' young children. The Korean *chaebols* were noted for their full range of benefits in additional to salary—housing or housing subsidies, subsidized mortgage, company hospitals, education loans, and subsidized cafeterias. In China such employment-based benefits have been referred to as the "iron rice bowl." Russia, under Communism also made the employer responsible for many of these benefits. It should be no surprise, therefore, that workers should have opposed privatization, for they correctly surmised that when their companies were in private hands, not only would redundancies be removed, but also the perquisites to which they had become accustomed would end. It is ironic, that similar programs are just becoming popular in the United States as the low unemployment rate is causing employers to vie with each other in providing benefits.

In those countries characterized as emerging markets, there is no unemployment compensation and very limited sick leave. These nations, however, do protect their workers in a different manner. Once the worker has survived the probationary period, a myriad of benefits accrue, some of which make it very difficult to fire a worker, particularly one who has been with a company for a protracted period. Here, the goal of worker protection is frequently thwarted by employers entering into sequential 89-day contracts, where the probationary period is 90 days. The worker winds up not being protected, and the employer benefits from the increased flexibility of his workforce. Many U.S. employers are amazed to discover that these are some of the differences with which they must cope; for failure to handle the matter appropriately can be the difference between profitability and losses.

Yet, we in the United States, have also attempted to cut the cost of our permanent full-time employees by engaging independent contractors and out-sourcing temporary workers. The Internal Revenue Service became very concerned over the increased number of so-called independent contractors and established clear-cut rules as to when a person could be so categorized, saving the employer from paying a myriad of benefits including workman's compensation, unemployment compensation, social security matching, health insurance, and so on. The IRS and the courts relied on a common law standard that basically spoke to who had control over the hours and work of the worker, where was the work undertaken, who provided the equipment and the nature of the supervision by the employer. If it appeared that the employer really controlled the work and supervised the worker, the worker would be deemed an employee and not an independent contractor.

Once this became clear, employers switched to the temporary worker, hired from an agency. Here too, the employer would not be responsible for a myriad of benefits; these would be the responsibility of the employment service which was paid a fee from which it paid the worker. As a result, employment services who would send in workers to those companies that needed their services enjoyed tremendous growth during the 1990s. In a sense, this is not different than the Mexican employer who keeps on rehiring probationary workers, but the U.S. employer may find this route somewhat more difficult after U.S. Ninth Circuit case. A number of individuals who had been classified either as independent contractors or as temporary workers because they were paid by an outside agency complained that they had worked for Microsoft steadily for a number of years. They alleged that because of their so-called temporary status or because they were "independent contractors" required to sign a document waiving company benefits they had been barred from participating in stock options and gifts of stock which were customary for permanent full-time employees who were their coworkers. The U.S. District Court in Washington State declared that Microsoft's practices were totally acceptable; the Ninth Circuit Court of Appeals, however, applied theories of common law employment which led to the decision that both classes of workers were indeed Microsoft employees and therefore eligible for these much prized benefits.[8]

Within the European Union, workers have long had much longer vacations and shorter work weeks than workers in the United States. Recently France was discussing the appropriateness of decreasing the official work week to 30 hours, in an attempt to create new employment opportunities. In Germany, six weeks vacation is usual. From an American perspective, the work ethic does not seem as strong in Europe as we have been taught. Socialist governments have provided such broad and apparently secure safety nets that governments now have difficulty in decreasing the unemployment rate and employers are loathe to commit themselves to all of the conditions which are part of the employment "contract."

Although this is not part of this chapter, U.S. businessmen should be aware that there are major differences between U.S. labor unions and those in other parts of the world. Here, the labor movement grew out of a desire to improve conditions in the workplace. As the government has taken over more surveillance and control of these issues— whether relating to safety conditions, minimum wages, hours of work, vacation and sick leave—unions have become less attractive to the worker. Until the recent successes of the U.S. labor movement with the UPS strike and the threatened strike of the America West stewardesses, there were many who believed that the unions had outlived their usefulness. In Europe and in Latin America, labor unions have long been associated with specific political parties and many of their goals were to assist the party to remain in power. As a result, strikes or work stoppages were frequently called for political reasons having nothing to do with conditions at the workplace. Although businesspeople who are used to this practice understand it, the U.S. businessperson must understand the differences in operation and in attitude. U.S. union-management relations are often referred to as confrontational, as compared to those in Europe; but it should be remembered that in European countries the labor union and the government are one, and if the employer takes on the union, he may well be taking on the government at the same time. Also, in Germany, there is labor participation at the board level, labor unions do not charge that they are being denied access to information or to people at the top, a claim made by some U.S. labor unions particularly during labor negotiations.

Increasingly as part of globalization, there is a movement of management personnel and highly skilled workers across national borders. It is essential to be aware early in the process of entering into negotiations to acquire a company, or establish a sales force, what the specific requirements are to move personnel from one nation to another. Just as in the United States there is no problem today, so too in the European Union, holders of a Community passport may accept a position in any other of the member nations. That is not the case for U.S. employees. Although the U.S. government permits some visitors to enter without visas for up to three months at a time, these travelers are not permitted to engage in employment while in the United States. There are visas which do permit certain groups of people to work in the United States as temporary workers for periods of up to six years, but these require advance paperwork and the approvals are subject to the vagaries of an increasingly inefficient and over-worked Immigration and Naturalization Service. If an employer wants his American staff or other employees to go overseas, the proper documentation should be obtained on a timely basis.

Anti-Trust Law

The United States was the first nation to legislate against monopolies and cartels in the 1890 Sherman Anti-Trust Act. As time progressed, additional laws were passed, the Federal Trade Commission (FTC) was established and the scope of control has continued to increase. The goal of protecting competition in the United States has been pursued differently by various administrations, which in the past century have balanced the imperatives of promoting economic growth and supporting innovation and making sure that no company or group of companies abuse their dominant position nor take such actions as will prevent or tend to prevent on-going competition. From the days of the Rockefeller cartel, the Standard Oil Trust, which was dissolved in 1910, to the AT&T consent decree which led to the divestiture of the Regional Bell Operating Companies in 1984, to the current law suit brought against Microsoft, the government has been attempting to foster competition.

Immediately following World War II, the United States exported the antitrust law concept to occupied Germany and Japan in an attempt to extirpate their prior practices of vertical and horizontal cartels. Over time, antitrust law has become accepted as a means of protecting one's citizen consumers against the activities of big business. It is not surprising, therefore, that the Treaty of Rome (1957), included competition policy, as antitrust law is known in Europe, as Articles 85 and 86.

As international trade and business have expanded, the United States has become even more rigorous in asserting its rights to charge any business with actions that have or tend to have the effect of lessening competition in the United States. A classic case was that of Pilkington.[9] A manufacturer of plate glass, Pilkington had entered into uniform agreements worldwide with its distributors. These agreements granted each distributor exclusive territories. One such distributor was in Arizona. The U.S. government brought suit against Pilkington alleging an anti-trust violation. This case was settled by a consent decree between the parties which covered Pilkington's worldwide operations. The extraterritorial impact was to prevent nationals of other countries from engaging in practices which were legal in their countries because of the potential adverse impact on U.S. exports to their territories. This is of particular significance in that the plate glass industry is one in which the product is generally not exported but manufactured near the customer. It could be said that the United States overstepped its bounds.

Although roundly criticized at the time by trading partners of the United States, the European Commission recently reviewed the proposed merger of Boeing and McDonnell Douglas and determined that the merger would be in violation of the European Competition Policy for it would tend to diminish competition within the Community. This in spite of the fact that these two companies were U.S. corporations. The concern was really to protect the interests of the European consortium Airbus, which would face stiffer competition from such a combination.

In this area also the European Commission has issued directives to implement the policy of the Treaty, but all of the member nations do not yet have competition policy laws that are in complete conformance with these directives. For example, although Finland is revising her competition policy to be in line with that of the European

Union, there are still significant differences. She has banned only vertical price fixing, not including violations of any other vertical arrangement. She has, however, for the first time included as a violation of competition policy, abuse of dominant power. Horizontal arrangements are banned unless they are in the interest of competition. The Finnish review of her competition policy was not something that was initiated solely at her own initiative, but rather was a response to a European Commission rejection of a merger between two Finnish supermarkets, Tuko Oy and Kesko Oy. The revised Finnish law, which for the first time addressed the issue of mergers, would only ban them in the event that a dominant position would be created or strengthened and result in "significant impeding of competition in the Finnish market or a substantial part of it."[10] Those nations that seek to become members of the European Union recognize that they must harmonize their laws to be in conformity with existing European policy, and are working toward this goal in the area of competition policy as in others.

Germany has also revised her competition policy a number of times since it was created. Nonetheless, in 1998, Germany felt the need to modernize it further, as the existing rules and regulations were perceived to make Germany less competitive vis-à-vis her European Community neighbors. As a result, she now has banned cartels absolutely, whether horizontal or vertical, but unlike Article 85 of the Treaty of Rome, she retains a distinction between them. She has ended the distinction between pre- and postmerger notifications and requires prenotification for all mergers which are valued at 1 million DM (Deutsche marks). It is for the Federal Cartel Office to approve or deny such merger; nonetheless, the Minister of Economics may override the decision of the Cartel Office. Germany has expanded the notion of dominant position expressed in 1957 in the Treaty of Rome and includes actual and potential competition from foreign multinationals. There is at least the remnant of nationalist concern in a nation that is the driving force behind European unification.

Emerging markets are also using competition policy as a means of protecting their own consumers. Mexico enacted such legislation in 1992[11] and India is approaching this issue through the Companies Bill which would prevent the creation of monopolies through consolidations and mergers.

Concern is growing both in the United States and in Europe as to abuse of dominant position. In the United States, the Department of Justice has brought suit against Microsoft for such abuse, in spite of the fact that the company alleges that there is, has been and increasingly will be competition in their industry, and the bundling of browser software does not and has not prevented other browsers from being used by the consumer. In Japan, in 1998 a suit against Microsoft was settled, but in that case, the government attacked the bundling of word processing and spreadsheet software as part of the presale installation package. By the time the agreement between the government and Microsoft was reached, the company was no longer engaging in this practice in Japan. The Department of Justice has also brought suit against Intel, the major chip manufacturer, but this suit was rapidly settled. There is some concern in the business community, that the present administration is really attacking companies for having achieved great success through continuous improvement in their product line, whether through innovation or acquisition. At the same time, mergers of major companies are being permitted, whether in banking, telecommunications, or petroleum companies. These are presumably acceptable because they are increasing competition although also increasing the not insignificant market share of the premerged companies. Businesspeople should be cautious in interpreting the future direction of the enforcement of antitrust laws in the United States, as well as in the rest of the world.

Although the European Union laws require premerger clearance, for certain acquisitions and takeovers, as does the United States, in the Hart-Scott Rodino filings, the European Union also has a process called "negative clearance." This procedure provides approval for vertical arrangements that otherwise would be in restraint of trade. It is only recently that other nations have begun to actively use this legislation, and some, like Finland even with a recent revision in its competition policy, do not provide for such procedure.

With the increase in cross-border mergers and acquisitions, we are even seeing the spread of extraterritorial application of antitrust law to protect national consumers but also as an effective means of assisting in economic development; a method which is deemed even better than regulation of domestic industries to achieve the latter goal. It is, therefore, incumbent on the American businessperson to

realize that although the United States was the prime mover for competition policy law, there are many aspects in which different nations
and regions have perceived it differently. Once again, the caution
must be given not to assume that because antitrust and competition
policy are similar that they are identical. In this area as well as the
others which have been discussed in this chapter, failure to carefully
study the ramifications of planned actions can lead to disaster.

Export Limitations

Limitations is of particular concern to businesses which export goods
from the United States whether U.S. companies or foreign companies
with offices in the United States. It also impacts those who hire foreign nationals to work in certain sectors. We in the United States have
had export bans for the purpose of national security for decades. It was
automatic that countries with whom we did not have diplomatic relations were barred from purchasing goods on this list. Among those
nations were the Soviet Union, People's Republic of China, Iraq, Iran,
North Korea, North Vietnam, Cuba, and Libya. As the Cold War
ended, there has been relaxation of the restrictions on some goods for
some of these nations. The kinds of goods for which the restrictions
were established were initially weapons of war which were clearly rec-
ognizable as such. Today with advances in technology, these restrictions have been expanded to include high-speed computers and
encryption devices, which could be used to program missile launches
or decode classified information or in a variety of other matters.

The most recent addition to the list of forbidden products are
sales of satellites and launch systems. These have now been classified
as "munitions" as a result of the discovery of the extent of alleged
Chinese spying over the past decades and the purported release of
classified information in connection with launching telecommunications satellites. Although the companies involved, principally
Hughes and Loral, have denied the allegations of the Cox-Dix Report released in May 1999, all companies will now have to get pre-
clearance even for telephone conversations about such matters, even
with our NATO and NAFTA allies. Whenever one is about to export a new product, it would be prudent to check with both the
Department of State and the Department of Commerce whether
this particular product falls within a prohibited class. It is always

better to do this prior to consummating a sale, and it would be advisable to do so prior to negotiating such a sale. There may also be problems if one has non-U.S. citizens working on certain projects, for this may also be a violation of U.S. law. It is incumbent on the business to make sure that it is in compliance with *all aspects* of U.S. export policy.

We in the United States are not the only nation which has such export prohibitions. For example, there are international agreements as to the ability to export hazardous wastes and certain types of chemicals. A businessperson must therefore be aware of the potential for such bans. This is an area which is under constant scrutiny and evolves depending on the international political scene of the moment. Information must be updated frequently to maintain compliance. A company may either assign this task to specific individuals or rely on outside experts for advice. It is also possible, in some circumstances, to get a presale clearance by a government. Regardless of the method chosen, it is essential to be in compliance. Failure to do so can result not only in significant fines but also in prison terms for the executives of the company.

Product Liability

In the United States, we have seen a steady movement in this law from *caveat emptor,* buyer beware, to consumer protection. One aspect of this change in attitude can be seen in the increasing scope of product liability for manufacturers. This issue, is just one of the areas in which consumer protection is salient, but has significant impact on business, whether engaged in solely domestic or international operations. Companies are held responsible for ever-longer periods of time for the proper functioning of their goods, even if such goods are not under their control. Recalls of vehicles 6 to 10 years after manufacture to replace parts that may have become potentially dangerous is just one manifestation of this. There are many who are concerned that this field of law will cause a decrease in inventions that are significantly different, rather than merely adaptations of existing products, for fear of untold future consequences in the use of these articles.

The potential for product liability has expanded significantly as the United States has become more litigious and as the courts have expanded the classes of individuals able to recover damages. Initially, only those in a contract relationship could recover for malfunction of goods; then the theory was broadened to include those whom it was logical and reasonable to assume would be using or affected by the use of the goods-based on the theory of negligence. The manufacturer knew or had reason to know that the product if used as intended could do harm. It is on this basis that attorneys are now attempting to create class action suits against gun manufacturers.[12]

A further step was taken when the courts decided that if a good was purchased based on a writing or representation made by the manufacturer, then there was an "express warranty" rather than the implied warranty which usually controls. This express warranty as to the quality and performance of the goods would further the responsibility of the manufacturer, as the user was acting in reliance on such statements. No longer is it necessary to be the purchaser of the product to recover; at this point, it is the purchaser, his employees, and family members and others who might rightfully use the product or be adversely impacted by it. The litigation against the tobacco companies has been conducted on both the implied and express warranties that presumably enticed smokers to begin using tobacco.

As manufacturers increasingly outsource products and frequently do so from international suppliers, it is imperative that they insure themselves insofar as possible against liabilities arising from malfunction of the product or the component. In many of the nations from which these components come, there may be no product liability laws; the producer probably does not have the financial resources to make the manufacturer whole; and/or insurance products are either not available or not affordable. As a result, it is essential for the U.S. manufacturer to make sure that he takes such steps as possible to limit his exposure.

One should be aware that the notion of consumer protection is becoming of increasing concern to governments worldwide. African nations have indicated that they are going to sue the tobacco companies and this has already begun in some Asian nations. Although one can posit that the tobacco situation is special, it may prove to be a harbinger of things to come. As a result, wherever sales are to take place, the manufacturer must exercise caution, particularly as the manufacturer never knows the final destination of his goods.

Dispute Resolution

As globalization proceeds, the number of cross-border disputes invariably also increases. Citizens of one nation are loathe to trust the courts of another, in part because they are different from what is known at home; in part because of the additional expense in having to conduct a case at a distance, and finally, in part because of lack of confidence in the outcome. These facts have made businesspeople and government alike look to dispute resolution mechanisms that can by-pass national domestic systems.

The most common form of dispute resolution is that of arbitration that must be called for specifically in the contract or transactional documents. However, merely stating that one wishes to have arbitration in the event of a dispute that cannot be solved by the parties themselves, is insufficient. There are a number of decisions that must be made prior to entering into a final agreement which will significantly impact the success of any arbitration effort undertaken thereafter.

Among the issues that must be confronted are whether the parties wish to engage in ad hoc arbitration, in which they themselves administer the process although they have indicated which rules of procedure they intend to use. Among the choices are the United Nations Commission on International Trade Law (UNCITRAL) Model Law on International Commercial Arbitration and the Inter-American Convention on International Commercial Arbitration. Each provides only procedural rules. The procedural rules of the International Centre for the Settlement of Investment Disputes (ICSID) may come into play when there is a dispute between a nation and a foreign investor, provided that the nation has become a signatory to the Convention establishing the Centre. Although the expenses may be less to attempt to conduct the ad hoc arbitration, if it is not carried out correctly, the award may not be enforceable. Since the goal of arbitration is to come to a speedy conclusion of the dispute, going to court after the arbitration is complete in order to defend the enforcement is not a desired outcome.

It is generally agreed that administered arbitration is the wiser course. The parties must decide a number of issues relating to this as well: the arbitral body must be selected.[13] Although each arbitral body has its own procedural rules, in some of them it is possible to choose other rules, and the decision must be made as to which should be selected. The substantive law governing the dispute must also be specified, and there is great freedom in making such a choice, so long as there is some connection between the nation whose law is being chosen and the subject matter of the case. Here, too, one must exercise extreme caution to make sure that the national law chosen is sufficiently developed that the arbitrator will be able to be guided by it. If the matter involves the sale of business goods cross-border, the Vienna Convention on Contracts for the International Sale of Goods (CISG) of 1980 will come into play if both nations are signatory. It is possible, however, in the initial agreement to opt out of this Convention.

Then there is a decision as to whether to have one or more arbitrators. There is greater expense with having more than one arbitrator, but having only one may create a bias, frequently obviated by declaring that the arbitrator may not be a national of either country of the parties. The matter is often left to the administrating body: If it determines the matter is very complex, it may require additional arbitrators. In any event, the expertise of the arbitrator should be spelled out depending on the subject area of the contract, so that specialists do not have to brief the arbitrator in the customs and practices of the field, which would only add to the costs.

The language of the contract must also be specified and this becomes the language of the arbitration. All documents must, therefore, be translated into the chosen language and these become the "official" ones. Any businessman who has dealt with translation knows how difficult it may be to get the nuances of an agreement into another language, and the more complex the matter the greater the likelihood that the translation will not be completely accurate. This is another worrisome problem that must be dealt with even in arbitration matters.

Finally, after the arbitration has taken place, the arbitrator must issue an award. The agreement should specify that a simple not a "reasoned award" be issued. A reasoned award requires that every finding of fact and determination of law be fully stated and adds to the time and to the cost of the procedure. Once the arbitral award is made, however, there is still the need to have it enforced, and a particular statement in the agreement should indicate where the award is to be issued as well as where the arbitration is to take place. There should be little difficulty, provided that the nation(s) where the arbitration takes place and whose law is being followed as well as the nation whose courts will be charged with enforcing the award have become signatories of the United Nations Convention on the Recognition and Enforcement of Foreign Arbitral Awards of 1958, also known as the New York Convention. As well over 100 nations have signed this Convention, it is likely to be the case. Here too, make no assumptions; have the matter checked out by professional advisers.[14]

Enforcement should be relatively simple, but be aware of the fact that even using an administered arbitration, the nation may refuse to enforce the award if so doing would be against public policy. Compare this, however, with the difficulties of enforcing a judicial judgment in Mexico, for example. There the courts may refuse to recognize a decision, unless it complies with all of the regulations relating to letters rogatory; personal jurisdiction over the national was obtained by the foreign court; the obligation on which the award was based is a matter for claims in Mexico; the judgment is a final one in the country of origin; and finally that it is properly authenticated. Authentication requires not only the translation of the decision into Spanish but also a number of other procedures which must be followed to the letter. Clearly, an arbitral award is easier to enforce.

A major factor that led Canada to request negotiation of a free trade agreement with the United States was an attempt to find alternatives to both the unilateral actions taken by the U.S. government under our trade policy and also to avoid U.S. courts when Canadian companies were sued by U.S. businesses for the impact these companies had on the U.S. business. A dispute resolution mechanism was incorporated into the Canada-U.S. Free Trade Agreement (1989) in which a number of formal procedures were established to handle trade disputes. In addition to the creation of procedures to be followed, the nations established expert panels from whose ranks the arbitrators could be chosen. In NAFTA (1994), which includes Canada, Mexico, and the United States, the rules for alternate dispute resolution were strengthened. There are special provisions for settlement of disputes that arise between a nation and an investor from one of the other member nations; in relation to financial services, temporary entry of businesspersons; and antidumping and countervailing duty matters. There is also a chapter which deals with the institutional arrangements and dispute settlement procedures to be followed by the members.

Negotiation of the Uruguay Round of the GATT which were contemporaneous with the negotiation of both the Canada-U.S. Free Trade Agreement and NAFTA, also covered the issue of dispute resolution. As a result, the World Trade Organization (WTO) also has provisions for the settlement of disputes under its rules and procedures which are very similar to those of NAFTA.

Other forms of alternate dispute resolution are also becoming more popular. These include mediation, in which an outside adviser attempts to help the parties choose an outcome satisfactory to both. It should be remembered, however, that nations are loathe to give up their ability to determine outcomes of events which have occurred within their territory. As a result, it is essential that all of these alternatives be thoroughly explored rather than have them treated as after-thoughts in contract negotiations.

Taxes and Accounting Principles

Globalization and the desire for economic development is causing a number of concurrent trends to be emerging on the international scene. There is an increasing number of tax treaties, in which governments try to protect their nationals from having to pay "double taxation." These treaties, however, generally are limited to those taxes that are denominated as income tax. The businessperson operating cross-border will frequently find that the least of his problems is the "income tax," for there are many transaction taxes, property taxes, value-added taxes, and so on which eat up revenues at an astounding rate.

As a result, in many nations it has been common practice to have two sets of books—one for the managers and one for the authorities. This has had disastrous results for those companies that find their properties expropriated and the officials in determining compensation look to the value of the assets as reported to them.[15]

As is widely recognized, there are a number of reasons to have generally recognized rules for accounting. It assists management to understand cash flow; it assists investors in understanding the financial condition of the companies in which they already have bought shares or those they are contemplated purchasing; it is a means by which taxing authorities can determine whether the taxes paid are the taxes truly owed. This does not mean that there cannot be two different ways in which the information is presented; one for compliance and one for the use of management. What it does mean, however, is that the two sets of books must have the same total assets and liabilities, or cash flow or profit. One may not have one set of books that shows that there are marketing costs for selling crude oil to one's own refinery for government purposes and have no such costs on the figures prepared for management.[16]

The United States has long had a fully developed Generally Accepted Accounting Principles which is the rule for publicly held companies within this country. The Security and Exchange Commission has also mandated that publicly held companies must use the GAAP in their disclosure statements. It is also necessary as part of the transparency and disclosures expected of these companies, that outside auditors review the financial statements and are required by law to advise as part of their evaluation whether the annual report has been prepared according to GAAP and whether there is any problem which may be potentially material (i.e., impact net income by 5%). This enables outsiders to compare companies with confidence.

In other countries, this type of disclosure is not available. It is one of the reasons so few foreign companies have sought to issue capital on the U.S. stock exchanges: They do not wish to have this type of scrutiny of their operations. Accounting principles in other parts of the world are for the insiders and not for the outsiders. As a result, the United States has not been successful in attempting to have its system accepted as the uniform accounting principles world wide. An International Accounting Standards Committee (IASC) was established in 1973 and has issued standards that it believes are appropriate for all nations. Many of the emerging market nations are conferring with the IASC to assure that their accounting requirements conform to IASC recommendations. Nonetheless, the IASC recommendations do not agree with standards currently in place in the United States, the United Kingdom, or Germany. The probability of a single, worldwide accounting system is, therefore, unlikely in the near future.[17]

The manager must also understand that the U.S. tax code and the accounting principles that exist are in conformity. Frequently, Congressional committees look to either the GAAP or to the Financial Accounting Standards Board (FASB) to see what language is being used by the companies and then write the tax law using the same language and/or formula. This is not the case in many other jurisdictions. As a result, one must use extreme caution in both the accounting methodologies used and characterizations of revenues and expenses chosen and be aware that the taxing authorities do not necessarily agree with the accounting principles of their own nation.

Conclusion

The purpose of this chapter was to alert businesspeople to the importance of understanding the impact legal issues have on their operations when they "go international." Some of these have been discussed herein to highlight the range of subjects in which one must consider legal implications. This chapter is not, however, a do-it-yourself manual. The entire legal environment is in a state of flux; it is therefore essential to maintain current information and rely on it in the legal field as one does in planning marketing strategies or seeking financial solutions. The manager who will be successful *will* include in his strategic planning and running of his business, consideration of the legal issues. He will also attempt to remain current in his thinking and ask his professional advisers to make sure that he does understand what is being considered by governments in whatever part of the world his operations take him. Failure to do so will inevitably lead to at the very best lost business, increased costs, and more crises than are necessary.

Notes

1. Daniel Yergin and Joseph Stanislaw, *The Commanding Heights: The Battle Between Government and the Marketplace That Is Remaking the Modern World* (New York: Simon & Schuster, 1998).

2. M. Juan Quintanilla and Mariano E. Bauer, "Mexican Oil and Energy," *Changing Structure of Mexico. Political, Social and Economic Prospects,* ed. Laura Randall, (Armonk New York: M.E. Sharpe, 1996), p. 125.

3. In addition, the U.S. and Mexican states and the Canadian provinces were given two years in which to list all of the exemptions which they wished to make. The list is so long that it requires several cds to contain them all.

4. At least these are the allegations of a number of U.S. businesses which until the Japanese economic recession appeared impossible to penetrate. One example was that in which Eastman Kodak took on Fuji declaring that it was unable to penetrate the Japanese market as a result of Japanese domestic practices. Recently, however, a number of U.S. companies have proven that they can be successful in Japan, by-passing the traditional distribution channels. These are the large distributors who use catalogs like L.L. Bean. Lester C. Thurow, *Building Wealth: The New Rules for Individuals, Companies and Nations in a Knowledge-Based Economy* (New York: HarperCollins, 1999), p. 28.

5. This occurred to a U.S. software company that had expanded into Europe and believed that it would be able to move its personnel at will.

6. *Public Report of Review of NAO Submission No. 9701.* U.S. National Administrative Office, Bureau of International Labor Affairs, U.S. Department of Labor. (January 12, 1998).

7. U.S. Family and Medical Leave Act of 1993 (FMLA), effective August 5, 1993.

8. *Viscaino v. Microsoft* 173 F3d 713 (9th Cir 1999).

9. *U.S. v. Pilkington* Civ. No. 94-345 (D. Ariz. May 25, 1994) 59 Fed. Reg. 30,604 (June 14, 1994).

10. Christian WikNina Isokorpi, "Finland," *International Financial Law Review,* Competition and Antitrust Law, 1997, Supp. (London, September 1997).

11. Mexico. Federal Law of Economic Competition. *Federal Official Gazette.* (December 24, 1992). It should be noted that in Mexico, laws do not become legally effective until published in the *Gazette,* unlike in the United States where they become effective immediately upon signature of the President.

12. Not only have individual cities, such as New Orleans and Chicago, brought suit against gun manufacturers, but there are lawsuits which have been brought as a class action by the victims of crimes involving guns. David Segal, "After Tobacco Success, Lawyers Pick Gun Fight," *The Washington Post,* (January 5, 1999), p. A01. In addition, it should be noted that in the June 1999 annual meeting of the American Bar Association, the Tort and Insurance Practice Section presented a panel on Gun Violence Liability to "educate practitioners . . . on the latest developments in this billion-dollar litigation." Available: http://scratch.abanet.org

13. There are several such organizations, some of which are older than others. Among the better-known are the American Arbitration Association in New York; the International Court of Arbitration of the International Chamber of Commerce in Paris, and the London Court of Arbitration. In addition, there is an arbitral body in Budapest, Hungary, in Zurich, Switzerland, in Stockholm, Sweden and in Moscow, Russia.

14. For a complete analysis of the language which should be included in arbitral clauses, see Roger W. Reinsch and Raffaele DeVito, "A Business

Person's Guide to Negotiating an International Arbitration Agreement," *Multinational Business Review,* vol. 6, (spring 1998), pp. 1–12.

15. Probably the most famous expropriation case involving such a use of differing valuations was that of *La Brea,* a field exploited by the International Petroleum Company, a subsidiary of Standard Oil in Peru. After years of conflict between London Pacific, a British oil company and the government of Peru, an international arbitration award issued in 1922 determined the extent of the concession. In 1924 IPC took over the company, but continued to pay taxes on significantly less property than it was supposed to. The Peruvian military government in 1968 attempted to set-off the past due taxes from the amount owed for the expropriation. The U.S. government contended that such set-offs were illegal and invoked the Hickenlooper Amendment against Peru for this action. Leopoldo Gonzalez Aguayo, *La Nacionalizacion de Bienes Extranjeros en America Latina II,* (Mexico City: UNAM, 1969), pp. 7–45.

16. This occurred in Venezuela during the 1950s and early 1960s causing that nation to be a leader in the creation of the Organization of Petroleum Exporting Nations.

17. James Don Edwards and John B. Barrack, "Reaching International Accounting Standards," Center for International Private Enterprise. Available: www.cipe.org/ert/e31/e31-5.html

9 | Global Financial Strategy for the Twenty-First Century

RAJ AGGARWAL

ROBERT E. GROSSE

Finance at the turn of the twenty-first century is once again truly global. In any medium- or large-sized firm, financial decisions must take into account the opportunities and risks offered by more than just domestic financial markets. Financial managers have before them an incredible array of financial instruments and arrangements. There is an ever-expanding range of funding instruments and sources, with both sides of corporate balance sheets becoming increasingly liquid. On both the asset and the liability sides, opportunities abound. Consider the range of alternatives available for funding the company's needs shown in Figure 9.1.

If the firm needs debt financing, the choices range from short-term bank loans or commercial paper, to medium-term financing facilities, to long-term bonds—all of these available at home or abroad. If the firm needs equity financing, the choices range from retained earnings to regular equity instruments to depository receipts—again available at home or abroad. These choices are considered in detail later.

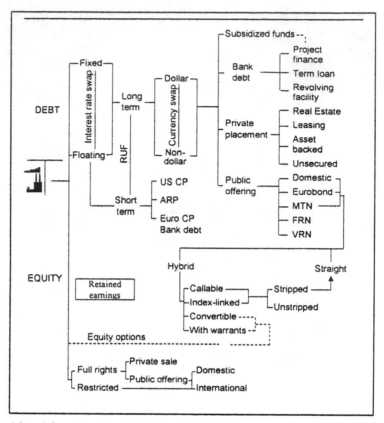

Adapted from Gunter Dufey, unpublished figure.

Figure 9.1   Financing alternatives available to major corporations.

Think Global, Act "Glocal": A Conceptual Framework for International Financial Management

There are many reasons why cross-border financial activity is different from financial activity within one country. These differences can be classified into two main categories: institutional and political. These differences give rise not only to exchange rate changes but also to international differences in the pricing and risk characteristics of financial instruments and activity. A key role of the finance manager is to identify and exploit arbitrage opportunities created by these exchange rate changes and by international institutional and political differences.

International Institutional Differences

The institutional structure of finance differs significantly from one country to another. Such differences arise for many reasons including historical evolutionary paths, cultural preferences and behaviors with regard to risk pricing and financial services, and regulatory and political structures for managing the economy. For example, financial (especially securities) markets tend to be much more important in financial intermediation in North America and other Anglo-Saxon countries such as the United Kingdom and Australia, while firms in other countries rely much more on banking systems. In addition to this difference in the relative role of markets versus banks, countries generally also differ with respect to the relative importance of the overall financial sector in an economy, with higher levels of relative importance generally associated with higher economic growth rates.

International Political Differences

Countries differ greatly in terms of their political structures, and these differences generally lead to differences in how the economy is managed by the government. Political systems generally differ with regard to the nature and importance of fiscal and monetary policies. As an example, prior to the adoption of the EU convergence treaty in the mid-1990s, German monetary policy was generally considered to be tighter than monetary policies in other European countries such as Italy. Governments may also differ in terms of a number of specific issues such as the importance given to social safety nets. International political differences are also very important in shaping national financial systems. Regulatory and other governmental influences on the financial sector vary greatly among countries. These differences in the management of an economy not only influence the nature of domestic financial systems and banking structure, but also influence cross-border flows of funds and other financial activity. They certainly also influence how interest rates and exchange rates change and evolve over time.

Implications for International Financial Management

Institutional and political differences not only shape the nature of exchange rate movements, they also influence how financial and business risk is evaluated and priced in a country. Astute financial managers can arbitrage and exploit such differences to reduce operating and financial costs and risks for their firm. For example, long-term deviations from purchasing power parity exchange rates mean opportunities for value creation through sourcing and market segmentation.[1] In addition, there may be opportunities to create value by hedging unexpected or undesirable exchange rate movements. Similarly, these international differences allow a company with access to finance in multiple countries to lower its financing costs by raising money in the most cost-effective country at any given time. Thus, astute financial managers in multinational firms must simultaneously account for both global and local goals and conditions, that is, they must be globally-local or "glocal" in all their actions and deliberations.

How Global Are Financial Markets?

Financial markets today have a scope that truly spans the world. That is, firms from around the world have access to domestic and external markets in many countries and currencies. Although there are barriers to overseas investing and borrowing in many countries and firms face different levels of taxation and other regulatory costs, nevertheless, financial markets are linked globally. From the sweep of stock market prices that affect each other across the globe as Tokyo closes and London opens, followed by New York opening and finally San Francisco closing—these markets interact. Indeed, they are more and more linked in terms of trading, such that investors in one stockmarket have increasingly broader access to markets across the globe. And companies themselves now often list their securities in multiple markets, making their equity or bonds tradable on domestic financial markets in several countries.

A measure of the globality of financial markets today is the foreign exchange market, which transacts more than $1.5 trillion of value each business day.[2] This market is centered in London, but trading continues all day and all night as banks pass their trading activities to their branches or subsidiaries from London to New York, San Francisco, Tokyo, Hong Kong, Bahrain, Frankfort, and back to London. It is truly a round-the-clock business, and by far the largest financial market in the world in value terms. (By way of comparison, world trade in goods and services for the entire year in 1998 was about US

$6.7 trillion, or less than the equivalent of foreign exchange trading for one week; turnover on the New York Stock Exchange was US $7.3 trillion in 1998, or about as much as is traded in foreign exchange during one week.)

Another measure of how global are financial markets is the level of participation of non-U.S. firms in U.S. financial markets. The number of foreign firms listed on the New York Stock Exchange, including ordinary stock shares and ADRs, is now over 400 (and continues to climb) from 48 countries. There is a great deal of foreign investment in U.S. securities and, conversely, of U.S. investment in foreign securities (both figures continue to rise faster than domestic investment). In all, the U.S. financial market is highly global, and global borrowers and lenders alike are active in it.

Yet another measure of the worldwide operation of financial markets is the spread of financial shocks. When the speculative crisis hit Thailand in July of 1997 and millions of investment dollars were shifted out of that country, not only did the baht fall dramatically in value, but it drew several other currencies along with it. First to be affected were neighboring countries such as Indonesia and Malaysia, but the impact spread to Latin America, where fierce speculation hit Argentina and Brazil. Economic downturns and speculative attacks also occurred from Japan to Russia to Ecuador, where currency devaluations and emergency government policies tried to stop the panic selling during 1998. It appears that the spread of the speculative shock has ended, but the economic impact has clearly been global.

These kinds of major financial shocks dramatically emphasize that financial management needs to be carried out on a global basis. Costs and risks must be evaluated and managed on a global basis. It does no good to measure and plan for risks in one country without taking into account the impact of conditions in other countries. The late 1990s Asian crisis strikingly illustrates this problem. Even in the domestic context, it is not sensible to deal with interest rate risk without considering inflation risk and exchange rate risk (plus their interactions). When interest rates change, this most often occurs because of or in anticipation of changes in inflation, and often in conjunction with initial currency revaluation followed by short-term devaluation. The risks of either one should not and cannot be managed in isolation from the other.

International Financial Markets and Institutions

International financial markets in the early 2000s will continue to offer businesses access to financing alternatives, investment alternatives, and various other financial services such as funds management and transfer, and so on, just as in the late 1990s. The roles of different institutions are changing, however, as financial supermarkets become more common, and as the Internet is more and more widely used as a mechanism for providing the services.

Financial markets around the world are becoming more attractive for international borrowers and lenders. Less than a decade ago most national financial markets were quite segmented from each other, with differing regulatory and tax regimes, ownership rules, and transactions costs. Outside of the United States, the United Kingdom, and a small number of other markets, foreign borrowers and lenders faced enormous barriers to entry and exit. International company treasurers' choice for locating their cash management and/or exchange risk management centers generally used to be London. Other locations were too burdened by regulatory restrictions and transactions costs.

Today, most OECD countries offer unrestricted entry and exit for funds transfers and other financial transactions, and the financial centers in emerging market locations such as Hong Kong, Singapore, Panama, and the Cayman Islands likewise offer low-cost, unrestricted financial activity. The choice of a regional corporate financial center today has more to do with the kinds of counterparties with which you want to do business, rather than with transactions costs or regulatory limitations.

For example, a firm from the United States interested in expanding its funding sources to investors/lenders outside of the United States may look to the euromarkets for new funding. By issuing a eurobond, the firm may find additional institutional investors in Europe who are not active in the United States, thus expanding its opportunities. Likewise, by issuing equity as Global Depository Receipts or as ordinary shares in London or another major financial market, the firm may gain new equity investors. By considering bank financing in London or elsewhere in Europe or Asia, the firm can develop new banking relationships and additional funding sources.

These same sets of cross-border opportunities await firms from other countries as well. Foreign firms have access to the large U.S.

financial markets through the use of traditional debt and equity instruments and through innovations available only to non-U.S. issuers, such as American Depository Receipts on the equity side, and yankee bonds or commercial paper on the debt side.

Costs and Risks in Modern Financial Markets

The problems that one faces in taking advantage of these powerful markets may come from several sources. First, in terms of accessibility, if the firm does not already possess a high credit rating, many of the financing alternatives are simply not available. Since the ability of firms to issue most of the instruments discussed here lies wholly in their perceived creditworthiness, smaller and less-known firms generally have a difficult time gaining access to them. Second, in many countries, there still exist government policy limitations on international financial activities, so some firms may find that desirable financing instruments are not (yet) legally possible. Third, upon accepting funding from an international source, the firm becomes exposed to new risks such as exchange rate risk and the commercial and political risks of operating in foreign jurisdictions. Fourth, once a firm becomes part of the international financing arena, it becomes in play, and subject to the risks of operating at this level (especially in terms of mergers and acquisitions).

Financial Institutions in a Global Context

Even with the phenomenon of disintermediation that has swept financial markets since the early 1980s, commercial banks have retained their role as significant suppliers of financial services. In the early 1980s in the United States, it appeared that commercial banks might be on their way to permanent decline. Commercial banks were being threatened successfully by financial innovations (such as money market mutual funds and financial management accounts at the retail level, and financing facilities such as commercial paper and revolving underwriting facilities at the corporate level) by investment banks such as Merrill Lynch and Shearson Lehman Brothers.

Entering the 1990s, it was clear that commercial banks in the United States had survived the death threat of their nonregulated peers from investment banking (even though the savings and loans had not). Through this decade the major movement in the United

States has been to merge commercial banks into nationwide financial service powerhouses capable of competing with not only domestic nonbank suppliers of financial services, but also with foreign multi-purpose banks (universal banks, such as Barclays and Deutsche Bank). These changes in the U.S. banking market are illustrated by Bank One's national expansion through its acquisition of small- and medium-sized banks in more than 20 states (principally in the non-coastal regions of the United States),[3] and by Chase Manhattan's expansion through the establishment of loan production and real estate lending offices throughout the country (as well as its acquisition of Chemical Bank in 1996).

This trend concluded the 1990s with creation of the current Bank of America, which results from a 1998 merger with NationsBank (in which NationsBank essentially won control of the combined entity, even moving the headquarters of BofA from San Francisco to Charlotte, North Carolina). This bank contains the merged set of former regional banks such as Crocker Bank and Seafirst on the West Coast, and Barnett Bank and Boatmen's Bancshares on the East Coast. Another example of the consolidation frenzy is the 1998 formation of Citigroup, in which Citibank joined Travelers Group to form a financial supermarket, with major presence in commercial banking, investment banking (Salomon Smith Barney), and insurance throughout the United States and abroad.

Looking at the provision of financial services at the global level, a U.S. company could consider any one of the following firms as a possible provider of financial services in dozens of countries.

As can be seen from Table 9.1, the range of global financial institutions is large and multifaceted. The list is certainly growing and is limited by the fact that it does not include nonbank centered financial services providers (such as Merrill Lynch, American Express, Ford Credit, and GE Capital).

Scope and Relationships of International Markets

The size of financial markets at the end of the twentieth century is truly impressive. Starting from the foreign exchange market, with its $1.5 trillion of daily turnover, the range of financial markets is indeed wide and deep. These markets are linked not only by transactions between them but also by intermediaries that have offices in

Table 9.1   Major Global Universal Banks, 1999

Financial Institution	Services	No. of Countries
Citigroup	com, inv, ins	98
Deutsche Bank	com, inv	50
Union Bank of Switz.	com, inv	40
Bank of America	com, inv	37
Barclays Bank	com, inv	76
HongKong & Shanghai Bank	com, inv	79
Lloyds Bank	com, inv, ins	40
Credit Suisse	com, inv	50
Dresdner Bank	com, inv	70
Bank of Tokyo-Mistubishi	com, inv	45
ABN-Amro Bank	com, inv	30

Note: com = commercial banking; inv = investment banking;
ins = insurance

Sources: *Hoover Handbook of World Business*, bank annual reports, analyst reports from investment banks.

many countries. For instance, the HongKong Bank (HSBC) can offer a client a checking account in New York (through its wholly-owned Marine Midland network of branches), a letter of credit in Hong Kong, and a cash management service in London (through its Midland Bank affiliates), not to mention other services in dozens of other locations around the world. Table 9.2 provides a relative perspective of the financing possibilities in various markets.

Financial markets now operate not only through organized markets but also through trading rooms and electronic markets that include commercial and investment banks in transactions that encompass an ever-expanding array of assets and liabilities (OTC and exchange-traded securities) on a continuous (24-hour) basis.

Securities and Instruments Available

The wide variety of financial instruments available on the various financial markets are discussed next in separate sections covering

Table 9.2   Key Financial Markets in 1998

Market	Daily Turnover ($US billions)	Capitalization ($US billions)
New York Stock Exchange	$22.8	$11,800
London Stock Exchange	8.150	2,370
Frankfort Stock Exchange*	4.289	1,094
Tokyo Stock Exchange	2.357	2,439
Hong Kong Stock Exchange	0.562	344
US total bank loans		7,061.8
UK total bank loans		1,806.7
ADRs total issues		392

* Frankfort data cover all German stock exchanges.

Sources: Federal Reserve System; Bank of England; Bundesbank; New York Stock Exchange; London Stock Exchange

funding instruments (sources of funds), investing instruments (uses of funds), and hedging instruments (risk management).

1: Funding Instruments (Sources of Funds) and Strategies

The main sources of funds available to the international firm include those shown in Figure 9.1. These alternatives need to be evaluated in terms of not only their costs, but also their exposure to interest rate, exchange rate, political, and credit risks, as well as their impact on the firm's default risk, corporate control, and impact on the ability to seek further financing later. For a U.S. firm to issue euro-denominated bonds in Luxembourg would imply access to European investors, currency exposure in euros, and higher default risk than previously, other things being equal. The cost of issuing these bonds and their interest rate may well be below that of domestic U.S. costs, but the new risks and the expanded investor pool cannot be ignored.[4]

Unquestionably, the basic consideration for choosing among financing sources is cost, largely the interest cost (or required return on equity instruments). This cost depends on the period of time being financed (more time, higher cost) and the choice between debt and equity forms (debt being almost always cheaper, but subjecting the firm to default risk). When this consideration is paired with the risk involved, a classic risk/cost curve can be constructed, as in Figure 9.2.

This risk/cost trade-off curve demonstrates the familiar upward slope, rising faster as the firm takes on high levels of debt financing. What the curve does not show, however, is the firm-specific risk generated by each instrument. For example, if yen-denominated eurobonds would enable the firm to hedge existing yen-denominated assets, then this funding source would appear at a lower risk level than shown in the figure. In fact, the risks in the figure are seen from the perspective of the overall financial market, rather than from the firm's internal perspective. Each firm needs to construct its own cost/risk curve to compare various funding sources, since each firm's situation is different. What the figure does show usefully is the approximate interest cost of each instrument, though even these will vary to some extent for each firm.

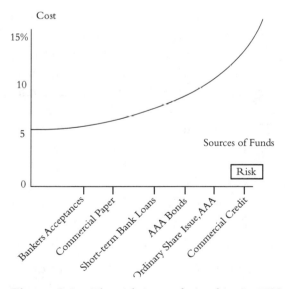

Figure 9.2   The risk/cost relationship (in US$ Instruments 1999).

Capital Structure Decisions

Capital structure decisions reflect choices of the proportions of debt and equity in the sources of funds used by a firm. Payments to debt holders must be made as due or the firm can be forced into bankruptcy. Equity holders have no such priority but can claim all residual income or assets. Debt is safer for an investor and its costs to the firm are tax-deductible, but it is generally cheaper but riskier than equity for the firm. To minimize its cost of capital and maximize its market value, a firm would like as much of the less expensive debt that it can service safely.

In addition, depending on a firm's investment opportunity set and management structure, debt financing can encourage managers to change the mix and extent of the firm's investments closer to its ideal investments. At the optimum debt level, additional risk-related and other costs of debt are just offset by the managerial and other advantages of debt financing such as the decline in average capital costs due to the use of a greater proportion of debt. This optimum level of debt that minimizes the average cost of capital would be different depending on the firm's investment opportunity set, management structure, stability of the firm's operating cash flows, the probability and costs of financial distress, and its tolerance for risk.

Thus, the optimum capital structure of a firm can be expected to vary not only by firm size and other corporate characteristics, but also by its tax rate, industry, and country. The capital structures of firms in the same industry but in different countries are often quite different. These differences generally reflect international differences in tax rates and regulatory regimes as well as differences in attitudes toward business distress. Higher tax rates imply a greater advantage for debt, and group business structures also favor debt, as members of a group are expected to help a group member in distress. Table 9.3 illustrates some international differences in capital structure norms. As this table shows, even among the largest companies in each country, there is a large international range in the proportion of total assets (TA) that are financed with equity (the rest are financed by debt).

Capital Structure Decisions for Foreign Affiliates

Capital structure decisions for a country subsidiary of a multinational firm often reflects three major influences: political risks, domestic

Table 9.3 International Differences in Capital Structure Norms (Large Companies from Selected Countries)

Country	Equity/TA (%)
Latin America	
Mexico	53
Chile	55
Brazil	40
Argentina	42
Europe	
UK	40
Netherlands	30
Germany	25
Sweden	24
France	18
Italy	12
Asia	
Hong Kong	67
Singapore	58
Taiwan	36
India	31
Japan	14
Korea	12

Sources: Raj Aggarwal, "Capital Structure Differences Among Large Asian Companies," *ASEAN Economic Bulletin* (July 1990): 39-53; Raj Aggarwal, "Capital Structure Among Latin American Companies," *Managerial Finance* (1/1987): 3–11; and Raj Aggarwal, "International Differences in Capital Structure Norms," *Management International Review*

debt ratio norms, and parent country debt norms. The first major influence is political risk in the host country, with the use of higher debt ratios and higher levels of local financing in countries with high levels of political risk and risk of blocked funds. Domestic influences on optimum debt ratios include tax rates and factors in the business environment that impact the stability of cash flows and the probability of financial distress. Home country influences on subsidiary capital structure include the need to conform to home country debt ratio norms in consolidated financial statements. Deviations from either set of debt ratio norms, domestic or home country, involves increasing costs. As these domestic and home country debt norms generally differ, the foreign subsidiary capital structure must balance these costs.

2: Investing Instruments (Uses of Funds) and Strategies

Multinational Working Capital Management

Working capital management involves decisions with regard to the levels of cash, receivables, and inventory. Too much working capital is costly, reducing profitability and return on capital. However, too little working capital can also be costly in terms of lost opportunities (e.g., lost sales due to inadequate inventory or too tight a credit policy) and the firm may suffer increases in its cost of capital due to too little cash if it cannot pay bills on time. Thus, like capital structure policy, working capital policies also involve a tradeoff between the risks of having too low a level of working capital versus the costs of having too high a level. Due to the difficulty of measuring many of these tradeoffs, determining the optimum levels of working capital cannot be completely scientific. In practice, it remains somewhat of an art form.

The costs and risks of a particular level of working capital depend on local norms and business conditions. For example, domestic bank clearing processes for payments processing and the predictability of cash inflows and outflows influence the optimum levels of cash, domestic and industry credit terms and collection policies influence receivables levels, and local availability and lead times and inflation rates have a significant influence on inventory levels. The strength of the local currency will also have some influence on working capital levels as discussed earlier. However, subsidiary levels of working capital cannot be too far out of line with home country norms to avoid problems with consolidated financial statements. As in the case of capital structure decisions for subsidiaries of multinational companies, optimum levels of working capital, cash, receivables, and inventory for a subsidiary of a multinational also must reflect a balance between both home and host country influences.

International Capital Budgeting

Capital budgeting is the process of funding projects that have long-term benefits (i.e., benefits that go beyond one year). Capital budgeting projects must add value (i.e., the present value of their incremental future cash flows and other benefits must exceed the present value of the investment with both discounted at appropriate risk adjusted discount rates). Thus, the capital budgeting process involves not only the estimation of appropriate risk-adjusted discount rates, but also the assessment of future project benefits and the conversion of as many of them as possible into cash flows, given uncertain competitor reactions and other changes in the future environment of business.

Many of the benefits (such as improved product quality or better delivery times or other improvements in customer service) may be very difficult to assess in cash flow terms. Some noncash future benefits may be in the form of real options that would position a firm for possible future profitable undertakings. In addition to these difficulties and uncertainties in assessing future benefits of a proposed project, capital budgeting also involves an assessment of the risks in these future benefits to estimate an appropriate discount rate for calculating the present value of these future benefits. Capital project analysis may use sensitivity analysis, scenario assessments, simulation, game theory, option pricing models, and other analytical procedures to assess these uncertain future benefits and estimate the appropriate risk-adjusted discount rate. In practice, assessing capital projects generally involves many approximations and subjective estimates especially for small projects with the assessment process for larger projects becoming increasingly more extensive.

Valuing real options that may be created by a capital project can be quite challenging. The first challenge is to identify the possible future business opportunity created and to recast it in terms of options terminology. For example, it is essential to determine what is the underlying asset and its riskiness, what is the exercise price of the option or what will be the required investment, and what is the maturity of the option or how long will this business opportunity be available? In addition, it is useful to note that the value of the option positively depends on the riskiness of the underlying asset and on the maturity of the option. The value of this future option must be discounted back to year zero.

The assessment of capital projects in a diversified multinational is further complicated by the fact that while corporate headquarters generally allocate funds for these projects, project proposals are prepared by division or business unit personnel who are likely to have better knowledge about the project risks and benefits. This information asymmetry leads to "gaming" between headquarters and business units and results in some residual intrafirm agency costs. The information asymmetry between headquarters and business units is generally worse for projects in foreign countries and funded (or rejected) because projects from different divisions, business units, or countries may not meet the same criteria. Appropriate intrafirm and interdivisional incentive systems and organizational structures for capital budgeting processes must be developed and implemented to minimize these agency costs.

All of these issues and challenges with regard to capital budgeting systems are accentuated for diversified multinational firms that often must compare project proposals from different industries and countries with different business and cultural environments, competitive intensities, inflation rates, and exchange rates. It is a challenge to make the assessment of project benefits and risks comparable across countries and industries. For example, this challenge for a diversified U.S. multinational packaging company was expressed in the question "How do you compare a capital request for a corrugated cardboard box plant in Mississippi to a request for a glass bottle plant in Ecuador?" There does not seem to be any one best approach to answering this type of question and diversified multinational companies have had to develop their own variations and techniques to evaluate and compare capital projects across countries and industries. Techniques to assess risk include informed but subjective classification categories, scenario analysis, and simulation to assess the impact of reasonable variations in at least the critical variables such as exchange rates, inflation rates, and discount rates.

In evaluating capital project proposals in a multinational firm it essential that the proposed project meet two hurdles for approval. First, it must be value-added for the domestic subsidiary in local currency terms reflecting the investment and benefits that accrue to the local subsidiary (e.g., it must have a positive net present value). In addition, however, for a capital project in a multinational firm that meets this first and primary hurdle, it must also be evaluated in terms of cash flows and other benefits to the parent company reflecting the parent's investment and benefits such as remittances. Should the second analysis come up short, the project structure and remittances to the parent may have to be adjusted, so the parent company also gets an adequate return on its investment.

3: Hedging Instruments (Risk Management) and Strategies

The main risks faced by firms operating at the international level are those encountered domestically, plus exchange rate risk and country risk. Even this statement needs to be hedged, because the domestic risks such as interest rate risk and inflation risk are expanded at the international level when the firm faces rates in different markets, thus with different degrees of risk. In all, international financial risks are more extensive than those encountered domestically, and they have additional nuances because of the mixing of multiple markets.

Sources of Risk in Cross-Border Business

Business and financial risks in cross-border business arise primarily due to cultural, institutional, and political differences. These differences give rise to differences in business practices and expectations that are often significant and may even be critical. A primary source of risk in cross-border business that can be straightforward to reduce or eliminate is the lack of familiarity with these international differences in business practices and expectations. In addition, international cultural, institutional, and political differences also influence the nature and predictability of changes in the business environment and, thus, the business risks faced in cross-border activity. Consequently, business plans and cost-benefit analysis for cross–border activity must take into account the costs and risks of managing these international differences in business practices, expectations, and changes in the business environment.

Operating and Financial Hedging Strategies

It is often contended that hedging is a zero-sum game and given that the financial markets are efficient, the costs of hedging must equal or exceed (due to transaction costs) the benefits of hedging. While this statement may be true in general, there are significant exceptions that argue that hedging can be a value-added activity in specific cases. Hedging can be a positive-sum game as markets are not always perfectly efficient and companies often face convex tax schedules and hysteresis in operating decisions.

There is considerable evidence of numerous short-term deviations from efficient markets in even the most actively traded currencies, with wider deviations for the less frequently traded currencies. In addition, there seem to be significant long-term deviations of numerous exchange rates from purchasing power parity rates. Many of these deviations from efficient markets may be traced to governmental actions, while other deviations may be caused by transactions and information costs that are not insignificant. Even in foreign exchange markets that are generally efficient, a company needs to engage in a number of transactions before exchange rate losses and gains average out to zero. Companies that do not engage in frequent foreign exchange transactions may find it useful to consider hedging exchange rate risks.

In practice, companies must also guard against extreme amounts of exchange rate and other losses to avoid costs of financial distress such as the costs of violating debt covenants and of perceptions of possible bankruptcy and inability to service customers, suppliers, and employees. Many operating decisions are not easily or costlessly reversible, and hedging of exchange rate changes can add value in such cases. Further, a company that faces a convex or progressive tax schedule with higher rates for higher income levels can reduce its expected tax bill by hedging and reducing extremes in its income. Similarly, a company that faces political costs of reporting high incomes (demands to share the largess with its stakeholders), can also benefit by hedging and reducing extremes in its reported income. Thus, in practice there can be many situations where hedging exchange rate risks may be useful. It would be useful for a financial manager to identify such situations for a particular firm in developing an exchange rate risk management policy for the firm.

Organizing for Hedging Currency Risks

As the preceding discussion indicates, there is no excuse for failing to seek out hedging tools when risks are large and/or they affect important corporate business. The problem is that you don't want to hedge every risk that comes along, especially when natural hedges often arise in multinational firms (for example, a French subsidiary may have net exposed assets in British pounds, but another subsidiary of the firm may have a net liability position in pounds that may offset part or all of the French exposure). Thus, before a firm undertakes hedging actions, it must determine what needs to be hedged (i.e., what is its net exposure). Information about projected cross-currency transactions and expected cash flows must be collected from each independent subsidiary and business unit and consolidated. Unlike traditional accounting systems, such consolidation must be by currency and not by country or business unit. This process of consolidating often-offsetting exposures in each currency allows a company to take advantage of self-hedging and offsetting transactions. Data necessary for determining net exposures is usually not available from a firm's accounting information system, as they involve future not past transactions. Exposures in highly correlated currencies may be further consolidated to determine the net exposures to be hedged in terms of a narrower set of the more liquid currencies.

In addition to the development of a currency exposure reporting system, a company must develop and implement an organizational structure to manage its currency (and other related) risks. The corporate officer responsible for hedging policies and decisions must be identified and a policy statement indicating the types of exposures to be hedged must be developed. Adequate and appropriate controls to limit derivatives positions must also be developed and implemented. If the company has many independent profit centers, the central treasury responsible for hedging must be prepared to sell hedging instruments at competitive prices to its independent business units and/or devise other procedures to take advantage of intracompany offsetting transactions and yet allow the business units to be independent.

Financial Hedging Strategies

A firm can manage its foreign exchange risks by engaging in transactions that will have offsetting gains (or losses) in the event of an unexpected exchange rate change. In other words, a firm may purchase or sell a financial instrument with a payoff that offsets an exchange rate loss on an underlying transaction. Examples of such financial instruments are futures and forward contracts and call and put options (actually there are many other more complex instruments also available to hedge an expanding range of financial, commodity, and event risks).

Futures, forwards, and options are all financial instruments that are issued for a specified time period. Futures contracts fix prices for future delivery of an underlying asset (or liability). These contracts are traded on organized exchanges for specific amounts and ending dates, and involve an up-front margin deposit and daily mark-to-market evaluation of the contract to ensure a minimum operating margin at all times during the life of the futures contract. Forward contracts also fix the price of an underlying asset (or liability) but are sold over the counter and are for customized amounts and ending dates. In a forward contract there is no exchange of cash until the date of expiration or exercise. Thus, compared to futures contracts, forward contracts involve higher levels of risk for the counterparties. A series of forward contracts with consecutive expiration dates are often combined in the form of a swap agreement.

Options also fix the price of the underlying asset for future delivery, with call options allowing the holder to buy at a fixed price and put options allowing for fixed price sales. Options can be exchange traded or traded over the counter. However, unlike futures and forwards, options do not require a contractual delivery (or settlement) of the underlying asset. Options can be exercised only when it is beneficial for the holder of the option and allowed to expire if exercise is not beneficial. Consequently, because of this flexibility, options are priced higher than futures or forwards.

If a firm wishes to hedge a foreign currency receivable, it may contract to sell the expected foreign currency receipts using a forward or futures contract eliminating any uncertainty in the future amount in terms of its home currency. To hedge a foreign currency transaction of uncertain amount or timing, as in the case of a bid involving a foreign currency commitment, a firm may use an option to hedge its currency risk. In practice, firms often face currency risks that can be considerably more complex than these simple examples. The field of financial engineering has grown greatly in recent years and financial engineers have devised various combinations of these simple hedging instruments to come up with exotic variations that can be designed to hedge specific risks precisely and efficiently.

A firm can also reduce its currency risk by changing its financial policies to respond to expected changes in currency values. For example, it can accelerate the collection of receivables in a weakening currency or of payables in strengthening currency. In general, a firm could accelerate cash inflows in a weakening currency and outflows in a strengthening currency. The cost-benefit analysis of such policies with regard to cash flows and monetary assets and liabilities should reflect not only the expected exchange rate change but also any offsetting opportunity costs of such changes. Similarly, policies with regard to inventories and other nonmonetary assets and liabilities should be evaluated taking into account exchange rate changes, inflation rates, and opportunity costs.

Operating Policies as Hedging Strategies

Longer term and persistent currency mismatches in cash flows must be hedged with operating strategies, especially as the availability of financial hedging instruments declines and their cost goes up sharply with their maturity. Conversely, because of their cost and irreversibility, operating policies are generally not suitable for hedging short-term currency exposures. Thus, the primary factor influencing hedging with operating policies are long-term changes in exchange rates and their deviations from purchasing power parity values.

In case of significant deviations from purchasing power parity, a firm may change its sourcing to take advantage of persistently weak exchange rates and try to increase its sales in areas with persistently overvalued currencies. Similarly, plant location decisions may also reflect the geographic distribution of its sales and the relative strengths of the currencies involved. For example, in response to the rapid rise of the Japanese Yen in the mid-1980s (and in response to U.S. protectionist policy), many Japanese auto manufacturers built plants in the United States to serve the U.S. market, greatly reducing or even eliminating the currency risks of a changing dollar-yen exchange rate. A marketing policy adopted by the Japanese auto manufacturers to combat the rising yen was to develop sales of products and brands that are less sensitive to price competition (market segmentation). This policy was reflected in efforts to expand sales of their new luxury divisions such as Lexus by Toyota, Infinity by Nissan, and Acura by Honda. In addition, the Japanese auto companies also moved away from serving the low-cost and price-sensitive segments for their other product lines emphasizing higher quality, styling, and other nonprice factors.

Global Portfolio Management: Real and Financial Diversification

International diversification can reduce risk as different national economies do not move up and down in tandem. In many circumstances, such risk reduction can be a value-added activity (e.g., in situations where total risk, not just systematic risk, matters); in situations where companies face progressive tax rates and political costs; and in other situations as described earlier when hedging can be a value-added activity. Thus, many large companies find that international diversification is a value-added activity especially if they can take advantage of market imperfections, government regulations and other policies, and opportunities that are not easily available to others.

International diversification of real assets is generally undertaken as part of the multinational company's process of foreign direct investment (FDI), where a firm invests overseas with the intent of exercising managerial control over these foreign operations. In contrast, foreign portfolio investment (FPI) involves cross-border investments in business securities without regard to managerial control. Compared to FDI, FPI has lower transactions costs and can have a shorter term perspective. Transaction costs for FDI are higher, necessitating a longer term perspective, but FDI generally allows access to opportunities that are not available to portfolio investors. Information costs are high for either type of foreign investment as information and expertise on foreign investments is relatively rare and expensive.

Alternatives for Foreign Portfolio Diversification

In undertaking FPI, one way to avoid these high information and transactions costs is to avoid direct purchase of foreign securities unless you are a large or institutional investor that can use economies of scale and scope in expertise in foreign investment opportunities. Because of the need to cross national legal boundaries, investments in foreign securities involve expensive and complicated clearing, settlement, and custody activity before title to purchased foreign securities can be confirmed. However, investing in foreign securities traded on foreign exchanges opens up the widest universe of investments with greater opportunities for finding good investments.

A second approach to FPI is to invest in foreign securities that trade in your home country in the form of depository receipts (DRs) such as global DRs (GDRs) or American DRs (ADRs). The depository receipts represent foreign shares held in a domestic depository (usually a large well-known bank or securities firm). Trading DRs avoids the legal complications of establishing cross-border ownership, and DRs can be traded on domestic securities exchanges with fewer accounting and disclosure requirements compared to listing the stock on a similar securities exchange. Further, investors can trade DRs just like any other listed security and more information is likely to be available domestically for such foreign securities. In recent years, the number of DRs and foreign shares listed and traded on domestic exchanges has risen considerably with a significant widening of the investment opportunity set in this category.

A third approach to FPI is to invest in the shares of domestically based or traded multinational companies (MNCs). Such companies are already internationally diversified in terms of their real assets, and their income streams generally reflect many of the advantages of international diversification. While individual investors have little or no influence on the nature and extent of international diversification in each MNC, they can get closer to their desired diversification by constructing an appropriate portfolio of MNCs.

A fourth approach is to invest in international (only foreign securities) or global (foreign and domestic securities), open-ended (new money is added to the fund) or closed-ended (fixed sum is invested and shares traded on an exchange) mutual funds. There has been a proliferation in international and global mutual funds in recent years, and investors can now find a wide range of international investment opportunities among mutual funds. Managers with varying abilities and cost structures run mutual funds, and the challenge is to pick the right mutual fund ex-ante.[5]

Global Asset Allocation

These different alternatives to global diversification are suitable for investors with different levels of knowledge and ability with regard to international diversification, their investment horizons, as well as their attitudes toward risks in such investments. For example, many individual and smaller investors should most likely be directed to appropriate mutual funds, while larger and institutional investors may consider investing directly in foreign securities. In addition, international investments should be considered as part of the overall portfolio of an investor and one of the first decisions, thus, involves asset allocation (i.e., the percentage of the overall portfolio that should be in foreign investments). The choice of the benchmark index (and its currency denomination) for these foreign investments is also important as it will greatly influence subsequent investment decisions.

Managing Strategic Events

In spite of all of the financial markets and instruments that have been developed during the past two decades, the financial world has not become any more stable or predictable. Hedging techniques require volatility for their existence, so perhaps the rollercoaster rides that could be traced back to the stock market crash of October 1987 in the United States may be seen as acceptable offshoots of this environment. It does not make financial managers any happier, however, when the volatility itself is unstable, and thus their hedging techniques often fail to properly measure this key characteristic of the markets.

Additional risks occur when problems in one market affect business in another. In recent years, the notion of global risk management has been greatly influenced by contamination effects or financial contagion especially in emerging markets. Financial contagion became particularly important after the Mexican Tequila crisis of 1994 and the Asian crisis of 1997, when domestic crises spilled over into other countries of the two regions and eventually into emerging markets in other parts of the world.

Finally, the global economic environment is characterized not only by many frequent small changes and fluctuations, but also by infrequent strategic discontinuities like the oil price shocks of 1973 and 1979, the Wall Street crash of 1987, the derivatives trading-related bankruptcy of Barings in 1992, and the Russian crisis of 1998–1999. Such major political and economic events can and indeed do have significant consequences for financial markets.

What can one do to *manage* what many have called *event risk* and we call risk due to strategic events? The first thing is to recognize that the markets will continue to demonstrate this volatility, assuming that governments continue to allow global finance to operate. Global financial markets continue to grow in importance relative to the goods and services economy, and such markets are governed by expectations about the future that can and have sometimes become unstable. Multinational companies must monitor markets and organize to anticipate, as far as possible, such strategic events. Firms must also use probable scenarios for such events in their strategic planning efforts. Second, it is best to build in some operating and strategic flexibility (e.g., allow for some spare debt capacity in financing so that sudden downturns do not force financial distress). And finally, managers must be ready to react immediately to the announcement of strategic events, with ready-to-go responses prepared in advance of the possible events that may materialize.

Conclusion

Financial managers must continue to develop lower cost and safer financing alternatives as well as higher return and safer investments. They must help assess and manage business and financial risks faced by their firms. Both sides of corporate balance sheets are now more liquid and there has been a veritable explosion in the range of financial instruments available to financial managers. Financial markets are now global, and increasing numbers of product markets are also becoming or are already global. These changes represent both unprecedented opportunities and interesting challenges.

This chapter has provided a short review of the challenging tasks faced by financial managers of multinational companies at the beginning of the twenty-first century. Such managers face financial markets that are increasingly global in nature yet continue to be influenced significantly by local regulations and norms. Such managers must think global but must act "Glocal" (i.e., with due regard to balancing both global and local needs and conditions).

Notes

1. For example, in Japan and Switzerland during the past decade, the currency has been persistently overvalued, making it more profitable, all other things equal, for firms to produce outside of these two countries and import into them to serve those markets.

2. See the tri-annual survey of national foreign exchange markets carried out by the Bank for International Settlements, which describes the volume and various disaggregations of foreign exchange activity in the main markets around the world. The latest survey is available at the bank's webpage: www.bis.org.

3. Bank One also has recently moved into acquisition of larger financial institutions, with the huge purchase of First Chicago-NBD in 1998. It has still maintained its noncoastal scope at this time.

4. While it is beyond the scope of this chapter to discuss the details or the fine points of specific financial instruments, we recommend a book such as *Financial Markets, Instruments, and Institutions,* by Anthony M. Santomero and David F. Babbel (Chicago: Irwin, 1997) for such details. For our purposes here, the point is to highlight the key considerations that should go into decision making.

5. Errunza et al., "Can the Gains from International Diversification Be Achieved without Trading Abroad?" *Journal of Finance,* (December 1999), have shown that in the 1990s, U.S. investors can reap almost all of the benefits of international portfolio diversification by purchasing instruments such as those discussed above (e.g., ADRs, country funds, multinational firms) in the domestic U.S. market.

Key Concerns
of the
Global Manager

10

The Key to Managing Information Globally: Flexible People

D. LANCE REVENAUGH

Change is constant. In the current hypercompetitive business environment, the old means of differentiation—quality, cost, innovation, and speed—have increasingly become commoditized. Similarly, competing globally and using new technologies are both becoming competitive imperatives. It would seem that we have returned to a time of keeping up with the corporate Jones', but the neighborhood is now a lot bigger.

The "New Economy," which is characterized by the revolution in information technology and the globalization of business, is a phenomenon that individual businesses are still trying to cope with. Similar to the Internet in its infancy, the applications and change that will precipitate from this trend are difficult to predict. This New Economy requires changes in companies' value propositions and major business paradigm shifts. In the hypercompetitive and

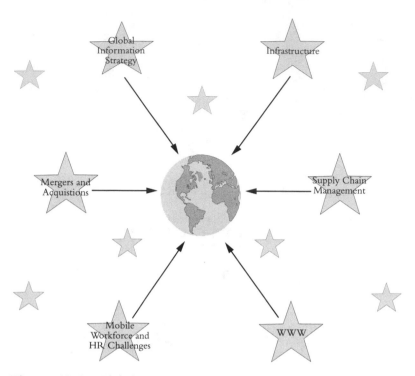

Figure 10.1   Global management of information.

time-constrained context, managers will need to trust employees who will be asked to take on more risk and be expected to understand more fully all aspects of the business. Therefore, more complex systems will be needed to support the business of business. People will be the difference in the adjustment to these new realities.

The intent of this chapter is to give managers an overview of six issues, which will have a significant impact on business in the next several years (Figure 10.1). The issues are a mix of emerging technologies and business ideas, which present opportunities that can be pursued with the use of information technology (IT). The importance of the issues examined is supported by many research perspectives, including a recent CEO survey performed by *Industry Week* magazine.[1] In this 1998 survey, CEOs from 78 manufacturing firms in Europe, the United States, and Japan were asked to give their top concerns for the near future. High on the list were:

- Rising customer expectations.
- The quality of their companies' information systems.
- The availability of a sufficient number of skilled workers.

These topics as well as many others are examined in this chapter, with a focus on how these issues affect strategy development.

We begin by looking at some current global information strategy drivers. These include competitive forces, networking, speed, and changing relationships. Specific to relationships, the nature of business relationships is currently being redefined, and thus requires new skills and forms of management. Relationships with customers, employees, suppliers, and competitors are becoming more dynamic and mutually beneficial.

Next, broad infrastructure issues will be examined including Enterprise Resource Planning (ERP) systems, supply chain management, and the World Wide Web (www). ERP is taking the business world by storm and changing the role of managers due to the automation of many tasks and a decrease in the amount of time spent on information gathering. In the back office, ERP systems will increasingly be linked to other systems within the supply chain, providing more transparent, timely data for managers to use in their decision making. ERP will also be a factor in the front office, capturing information input by customers on company web sites, thus automating the sales process. Supply chain management is a clear example of the changing relationships. With the Internet, intranets, and extranets, we do not yet know all the ways the www will impact business and strategy. What is hype and what is probable reality?

Many projections suggest that perhaps the most critical issue facing top companies is their relationship with employees. The next section of the chapter analyzes the tightening of labor markets, especially in the Information Systems field, and how it can affect a firm's ability to even consider, much less pursue, certain strategies. Also, as the nature of work evolves, employee mobility becomes more of a factor. Telecommuting and the management of this new employee relationship become a topic worthy of management attention.

Finally, in the past few years we have seen an increasing amount of consolidation within many industries due to deregulation and the opening of new markets. For a firm to take advantage of the synergies created by mergers and acquisitions, they must plan and quickly harmonize their existing information systems.

If we generalize the role of the senior managers, their characteristics can be boiled down to people who (1) can lead, (2) have big-picture perspective, and (3) can deal with uncertainty. Here, we attempt to provide clarity and assist in broadening the vision of the strategic impact of IT on the future of business. The focus on IT in this chapter should not be interpreted as a call to remove the human component from the business process; rather, the argument made is that the human element continues to be the most important aspect of the competitive enterprise of the future. People will be the difference in the successful use of technology to achieve a firm's strategic objectives. We see the emergence of a paradigm where superior IT and human capital management can offer significant competitive advantage. This chapter's aim is to bring attention to the increasingly important role of IT and to raise questions of how IT can and will affect your business. In addition, its goal is to provide an understanding of how IT is transforming business and why new technology has to be synchronized with global business strategy.

Global Information Strategy

Technology in general and information technology specifically have been viewed historically as a facilitator of corporate strategy. The proposition offered here is that IT will be increasingly seen as a driver of business strategy. The role of this discipline now is not only to enable a firm to make better, faster decisions, but also to enable a firm to create new forms of relationships and to open up opportunities for the firm to compete in new arenas. The keys to capitalizing on these opportunities are:

- A well-developed IT infrastructure.
- Information-rich products.
- A flexible organization made up of creative people.

This is the goal. But, how does an organization get there? Where does one find examples of firms with such attributes? There are few firms that can claim all of these attributes, but there are many moving in this direction.

Managers can look to many different industries for examples of companies pursuing the attributes just mentioned: financial services is an industry known for its fast adoption of new technology; consulting, for its organization and management of a knowledge-intensive, mobile workforce; software, for its innovative marketing and business models; and the auto industry, for its management of large and complicated manufacturing processes. These industries' combatants are pushing the envelope of business process with wide-ranging applications that can be adopted by other industries. Keeping abreast of the activities of these industries will give managers ideas of how they can innovate in their own industry. Additionally, a good source for benchmarking a firm's IT innovation is the annual issue of the *Informationweek 500*. The magazine ranks companies in 21 industries on their technology innovation and use of corporate information systems.[2]

Competitive Forces

We see an ever-increasing complexity to the nature of competition. Changes in technology affect all five forces of Porter's model: power of buyers, power of suppliers, threat of substitutes, threat of new entrants, and degree of industry rivalry. Technology already is enabling and will likely further enable the creation of substitute products and ease the path for potential entrants to compete in new industries. Managers will need a dynamic strategy to adjust and take advantage of these shifting market forces.

Barriers to entry in many established industries are disintegrating. Economies of scale are becoming less of a factor in a world of oversupply, overcapacity, and mass customization. The key to new competition is possessing the agility to react to changes in the market. With outsourcing and new channels of distribution, from the direct sales model of the Internet to the mass merchandiser model of Wal-Mart, capital requirements are less of a factor than in the past. We are also seeing deregulation in nearly every market, enabling new entrants to enter existing markets; for example, allowing telephone operators to compete in the cable industry or banks to compete in the insurance industry. Additionally, globalization is allowing foreign competitors to enter new markets. A firm's ability to raise prices and earn greater revenues will be limited by the increases in number of competitors and the increase in customer power, garnered from use of the Internet for comparison shopping.

All these forces add up to a requirement for new strategy formulation. With increases in automation, management's use of time will theoretically move toward more strategic roles and away from tactical duties. They will need to see what Stan Davis and Christopher Meyer refer to as "blur," the constant redefinition of buyer and seller, of product and service, and employee.[3] Also crucial is the development of an understanding that advantage is temporary. A fine example of this understanding can be seen in Dell Computers, whose strategy changed from a low-cost leader to a technology leader and then changed again to a service-based competitor. This strategy metamorphosis enabled Dell to find new opportunities and profits within their industry. A focus on recognizing and capturing value and finding innovative ways to deliver this value through the value chain is and will continue to be a strategic imperative. For example, Dell used IT to destroy the previous distribution paradigm and create a revolutionary new model.

Network Concept

Most concepts in business today revolve around the analogy of a theme commonly associated with computers—the network. From the value chain to supply chain, from the World Wide Web to distribution channels within a customer network, the term is ubiquitous and will grow even more so in an information-driven service economy.

As theorized by Carl Shapiro and Hal R. Varian in their book *Information Rules,* there is a critical mass component to any network.[4] The value of a network is enhanced by the number of people who use it. This can be seen today by the economic impact of corporate enterprise networks and the Internet and is similar to that of earlier "networks" such as the railroads, telephones, and bank machines. The exponential growth of the Internet has demonstrated the self-reinforcing feedback-loop characteristic of network economics, for which Shapiro and Varian coined the term "network effects."

Shapiro and Varian have also put forth the idea that the information economy is "driven by economies of networks, which tend to create monopolies." They emphasize that the key to companies trying to build markets is to "look at the industry and gauge the extent to which there are network effects and the extent of switching cost, and build your strategy around this."[5]

What does this mean for strategy formulation? It would suggest that companies could benefit by proliferating their IT vision. By convincing their suppliers and customers to follow suit in development of IT infrastructure, leading companies can develop a richer network of information and a more effective transfer structure within the group. It would also suggest that a firm should move to establish standards both in its industry and throughout its value chain. This standards development concept can also be applied to product or service development. If we look at Microsoft as an example of a standard setter in software, how can your business process or product be developed into a standard and how can you derive profits from this position? This may be easier to conceptualize as more and more products tend to contain a software component. The challenge of developing a sustainable standard may be very important to future new product introduction and market success.

As stated earlier, information goods drive a network economy. New technologies are dramatically changing the world by linking economies, empowering consumers, and altering the structure of global corporations. In this environment, adaptability is paramount as more companies build permeable networks of business relationships with their suppliers, distributors, employees, and competitors. One of the benefits of an open information system on a fairly standard platform is that it increases the dimensions of accessibility to member input and creation.

In summary, be a leader in information distribution and process innovation. A company can benefit from the development of an information infrastructure based on standards either common to its industry or its value chain. It should proliferate that vision throughout the market. This infrastructure should be based on the idea of open systems.

An example of this idea of industrywide open information systems is the Automotive Network eXchange (ANX). This network, developed jointly by the big-three American automakers, Ford, DaimlerChrysler, and GM, is an industrywide extranet. It handles many kinds of data on a standard platform from computer-aided design (CAD) files to purchase orders and electronic payments.[6,7] Efficiency is gained from the decrease in massaging of data to fit into proprietary data formats.

By the year 2005, the auto community, according to personnel at Ford, DaimlerChrysler, and General Motors, will heavily rely on ANX for the following:

- Engineering & Design—Suppliers and OE partners utilize ANX to collaborate on design and manufacturing issues instantaneously, saving travel time and inadvertent cost.
- Purchasing—Accounting practices are enhanced via the secure, supervised, access-only communication methods assured via ANX.
- Parts Distribution & Project Management—Overall manufacturing efficiency is already being realized by ANX.[8]

Thus, the value chain for each automaker is made more valuable through connectivity and integration across companies.

Speed

If, as asserted in the beginning of this chapter, past means of differentiation—high quality, low cost, and continuous innovation—have become less effective in a world of time-based competition, then *speed* seems to be the "last" means of differentiation. Taking this information into account, companies will need to make faster decisions and be real-time reactive to changes in the market as a means of remaining competitive. IT investment is a means for increasing firm reflexes. Investment in advanced ERP (Enterprise Resource Planning) systems with links to the web and to other partners in the value chain should enable managers to analyze and respond to dynamic market shifts. This is discussed in the next section.

The dramatic acceleration of pace is forcing business to restructure toward fewer layers of management. This brings us to the fact that corporations will have fewer people who will be filling wider roles. These people will need to be dynamic, flexible, and adaptive. They will not only need to be empowered, but intensely informed. To be sufficiently informed, the organization needs to be at least quickly reactive, if not proactive, to changing markets. The concept of speed will run throughout the rest of this chapter, for it is a major consideration in all topics discussed.

Relationships

Technology is changing relationships between companies, their customers, and suppliers, and changing the way firms organize themselves. Companies and industries assume the form they do largely due to cost avoidance. Historically, information collection and dissemination were very expensive. In today's economy, this is no longer the case. As a consequence, cost structures have changed across many industries. As these cost structures change, industry structure changes as well. Firms enter new fields and, over time, the boundaries that exist between companies will be redrawn and redefined. This will in turn call for a redefinition of a company's value chain. For example, Xerox has had to alter its structure due to the continual increase in electronic transmission of documents versus paper transmission. Not only is Xerox's relationship with customers and suppliers transformed, but so is the way the company functions internally.

The idea that a business ecosystem of partner relations exists and that a firm's business environment is often broader than earlier considered continues to have more adherents. This wider ecosystem consists of a company's suppliers and customers but also extends to the supplier's supplier and your customer's customer. To ease the visualization of this ecosystem and its components, interrelation software companies are developing tools that allow firms to graphically represent a company's relationships. These relationships can then be viewed based on geography, market segment, product, or business process. The purpose of the software is to greatly increase understanding of the ecosystem and thereby ease related decision making. If a company is already looking at customers and suppliers as allies whose interests need to be considered, then this software might not add much. If not, this software could help build this critical recognition.

There is also a movement toward what can be termed as an "agile web" philosophy.[9] This idea looks at changing the nature and definition of relationships (Figure 10.2). The trend towards outsourcing falls solidly into this camp. However, this trend is simultaneously making companies more specialized in some aspects and allowing for more diversification in others. Nike is often thought of as a marketing

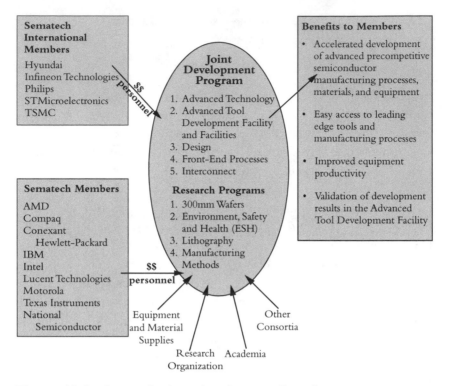

Figure 10.2 Sematech: A semiconductor agile-web.

machine. A major portion of its functional disciplines is outsourced, as is its manufacturing. Therefore, in some ways Nike could be considered very specialized. However, the company can exploit its small base of fixed costs to venture into new territory, beyond the sneaker world and into apparel, skis, and other sporting goods.

 This agile web philosophy goes beyond outsourcing to alliances and partnerships set up to take advantage of short-term market opportunities or limited objectives. Sematech, a consortium of semiconductor manufacturers, is a good example of this (Figure 10.2). The consortium of 10 companies was developed with the aim of increasing the efficiency of the semi-conductor manufacturing process. The firms pay dues and offer employees to the project on a limited basis. By funding suppliers to the industry's research and development, the group has achieved great increases in efficiency which none of the members could afford alone.[10]

Management guru Peter F. Drucker emphasizes the need for relationship development in the evolving business environment. "Information technology and a global economy are dictating that organizations outsource tasks and develop ever-changing alliances and partnerships with businesses, universities, and research departments to continue to be competitive."[11]

Infrastructure

Assembling an information system is a dynamic process driven by continuous improvement efforts and new technologies. As systems are increasingly linked throughout the value chain and to customers via the web, management and employees will likely be dealing more with issues of information overload. Attention will be the limited resource with the most demand.[12] Due to this factor, we will likely see in the future the proliferation of agent technologies and protocols built into systems enabling management by exception. Targets will be established for critical indicators, and management will be notified if data falls outside of the prescribed range. This data will likely be presented graphically for ease of understanding as well as easy trend identification. Managers in many positions will likely move toward functioning as monitors or drivers of business, having company key indicators presented in a dashboard or cockpit environment. But that is a glance at the future; let's look at what is here today.

Enterprise Resource Planning Systems

An Enterprise Resource Planning (ERP) system is software designed to model and automate many of the basic processes of a company, from finance to the shop floor, with the goal of integrating information across the company and eliminating complex, expensive links between computer systems that were never meant to talk to each other.[13] These systems offer online real-time information, which reduces processing time and frees managers and analysts from taking time to gather decision-making information.

ERP systems are becoming ubiquitous in the corporate world. They will also invade the small- and medium-sized company as firms like SAP, Baan, and Oracle go after these large markets. Although the benefits of these systems are manyfold, businesses today seem to be moving toward this technology primarily because the systems are considered to be a source of competitive advantage or at least a way to keep up with the competition. However, these systems bring with them their share of problems. Implementing these systems usually involves a significant amount of process change and often dictates changes in organizational structure. In fact, ERP implementations may be used as a means for re-engineering the firm. Management has a big role in the success and acceptance of these systems. As with the other technologies mentioned, the business process redesign inherent in ERP implementations requires major technical, organizational, and cultural change. The biggest associated challenge is fostering a new culture and managing the changes with consistency and coordination.[14]

When implementing information systems, there are usually two paths to take: adapting the inherent process to the people, or the people to the process. The former view stresses people as a firm's fundamental resource, while the latter view emphasizes consistency and coordination of corporatewide information. Neither path has been proven better, however. More frequently today, these large ERP systems, which are designed around best practices, are being used as a facilitator of change in companies. This point is supported by Dwight Klappich, vice president of industry marketing at Ross Systems Inc of Atlanta: "The key thing when you look at the success or failure of software implementation is whether the client is implementing software or are they implementing change within their business."[15]

In addition, client-server ERP systems feature many advantages over their mainframe counterparts. Most importantly, they can transfer data in real-time between locations worldwide. They can also support multiple currencies and multiple languages so they can be used at various global locations. The move to these systems has been fostered in a large part because they are Y2K and euro compliant, giving many companies the ability to avoid the costly conversion processes of their legacy systems associated with these events.

ERP Impact

Recognizing the firmwide impact of these systems, ERP market leader SAP started the trend of selling information systems to CEOs. Other technology companies will likely follow this marketing trend in the future, due to the fact that IT is having a greater impact on strategic capabilities and the bottom line. This strategy also protects against two of the key components of failure for IT projects; namely, lack of congruence between a company's business strategy and its IT goals and lack of upper management support.[16]

The name of the game in today's business environment is speed and flexibility. Companies in every industry are constantly under pressure to perform their service or production faster while tailoring it to the needs of the customer. To accomplish this, companies need to streamline operations from the time an order is placed to its delivery. ERP enables this.

ERP Problems

ERP systems do present many problems for companies, however. The first has to do with the fact that they are usually part of a larger re-engineering effort. Therefore, the costs and time expectations of implementation are usually exceeded. Second, many companies purchase ERP systems to satisfy what they perceive will be a single integrated solution to all their data processing needs. ERP systems are not IT silver bullets. ERP systems are not good at everything and cannot perform all the processes that a firm may already have in place. This requires firms to either change processes or use additional applications, the idea of which runs counter to a single-solution philosophy.

No ROI

Early ERP implementation projects ran into the problem of not providing an easy means for determining the project's return on investment. Since the typical ERP implementation costs can be anywhere from $30 million to $60 million, managers were very concerned with a means to measure their investment. However, today these projects are not being viewed as measurable purely by traditional financial analysis. Rather, intangibles are often being used to measure their success. Commenting on SAP, John Donovan, chairman of Cambridge Technology Group, says, "There is no return on these projects. Everyone is looking at this investment the wrong way and doing the wrong analysis, calculating the replacement of one system for another. SAP is the infrastructure. What is my return on putting electricity in this building? There is none; I just have to do it."[17] Examples of some of the intangible measurement criteria being used include customer satisfaction, employee morale, and employee turnover. These factors are all difficult to link directly into an IT project and are difficult to measure. Revenue improvement goals are a commonly used financial target.

Supply Chain Management

Today the success of a product or service is increasingly being influenced by its time to market. Cycle-time reduction is one of the main benefits of implementing an integrated supply chain. These systems are characterized by viewing suppliers as partners to help in design, technology development, cost reduction, and management of inventory.

Seamless Transaction Automation

The team concept of the supply chain has been extended to not just include your direct customers and suppliers, but also your customer's customers and your supplier's suppliers. IT is the catalyst that enabled the migration to supply chains. New technologies are allowing the supply chain to become more automated. These systems began to flourish with the introduction of Electronic Data Interchange (EDI). EDI is defined as the ability of two or more companies to electronically process orders, send invoices, and share forecasts to help shorten the supply chain. The problem with EDI is that it is fairly costly and the uses are fairly limited.

Extranet, a term used to describe transactions with suppliers and customers within a firm's ecosystem using the public Internet, is slowly replacing EDI. Extranets allow for extended automation of the integrated computer system at a lower cost. An e-mail can begin the process that starts the supply chain communication. Bob Beckett, corporate vice president of supply chain management at EMS, explains, "When an order comes in, it should be disseminated through the system to our partner and to the manufacturer, if required, or to its storage facility for shipment automatically without manual intervention."[18]

To complicate things further, just as the supply chain has been lengthened, the synchronization of demand planning has moved from monthly or weekly to a daily cycle. This is a change which the whole supply chain must adapt to. Trends toward make-to-order and just-in-time manufacturing are fueling this necessity. The transparency of information, alluded to above, allows both customers and manufacturers to plan better, which in the end enables better customer service and timely delivery. The end plan is to integrate and automate the information systems of the supply chain so closely that they operate as one seamless machine.

What Are the Facts?

This kind of supply chain management sounds great, but is it too hard to actually implement successfully at a reasonable cost? The numbers seem to indicate that it's worth the trouble. Industry analysts Pittiglio Rabi Todd & McGrath (PRTM) of Weston, Massachusetts, have estimated that a "$600-million company could save as much as $42 million annually in inventory and other costs by building a chain."[19]

A 1997 study of 165 blue-chip technology companies by PRTM indicated that on-time delivery performance of median companies improved by 15%, order fulfillment lead times were reduced by 25% to 35%, and value-added productivity of median companies increased by 10%. Overall, companies shaved 10% off their total supply-chain management costs as a percentage of revenue. Jeffrey Berg, a PRTM director in Stamford, Connecticut, states, "Customer satisfaction metrics, such as on-time delivery, have shown dramatic improvements over the two-year period. The ability to flex production to meet changing customer demand without investing capital in inventory is a core competency for business today." When a firm begins to quantify what supply chain spending is—12% to 14% of revenue—it starts to be an area of consideration. Additionally, the study found that best-in-class companies have a 40% to 65% advantage in cash-to-cash cycle time, maintain 50% to 80% less inventory, and realize a 3% to 6% revenue advantage in total supply chain management. Simply put, for a company to remain competitive in a business that has decreasing product life cycles, it has to improve the supply chain.[20]

Culture

Like most all of the topics approached in this chapter, the move to supply chain requires a significant shift in current business process and what would traditionally be called a "leap of faith." This "leap of faith" may be better classified as *trust in your partners*. "In supply chain management, current best practices comprise a blend of new technology and a radical rethink of basic business concepts."[21] "The successful implementation of new business models depends heavily on the ability to break down barriers among business partners all along the supply chain. Implementing electronic commerce is a critical part of realizing that vision."[22] Again, Bob Beckett of EMS explains, "There has been a lot of focus on the manufacturing and engineering process but not on the supply process when it comes to cycle time. Few people are doing it because the paradigm shift involves a cultural change in business practices, which doesn't come easy."[23] Cultural resistance occurs inside the company and at suppliers. While corporate culture is too often ignored when planning the supply chain, it is never ignored in *successful* implementation.[24]

Resources

Critical challenges to global supply chain management are language barriers and a lack of standards. Language barriers make communicating and maintaining an internationally diverse supply chain particularly difficult. This, coupled with the fact that there is no standard terminology or methodology for communicating well throughout the supply chain, increases the challenge. As a first step in answering this challenge, several major companies banded together and formed the Supply Chain Council. One of the Council's first acts was to develop and (now) maintain the Supply Chain Reference (SCOR) model. SCOR consists of four main components: common definitions of supply chain management processes; benchmarking performance data associated with these processes; descriptions of supply chain best practices; and information on selecting supply chain software products.[25] While SCOR is a step in the right direction, standards, language, and culture issues will be a continuous challenge for effective supply chain implementation.[26]

The Role of the World Wide Web (www)

Another integrated component of the IT value chain is the World Wide Web. This technology enables improved communication with many different stakeholders including customers, employees, suppliers, and shareholders. It can be used both as a feedback mechanism and a means of gathering marketing data such as demographic information, as well as a way to change distribution and the selling function. The technology is also very versatile in strengthening a firm's relationship with customers. Internally, the web can be used to increase employee communication by implementing an internal Internet called an *intranet*. It can also be used to increase communication with suppliers in a form called an *extranet*. Finally, the Internet can be used as a means to strengthen the relationship with shareholders. In fact, the Nasdaq exchange recently announced an initiative to persuade Nasdaq 100 companies to offer non-institutional investors quicker Internet-based access to financial briefings. The initiative includes using "webcasting" technology, which "streams" live and on-demand audio and video programs over the Internet to allow individual investors access to company presentations.[27]

Here we will focus on the web's ability to change the relationship with the customer using the example of Dell computers as one of the most innovative and successful users of this new technology. First, let us examine how this medium changes the nature of the customer relationship. The web enables a means of increasing the level of service a firm can offer to consumers by allowing more flexible and timely interaction between the provider and the customer. An innovative service ability may lead to differentiation within the consumer's mind and thus the ability to achieve higher margins. The web may be seen as a way to streamline the business process and extend worldwide personalized service to every customer at virtually no added cost.

Service is the most important component of an online strategy. While customers, in theory, will receive more power in the purchasing relationships due to their improved access to information enabled by the web, they will likely be willing to spend more for a product supported by a strong service component. As made clear earlier, the speed and convenience of delivery is a large factor in the perceived service received. Firms will need to use the web to aggregate customer preferences and develop service strategies that target the highest perceived value. This in turn will require a shift in thinking, away from a cost-plus target pricing toward higher margin value pricing.

Current business journals often cite Bill Gates' quote about "frictionless capitalism," where comparison shopping by consumers will make it harder to make money using traditional business models. The suggestion offered here is that firms should move to be innovative in their value proposition; their product bundle and its related service must be unique and timely.

Direct Sales Model

The web is allowing more and more firms in many different industries to migrate to a direct sales model. This requires a radical change in the way many firms do business and also requires a change in thinking. To operate in this environment, the understanding of the customer must deepen. This intimate understanding of the customer is made possible by the use of IT. By tying the web front into back-end systems such as ERP systems discussed earlier, a more value-added transaction can be rendered. Through the use of stored information, the service interaction or dialogue can be customized. Using this information, a firm is capable of providing a convenient value-added experience for the consumer. By using a combination of demographic information, historical interactions, and purchasing behavior, American Express, for example, is better able to tailor its promotions to individual customers by placing targeted advertisements in the monthly billing packet it sends to card members.

Not only does this model allow for a better interaction with customers, it also enables a more efficient and possibly cheaper alternative to the model of service. As the selling function is automated and effectively outsourced to the customer, a situation referred to as coproduction occurs. This self-service model brings the customer deeper into the relationships and reduces the need for costly customer service staff.

To create an effective web strategy, a firm cannot consider its web site as a static instrument; the technology and customer expectations change too often. The firm must be thinking in terms of generations of their web site offering. The site must be constantly redesigned to take advantage of new technologies and organizational learning on how to affect the firm's encounter with the customer. Design should be attacked with growth and change in mind.

Following in Dell's Footsteps

The web has effectively changed the way Dell does business. This is a very progressive company that understands the opportunity provided by the web and the need for speed. In fact, Dell has made speed of delivery an integral part of its business model. In an interview with *Industry Week,* Dell Computer's CEO Michael Dell explained that the company focuses on how fast they can deliver the product.[28] Dell has designed the manufacturing process to be a "continuous flow with customer-specific aspects such as loading proprietary software built into the process." Dell is a shining example of how to use the Internet and a new business model to alter the nature of global competition by tightening the integration of suppliers, customers, and manufacturers. The company has a strong customer focus with an emphasis on efficiency, speed, and convenience. Currently, Dell's Internet sales are approximately $6 million a day and $2 billion a year. Quoting Mr. Dell, "The Internet is the ultimate form of the direct model. These are zero-variable-cost transactions."[29]

Dell is setting its targets higher. The company has set a goal of making half of its sales from the Internet by the end of the year 2000. With its emphasis on convenience, the company has created unique web sites in 36 countries and in 18 languages. Dell's emphasis on the customer has translated into 6,000 password-protected web-customized web sites. These pages, called Premier Pages, consist of information and purchase order processes unique to each customer. To quote Dell again, "These pages provide the opportunity to deliver critical service and support information directly to our customers based on the specific products they use and buy. This allows for a whole new level of intimacy with customers."

The importance of relationship-building through IT is supported by Dell's experience. He claims "the real potential lies in its (the Internet's) ability to transform relationships within the traditional supplier-vendor-customer chain . . . and to create value that can be shared across organizational boundaries. The companies that position themselves to build information partnerships with suppliers and customers and make the Internet an integral part of their strategy have the potential to fundamentally change the face of global competition."[30] This requires a high level of information-sharing that may make executives nervous, though they really shouldn't be.[31] Dell claims that "by sharing with suppliers the intimate details of our company and our plans, we literally bring them into the business."[32] These partnerships are obviously paying off.

Dell would suggest that a new consideration of relationships is necessary. He argues that collaboration is the new competitive imperative. An Internet strategy is really a question of survival. He feels that companies that fully take advantage of the Internet by looking at their business as "more than building and selling products and services" will be the market leaders and survivors because the traditional paradigm is not how the world works today. He goes on to state, "Both suppliers and customers must be treated as partners and collaborators, jointly looking for ways to improve efficiency across the entire spectrum of the value chain, not just in their respective business." Dell's example would suggest that the web can have a significant impact on company operations and profits. The ability to capitalize on this new medium is enhanced by the depth and breadth of relationships developed within the value chain.

Mobile Workforce and HR Challenges

The role of IT is becoming more and more the backbone for strategy implementation. Its ability to develop new relationships with suppliers and customers and help a firm enter new markets is vital to business in the twenty-first century. However, the market for IT professionals is extremely tight currently, and predictions see this trend continuing for quite some time. This tendency may hinder a firm's ability to pursue certain strategies or the development of their business. This is especially true if a firm wants to pursue an implementation of newer technologies such as an ERP or e-Commerce initiative, where the people with the needed skills are extremely hard to find. Here we look at some of the ways companies are increasing the retention of their IT employees.

The hardest pill for many firms to swallow is that IT professionals, because of the market demand for their skills, often do not fit into preordained company pay scales for the positions they fill. Human Resources will have to adapt to the idea that there is a fair market value for the skill set that these professionals possess. Otherwise, these positions will go unfilled for a long time. A related problem is the fact that many of the people are young and many managers have a hard time paying a 25-year-old $75,000+ annually. Firms must break out of the equity-based pay system. Simply put, how does a company with a traditional hierarchical culture deal with the hot-shot technology guys who are making more than their manager or the boss in the corner office? This is a very difficult question to answer.

Currently, organizations are pursuing two main solutions. In the first solution, a firm either moves to a more flat corporate culture, putting everyone in cubicles and trying other methods of removing status within an organization. This may be an effective model to deal with this problem due to the fact that many technology firms have assumed this type of nonhierarchical structure. A second solution that many firms are using is to use outsourcing for their IT personnel needs. Although this option would not likely change the high expense of these workers, it may eliminate the perceived inequality of other workers.

Keeping Your IT Employees

Another issue to consider is retaining the IT employees you have. As stated earlier, compensation is obviously important and, due to the market nature for IT skills, many employers have gone to quarterly reviews to keep salaries current. However, factors other than compensation need to be considered. Many companies have begun to dedicate significant attention to improving the work environment. Flexible work schedules, casual dress codes, and teleworking all have a strong effect on employees' perception of their work environment.

Training on new technologies can also be an effective means to keeping IT employees happy. To this end, a New York bank set up a "technology playground"—a conference room filled with cutting-edge tools and technologies—so that their employees would not feel they would have to go work elsewhere to get their hands on the latest and greatest technology.

Tenure-based bonuses rather than one-time signing bonuses are also an effective way of retaining top IT staffers. Getting your IT people involved in other facets of the business can also help retain their interest as well as increase your effectiveness in dealing with clients. Allow technology employees to see how the technology they develop benefits the business. "One company put a group of technologists with the sales and marketing department so they could observe first-hand how technology impacts users, external users, and ultimately revenues."[33]

Finally, there is a movement toward hiring foreign IT workers to make up for the gap between supply and demand in the United States. Though still relatively uncommon, some American companies are migrating to this practice. While these workers are *not* a source of cheap labor when imported into the United States—a federal law calls for skilled immigrants who enter the country on an H–1B temporary work visa to be paid the prevailing wage—one of the important benefits associated with this practice is the loyalty these workers have to their employers. H–1B visas are valid for three years and can be renewed for an additional three years.

Companies can also use special "telecommuting" visas, which allow Canadians and Mexicans to work from their homes and to travel to the offices of their American employers for short visits on a monthly basis.[34] There are many employment companies that specialize in recruiting foreign workers, which can save employers money and time.

Telecommuting

Though most managers would consider telecommuting a perk, here it is suggested that telecommuting is a means of achieving broader strategic goals and can be a contributor to better company performance. Find/SVP, an Ithaca, New York-based technology research firm, annually measures the number of telecommuters in the United States. For the last several years, the number has been growing at a steady 15% rate to the current mid-1998 total of 11.1 million telecommuters.[35] The reason companies are increasingly moving to this form of work can be boiled down to three factors—people, productivity, and cost.

People

In the tightening market for knowledge workers and skilled employees, employers are increasingly turning to telecommuting as a means of retention and recruiting. When competing for the services of people who have the skills to be able to choose where they want to work, the perceived quality-of-life advantages offered by telecommuting often is enough to sway new employees to a firm. The increased use of telecommuting may allow you to keep the star employees you have currently and may also allow you to recruit outside your local region, perhaps even globally. The argument could be made that availability of programmers in Seattle is tight, but that the market for programmers in Arizona or India may offer many more available employees who are not willing to move. Telecommuting may allow employers to tap these markets, enabling projects to be pursued at lower costs.

Perhaps the most compelling argument in support of telecommuting is that the cost of continually recruiting and training staff can dwarf the cost of initiating a telecommuting program, especially when intangible factors such as experience are factored into the equation.

Productivity

Managers and employees involved in telecommuting programs broadly agree that significant productivity improvements result from telecommuting programs.[36] When productivity in the standard work environment is difficult to assess, it should be no surprise that the extent of these telecommuting productivity gains are also hard to quantify. However, the drivers for this increased productivity appear to be higher employee morale and fewer unnecessary meetings and interruptions.

Costs

The anecdotal evidence is compelling. When IBM initiated a telecommuting program, they did so within the larger strategic goal of cutting costs. By mandating that 10,000 of their consultants and sales people telecommute, the company was able to cut spending on land and facilities by $75 million annually.[37] These sorts of figures may not be attainable by every firm and require a shift in corporate culture, but even for a small company the overhead savings could become significant, even if fewer than five employees participate.

Problems

Some of the most common problems surrounding telecommuting programs include:

- Poor technology planning.
- Unrealistic expectations.
- Culture shock.
- Lack of trust.

As with any major technology initiative, upper-level management buy-in and "realistic" expectations on results are key factors. With telecommuting, the real change must come in middle managers. They are the people who must manage the culture shock, change their management style, and give the trust to develop the loyalty that allows these programs to work. Most importantly, management must choose the right people to participate in telecommuting programs. This point was highlighted by participants in a telecommuting test program set up in Silicon Valley. These managers concluded (at the end of the project) that the success of telecommuting is partly driven by the telecommuter's self discipline and ability to adapt to a new work style and that telecommuting is not for everyone.[38]

Change in Management

What is necessary to make these programs work is for managers to "expand their notion of how to supervise people," says Merrill's chief technology officer and senior VP, Howard Sorgen.[39] Managers have to learn to trust their employees. This trust is most effectively gained instituting a training program that involves both managers and employees. Telecommuting programs also require a change in the way managers and employees communicate. Adaptation is also needed in the roles that develop from these programs. Due to the lack of face-to-face time with fellow employees, managers often have to take on the role of social activity organizer and company culture facilitator to replace the informal information exchange that traditionally happened at the water cooler.

Case evidence suggests that telecommuting can be successful in helping a company reach its broader strategic goals. The main benefits that can be achieved from these programs are higher productivity, employee retention, and decreases in overhead costs. An institutionalized program with willing management and adaptive employees are the most significant factors in determining when and where telecommuting can work for an organization.

Mergers and Acquisitions

Merger mania continues and shows no sign of stopping. The number, size, and value of mergers and acquisitions have increased dramatically in the past decade. Total merger activity in 1991 equaled $50 billion; in 1996, merger volume totaled $500 billion. And the trend continues—1997 saw a total of 10,700 merger deals totaling in excess of $919 billion.[40] This increase in mergers and acquisitions has impacted global information management, as systems and personnel are often merged as well. Often, this later part of the merger is fraught with problems.

Some of the opportunities and pressures that are frequently listed as reasons for so many mergers and acquisitions include globalization, the cost of technology, deregulation, and the growing importance of global brands.[41] Others have theorized that it is just a craze or mania that is self-replicating, that mergers seem to precipitate mergers. Mergers beget mergers, due to competitors trying to make up for perceived inadequacies stemming from their relative lack of size. As with many of the topics thus far discussed, mergers seem to be a means of survival rather than a means to competitive advantage.

Does Size Really Matter?

Are companies really benefiting from all these transactions? Analysis by Mercer management seems to suggest that they are not. The study conducted by Mercer found that two out of every three mergers tend to underperform their peers in the years after the combination. The most common symptom of demise seems to be that the mergers are based on a vision of opportunities to be capitalized upon, but lack supporting detailed *implementation* plans.

Global Mergers

Global mergers seem to be the next logical step in the merger trend. The merger of Daimler-Benz and Chrysler may just be the beginning. The global aspect of global mergers brings additional issues to bear such as differing national cultures, languages, legal and tax issues, currencies, and perhaps additional logistics issues. Part of a solution to these issues comes from the growing use of industry intranets and ERP systems. Industry intranets coupled with ERP systems provide firms with the ability to handle multiple currencies and several languages. These capabilities should make the IT consolidation in mergers much easier in the future. But, . . . as IT is an increasingly integral part (of both the problem/opportunity and the solution) of these new issues, the complexity of IT consolidation will grow and will most likely grow quickly. Thus, again the critical need is for a firm to have a creative and flexible IT staff supported by a physical IT infrastructure.

Virtual Ventures

Using recent developments in IT such as web pages and electronic commerce, companies may be able to exploit the benefits of a merger without actually merging. Firms in the near future will likely move to *virtual ventures,* where the only real shared asset is a combined web site and content. The companies would likely share the advertising and maintenance costs but little else. This scenario would be applicable only in industries that are best facilitated by Internet commerce (for example, retail sales of books or toys) and would require a dramatic increase in the amount of commercial business being conducted on the net.

An example of one mega-merger that might have been rethought if the partners had considered a virtual venture is Travelers-Citicorp. In the Travelers-Citicorp merger, one major sought-after synergy was new access to sales channels by both former companies. Travelers hoped to sell its insurance through Citicorp's bank branches, and reciprocally Citicorp believed it could increase the volume of its student and consumer loans through access to Travelers' sales channels. This strategy fits the "bricks and mortar" model.

The new economy model facilitated by the Internet appears to be making the merger synergies evolve in a manner that was not anticipated. The move in banking to fewer branches and in insurance to the use of competitive price comparison (of insurance benefits and premiums) is pushed to the extreme on the Internet. In this strategy, both insurance and banking customers could transact business via the same web gateway. The sought-after access to both sales channels is being achieved, albeit only to "electronic-oriented" customers at this point.

Conclusion

The most important aspect of what is being presented here is that the role of IT is changing in business, from enabler of strategy to driver of strategy. This shift requires a fundamental change in thinking. It pushes us to consider questions such as:

- How can we use information technology to better compete?
- How can we create and maintain better relationships with our customers, suppliers, and employees?

- How will the process of communication change in the next two, three, and five years?
- Finally, how can we capitalize on these changes?

In looking at IT's new role in strategy development, a manager needs to include a broader base of inputs. The assertion here is that IT and HR (Human Resources) will be the key contributors to the strategy development process, letting management know what constraints exist and what opportunities can be exploited. IT can provide the means for developing an integrated infrastructure linking current information systems with those of suppliers and out to customers via the web. IT can enable the relationships that we describe here as fundamental to a networked organization. IT can provide the connectivity to the market which will be crucial to the future. People will be the drivers and facilitators of moving to the new business models that IT enables.

In addition, management needs to consider speed in all its strategic decisions. Speed will be the differentiator of the information economy. In the future, an enterprise's ability to compete will be very dependent on its ability to predict and react to changes in market forces. Management must see this relationship. As observed by Tony Jackson in an article in the *Financial Times,* "Unless senior management has a clear understanding of digital technology in its various aspects, the company's real core competencies may prove ever harder to develop and sustain."[42]

The key to all of the ideas put forth here is flexibility in systems and people. This is what will allow a company to compete and take advantage of new opportunities. While flexibility is an easy word to say, the implications to management run deep. Greater flexibility is made possible only by greater trust. With the increasing complexity (and associated IT) of tomorrow's global organizations, successful firms will not only build this trust, but will glory in it.

Notes

1. John S. McClenahen, "Top CEO Concerns," *Industry Week,* (November 16, 1998), p. 39.

2. See www.informationweek.com for latest update on Informationweek 500 rankings.

3. Stan Davis and Christopher Meyer, *Blur, the Speed of Change in the Connected Economy,* (Ernst & Young, 1998), p. 17.

4. Carl Shapiro and Hal Varian, *Information Rules: A Strategic Guide to the Network Economy,* (Harvard Business School Press, 1999), p. 137.

5. Louise Kehoe, "Interview: Carl Shapiro and Hal Varian," *Financial Times,* (October 13, 1998), p. 11.

6. "Future Three Partners with Ideal Technology Solutions, U.S. for Total Automotive Network Exchange (ANX) Capability," *PR Newswire,* (Northville, MI: Financial News, July 9, 1999).

7. Kevin Brown, "Sectors in Each Others Pockets," *Financial Times,* (October 20, 1998), p. 14.

8. Mike Brennan, "Auto Industry Looks to Establish Worldwide Computer Network," *Detroit Free Press,* (August 31, 1999).

9. "You Need an Agile Web of Suppliers," (December 3, 1998). Available: www.agileweb.com

10. For more information on Sematech, see www.sematech.org

11. Michael A. Verespej, "Only the CEO Can Make Employees Kings," *Industry Week,* (November 16, 1998), p. 22.

12. John Beck. See Beck's Chapter 13 of this book.

13. "ERP/Supply Chain Research," *CIO,* magazine web page (January 5, 1999). Available: www.cio.com/forums/erp

14. Sarah Cliffe, "ERP Implementation," *Harvard Business Review,* vol. 77, no. 1 (January/February 1999), pp. 16–17.

15. Diane Trommer, "SCOR Sets Supply Chain Standard," *Techweb News,* (September 29, 1997).

16. Cliffe, "ERP. . . ."

17. E.B. Baatz, "Marketing Genius," *CIO,* magazine web page (June 15, 1996). Available: www.cio.com/forums/061596_sap_sidebar.html

18. Gina Roos, "How to Buy Connectors," *Techweb News,* (April 1998).

19. Hillery Rettig, "Supply Chain Management—VARs Link Up with Companies Automating Supply Chain Systems," *Techweb News,* (September 15, 1997).

20. Jennifer Baljko, "Customer Service Efforts Pay Off for Supply Chain—Companies Shave 10% off Supply Chain Costs, Study Finds," *Techweb News,* (November 24, 1997).

21. Malcolm Wheatley, "Lighten Up," *CIO,* (February 15, 1998).

22. Peter Fabris, "Electronic Commerce—E.C. Riders," *CIO,* (June 15, 1997).

23. Roos, "How. . . ."

24. D. Lance Revenaugh, "Implementing Major Organizational Change: Can We Really Do It?" *The TQM Magazine,* vol. 6, no. 6 (1994), p. 38.

25. Diane Trommer, "SCOR Sets Supply Chain Standard," *Techweb News,* (September 29, 1997).

26. Supply Chain Vendors:

Baan USA Inc., Menlo Park, California (650) 462-4949. Available: www.baan.com

Chesapeake Decision Sciences Inc., New Providence, New Jersey (908) 464-8300. Available: www.chesapeake.com

i2 Technologies, Irving, Texas (800) 800-3288. Available: www.i2.com

Manugistics, Rockville, Maryland (301) 984-5000. Available: www.manugistics.com

Oracle, Redwood Shores, California (415) 506-7000. Available: www.oracle.com

PeopleSoft Inc., Pleasanton, California (510) 225-3000. Available: www.peoplesoft.com

SAP America, Wayne, Pennsylvania (610) 725-4500. Available: www.sap.com

Supply Chain Solutions Inc., Marietta, Georgia (770) 980-1111. Available: www.supply-chain-solutions.com

SynQuest Inc., Norcross, Georgia (800) 844-3228. Available: www.synquest.com

Council of Logistics Management, Alexandria, Virginia (703) 838-1935. Available: www.clm1.org (a trade organization)

To view the SCOR model presented in the text, see Supply Chain Council web site. Available: www.supply-chain.org

27. John Labate, "Nasdaq in Move to Offer Retail Access on Internet," *Financial Times,* (December 10, 1998), p. 23.

28. Michael A. Verespej, "Michael Dell's Magic," *Industry Week,* (November 16, 1998), p. 57.

29. Verespej, "Michael . . . ," p. 58.

30. Verespej, "Michael . . . ," p. 60.

31. People, including executives, often do worry about releasing information which they have primary/exclusive control over because they are afraid of losing power.

32. Verespej, "Michael . . . ," p. 60.

33. Megan Santosus, "Best Practices Retention Tips," *CIO,* (January 1, 1998).

34. Mindy Blodgett, "Foreign Entanglements," *CIO,* (May 15, 1998).

35. Stuart Gibbel, "U.S. Telecommuting Trend Surpasses 11 Million," ITAC-International Telework Association and Council web site (November 3, 1998), p. 1. Available: etrg.findsvp.com/prls/pr97/telecomm.html

36. Susan Sears, "ITAC Launches Telework America '99—The Year of Telework," ITAC-International Telework Association and Council web site (January 7, 1999). Available: www.telecommute.org/twa_102898.htm

37. Jennifer Bresnahan, "IBM: Saving Money," *CIO,* magazine web page (January 8, 1999). Available: www.cio.com/archive/enterprise/011598_work.html

38. "Smart Valley Telecommuting Pilot Project Report," (October 24, 1994). Available: smartone.svi.org/PROJECTS/TCOMMUTE/TCGUIDE/#results

39. Jennifer Bresnahan, "Merrill Lynch: Earning Loyalty," *CIO,* magazine web page (January 8, 1999). Available: www.cio.com/archive/enterprise/011598_work.html

40. Mary Mosquera, "[The Making of a Merger] Merger Deals Constantly Dominate the Headlines. But What Does It Take to Push a Deal Through?" *Techweb News,* (March 3, 1998).

41. Richard Waters and Tracy Corrigan, "The Cult of Gigantism," *Financial Times,* (April 11/12, 1998), p. 7.

42. Tony Jackson, "Common Sense and Your Core Competency," *Financial Times,* (October 22, 1998), p. 9.

11

Managing Intellectual Property Abroad: The Limits of Protection

ROBERT S. TANCER

Scarcely a day passes without reading about misappropriation of unauthorized use of intellectual property. The International Chamber of Commerce (ICC) concludes that counterfeiting and piracy represent 5% to 7% of world trade.[1] Some industries are affected more than others. At the international level, 46% of all counterfeiting and piracy is accounted for in the software industry. Other industries that witness high incidence of piracy are data processing (35%), audiovisual (25%), toys (12%), perfumes (10%), pharmaceuticals (6%), and the clock and watch industry (5%).[2] Corporate wealth is no longer measured by controlling raw materials or in manufacturing capability; it is knowledge-based industry that dominates the world economy. Lester C. Thurow has noted "Today it is both more important than ever to protect intellectual property rights—and more difficult to do so."[3]

How companies protect their intellectual property abroad under national laws, international agreements, and the limits of this protection are the subjects of this chapter.

Intellectual Property: What Is It?

Intellectual property is often referred to or described as "intangible," the product of the mind. It can take the form of a published work, a book or a poem and be protected by copyright, or it can be a product or process manufactured as a result of new discoveries or inventions and be protected by a patent. The resulting rights of copyright or patent protection are similar to the more familiar property rights we claim over the real or personal property that we own. Just as the owners of these rights can protect their property from trespasses and unauthorized use, owners of intellectual property should be able to protect their property from comparable violations abroad. The World Intellectual Property Organization (WIPO) comments on the broad dissemination of intellectual property. It notes:

> Globalization of trade means that "works of the mind," or intellectual property, such as inventions, designs, trademarks, books, music, and films, are now used and enjoyed on every continent on earth.[4]

The major purpose of providing intellectual property protection is "to ensure that the rights of creators and owners of intellectual property are protected worldwide and that inventors and authors are, thus, recognized and rewarded for their ingenuity."[5] In addition to recognizing and rewarding the creative process, there is a broader public interest involved: the universal belief in the value and importance of sharing and disseminating knowledge and information. Intellectual property rights, therefore, are not monopolies and are not granted in perpetuity. Patent protection is available only for 20 years from the date of filing with the appropriate national authority and copyright protection lasts only for the life of the author plus 70 years. Once the period of protection expires, the property rights enter the public domain and are available to everyone at no cost. Even more important is the dissemination of information. Once a patent is issued, or in some countries, 18 months after the application is filed, the patent is published so that interested parties can obtain copies to study and hopefully add to human knowledge by further developments and inventions. Interest in new inventions is so great that *The New York Times* publishes an article every Monday discussing key aspects of new patents issued by the U.S. Patent and Trademark Office (PTO).[6] Copies of patents can be obtained from the PTO for three dollars or are available at the web site: uspto.gov. The expansion of new kinds of technology has led to a proliferation in the quantity and availability of intellectual property raising new issues of coverage and protection.

Who Are the Global Players?

The establishment of the World Trade Organization (WTO) in January 1995, created for the first time an international agency empowered to monitor, implement, and enforce a worldwide trade policy. The WTO was created at the conclusion of the Uruguay Round of GATT negotiations, which resulted in a series of agreements between member states. One of these, the Agreement on Trade-Related Aspects of Intellectual Property Rights (TRIPS Agreement) recognizes:

> the need to promote effective and adequate protection of intellectual property rights, and to ensure that measures and procedures to enforce intellectual property rights do not become barriers to legitimate trade.[7]

All members of the WTO must have agreed to accept the terms and standards of the TRIPS Agreement.

In addition to having over-all jurisdiction over international trade issues, the WTO provides a dispute resolution mechanism binding on all members. Working closely with the WTO is the World Intellectual Property Organization (WIPO), an agency of the United Nations. WIPO serves as the Secretariat for the WTO in administering all intellectual property treaties as well as providing much-needed technical assistance to permit developing and least-developed countries to establish the necessary infrastructure to comply with the requirements of the TRIPS Agreement. Both the WTO and WIPO are located in Geneva.

The TRIPS Agreement offers minimal standards of intellectual property protection, which each signatory is obligated to provide under its own national law. For example, the TRIPS Agreement establishes a term for trademark protection ". . . of no less than seven years."[8] Yet many countries provide for longer terms. The United States grants trademarks for 10 years. Further differences under national laws exist as a result of the effective date of the TRIPS Agreement. Members are allowed one year from the inception of the WTO, or until January 1, 1995, to comply. Yet developing countries are granted an extension until January 1, 2000, and least-developed countries until January 1, 2005. A further extension of five years is available to developing countries that do not currently provide for "product patent protection," so compliance is not required until 2005.[9] These variations in compliance dates result in differences in national laws. India, for example, could sign the TRIPS Agreement and still not provide pharmaceutical product patent protection until 2005 while receiving all of the advantages of WTO membership. The TRIPS Agreement was never intended to be an international intellectual property law, binding equally on all member countries, but over time it will lead to harmonization as national laws governing intellectual property will become more alike in each of the participating countries.

The TRIPS Agreement is not the only mechanism for protecting intellectual property rights abroad. Other international agreements offer protection on a multilateral level, although on a smaller scale. For example, the North American Free Trade Agreement (NAFTA) has an extensive chapter on Intellectual Property rights,[10] binding on its signatories, Mexico, Canada, and the United States. The NAFTA standards of protection are extensive and in some areas are even more stringent than the TRIPS Agreement. The European Union (EU) has recently authorized a community trademark (CTM)[11] enforceable in all 15 countries. Increasingly, bilateral treaties include provisions to protect intellectual property. The current form of agreement negotiated by the Department of State, Bilateral Investment Treaties (BITS) provides for full intellectual property protection.[12] In the event of expropriation of these or other property rights, the parties agree to arbitration outside of the country and subject to international law.[13] Thus, the investor or owner of intellectual property is spared the difficulty of litigating in a foreign country where he is unfamiliar with local laws and business practices.

National laws sometimes extend beyond national boundaries in an effort to protect intellectual property rights of its citizens. The United

States has effectively utilized Super and Special § 301 of the Trade Act of 1974, as amended. These provisions enable the United States Trade Representative (USTR) to impose trade sanctions against nations that practice unfair trade practices or violate intellectual property rights of U.S. citizens. The USTR conducts annual reviews of foreign countries' performance in these areas, undertakes negotiations to eliminate violations, and, if unsuccessful, imposes trade sanctions. One of the most recent confrontations was with China over the issues of compact disc piracy. The United States threatened to raise tariffs on Chinese imports unless China was willing to enforce intellectual property rights and shut down the factories manufacturing the counterfeit compact discs. Just on the eve of imposing sanctions, China and the United States reached an agreement resulting in a Memorandum of Understanding (MOU) providing for a broad range of intellectual property protection for U.S. firms doing business in China.[14]

The United States is not alone in negotiating intellectual property rights with its trading partners. The EU requires harmonization with its intellectual property laws before admitting any new member. Countries with diverse backgrounds such as Turkey and Poland must establish strong and effective intellectual property regimes before they will be accepted for membership in the EU. These negotiations can, and as with the case of Turkey, may take years. These negotiations occur on many different levels. If a country does not have intellectual property laws, they will be urged to enact them. If they have intellectual property laws in place, but are lax in their enforcement, they will be urged to improve enforcement. In all negotiations, threats of sanctions or withdrawal of trade preferences are standard. More countries are enacting and implementing intellectual property laws. An example of the detail with which the United States tracks progress in the enactment of new intellectual property laws and their implementation can be found in excerpts from USTR press release announcing results of special 301 Annual Review, April 30, 1999:

January 1999

- Estonia enacted new copyright and customs legislation and amended its code of criminal procedures to strengthen IPR protection.
- Turkey extended patent protection to pharmaceuticals.

February 1999

- The government of Colombia issued a presidential directive on government use of software on February 25.

March 1999

- The Kuwaiti Cabinet approved the draft copyright law on March 21.
- The government of Lebanon passed amendments to its Copyright Law, including adequate protection for computer programs, stiffer penalties for infringement, a term of protection for the life of the author plus 70 years, confiscation of illegal products and equipment, and Berne-compatible evidentiary presumption of copyright ownership.
- The United States and Honduras concluded negotiations on a bilateral IPR agreement.
- The Economic Minister of the Palestinian Authority on March 10 brokered an agreement between Israeli music industry representatives and the owner of a pirate CD plant in Hebron to end illicit production in the Palestinian-controlled area.
- The Taiwan Semiconductor Industry Association put forward a proposal for marking semiconductor chips manufactured in Taiwan with source identification (SID) Codes.

April 1999

- The government of China issued a high-level decree requiring the use of only legitimate software by government ministries.
- The government of India enacted legislation and drafted implementing regulations establishing mailbox and exclusive marketing rights systems for pharmaceutical and agricultural chemical products.
- Malaysia undertook a series of constructive steps toward developing and implementing a regulatory regime to control pirate optical media production, and to strengthen manufacturing and retail level enforcement efforts.
- Jordan signed the instrument of ratification of the Berne Convention, giving U.S. copyrighted works legal protection in Jordan.
- Mexico passed new antipiracy legislation that is a key part of its overall enforcement initiative announced in 1998.
- Hong Kong announced the formation of a new task force, staffed by an additional 100 customs officers, to strengthen enforcement efforts against copyright piracy.

Bases of Intellectual Property

In the European countries and the United States, intellectual property developed differently, thereby producing some substantive differences that remain today. The United States recognized intellectual property rights from the country's inception. The Constitution provides in Article 1, Section 8:

> The Congress shall have Power . . . To promote the Progress of Science and useful Arts, by securing for limited Times to Authors and Inventors the exclusive Right to their respective Writings and Discoveries.[15]

This short statement captures the essence and scope of intellectual property protection. Promotion of the sciences and arts is achieved through rewarding the creators by granting them periods of exclusive rights. Yet exclusivity is limited, thus ensuring that the public will ultimately benefit from these accomplishments. The Constitutional grant is sufficiently broad to anticipate copyrights (Authors) and patents (Inventors). Trademarks are not included in the Constitution, but became part of the federal system in 1905 with the enactment of the Lanham Act.[16] In Europe, the origins of intellectual property can be found in concepts of "natural law," a major influence in European thought. Natural law sought to achieve what was fair, just, and equitable. Thus it was only fair that an author be awarded copyright protection for his efforts. These observations are expressed by Cervantes early in the seventeenth-century Spanish classic, *Don Quixote*.

Intellectual property protection was examined at the international level at the end of the nineteenth century as a result of the Industrial Revolution, which created a plethora of new inventions and ideas eager to spread across Europe and the rest of the world. In individual European countries, protection was available for intellectual property, but this protection expired at the borders. Protection was granted on a national basis as the scope of law was territorial, limited to the nation state where the intellectual property was created and under whose laws it was originally protected. A need was felt to extend protection beyond national boundaries both to benefit the owner of the intellectual property, the inventor, and the foreign country where the new knowledge could be available instantly. With these goals in mind, a group of European nations convened in Paris in 1883 and established a Union resulting in the enactment of The Paris Convention for the Protection of Industrial Property (Paris Convention). Industrial property includes inventions (patents), trademarks, and industrial designs. By today's standards, the achievements of the Paris Convention were modest, but they were revolutionary at the time. The Paris Convention enabled the owner of a German patent to register his patent in France and obtain protection there under the same terms as a Frenchman. Registration was available in any participating country in the Union any time within one year from the original registration date in the home country.

National treatment became the standard for intellectual property protection abroad and was incorporated later into the Berne Convention (1886) for the Protection of Literary and Artistic Works and into the TRIPS Agreement. The Berne Convention differs from the Paris Convention in that multiple registration is not required. Protection in one Berne Convention country extends to all members of the Union. The United States adhered to the Paris Convention in 1903 and to the Berne Convention in 1989. Prior to adherence to the Berne Convention, U.S. authors seeking protection in Berne Convention countries, notably Europe and their former colonies, would publish their works simultaneously in the United States and in Canada or England, both Berne Convention members.

An awareness of the Paris and Berne Conventions is not solely a matter of academic interest, but it is important in following intellectual property trends. Both Conventions have been incorporated into the TRIPS Agreement, and adherence to both Conventions is a prerequisite to becoming a signatory. India, a member of the WTO, has not become a signatory of the TRIPS Agreement because of differences over the granting of product patents for pharmaceuticals. These differences were also reflected in India's failure to adhere to the Paris Convention. India's adoption of a new patent law to comply with the standards of the TRIPS Agreement remains a subject of debate there and in her trade negotiations abroad. In October 1998, when India advised WIPO of its adherence to the Paris Convention, observers believed this was but a first step to compliance with the TRIPS Agreement.

Intellectual Property Protected in the
TRIPS Agreement

Definitions of intellectual property vary as result of the different characterizations originating in the U.S. Constitution and the Paris and Berne Conventions. The U.S. Constitutional grant does not use the term *intellectual property,* but clearly encompasses both copyrights and patents. The Paris Convention protects *industrial property,* a term not used in the United States but widely used in Europe, Latin America, and countries in Africa and Asia with European derivative legal systems. The Berne Convention protects *literary and artistic works,* more fully defined to include items such as movies, recordings, photographs, sculptures, and architectural works. Yet the inclusion of these European terms rarely causes confusion with patents and copyrights in the United States. The TRIPS Agreement attempts to incorporate these three sources of intellectual property and offers protection for the following:

- Copyright and related rights.
- Trademarks.
- Geographical indications.
- Industrial designs.
- Patents.
- Layout-designs (topographies of integrated circuits).
- Protection of undisclosed information.

A brief examination describing the principal forms of intellectual property follows, including some comments on current international issues of enforcement. Industrial designs and layout-designs are not covered for discussion since they are rarely included as separate concerns internationally. Although industrial designs are recognized as a distinct form of intellectual property in the Paris Convention[17] and are the subject of the 1925 Hague Agreement, they are not a matter of international concern. Adherence to the latter international agreement has been minimal and most countries include protection of industrial designs within their patent laws. For example, in the United States, industrial designs are part of the patent laws and protection is granted for a shorter period, 14 years. WIPO is currently attempting to gain greater treaty compliance by amending the original Agreement to facilitate its acceptance by a greater number of WTO members. Only 29 countries currently participate in this Agreement while WIPO has 179 member countries.[18] The Hague Agreement of 1925 is not included in TRIPS as one of the international agreements for which compliance is required. Integrated circuits are covered by a separate international agreement, the Treaty on Intellectual Property in Respect of Integrated Circuits (IPIC Treaty) adopted in 1989. This Agreement allows member states to apply existing, national intellectual property laws to the semiconductor industry. Most countries have elected to provide protection for integrated circuits under existing copyright or patent laws.

Copyright and Related Rights

The TRIPS Agreement incorporates familiar provisions found in national copyright laws. Specifically, it focuses on *expression* and not on ideas.[19] You cannot claim copyright protection for the idea of a poem, you must write it out. Intellectual property rights are not granted for mere abstractions. Historically differences have existed between the United States and European countries over the "moral rights" of authors. The concept derives from the Berne Convention where the right of the author to claim authorship of the work even after the copyright has been transferred to a third party remains as well as his right to protect the work from mutilation or destruction. These moral rights are sometimes referred to as that of "paternity" and "integrity" of the work.[20] These notions have never been accepted in the United States where the owner of the copyright has absolute control over the work. It is over this issue of moral rights that the United States did not adhere to the Berne Convention until 1989, when changes in U.S. law to provide for moral rights were no longer demanded of the United States by other members. The differences between the U.S. view and the French surfaced, however, when Ted Turner purchased the black-and-white MGM film library and decided to color or tint some of the old black-and-white films. One such film by John Houston, *The Asphalt Jungle,* was released in its new version and licensed to be telecast on French television in 1989. Purists were outraged but powerless to intervene in the United States because Turner was the owner of the copyright. The Houston heirs waited quietly and shortly thereafter the new version of the film was shown in Paris. The heirs, joined by the screenwriter Ben Maddow, sued and won claiming the "integrity" of the work had been violated and the author's (director's and writer's) moral rights had been violated. Thus, the colored version could not be shown on French television.[21]

Authors, particularly those who publish their works both in Europe and the United States, are not unaware of these differing views. The late Stephen Spender sued the American writer, David Leavitt, for writing a novel, *While England Sleeps,* using scenes taken, without authorization or acknowledgment, from Spender's autobiography, *World Within Word.* These incidents involved a homosexual relationship between Spender and a friend and their trip to Europe in the 1930s, prior to Spender's marriage. Following his marriage, Spender's friend enlisted in the Spanish Republican Army, attempted to desert, was captured and threatened with court-martial. Spender went to Spain to help obtain his release. This incident is a minor story within the confines of the longer autobiography, but it is the basis of the complete Leavitt novel. In the autobiography, the relationship between Spender and his friend is treated with the greatest discretion, while the Leavitt novel describes the relationship between the two men in sexually explicit terms. In describing why Spender brought suit in England, he noted:

> Although American and British law equally defend an author's copyright In the general principles described, British law also extends to the *author's moral right not to have his work "adapted," distorted, or trivialized.*[22] [italics added]

Current issues in protecting copyrights abroad center on unauthorized or pirated production of optical media including CDs, VCDs, DVD, and CD-ROMs. In its *Annual Review of Special 301,* the USTR on April 30, 1999, noted that:

> Reports indicate that approximately 90 optical media (CD, CD-ROM, VCD, and DVD) production lines are operating in Malaysia. The combined production capacity of these lines far exceeds local demand plus legitimate exports. Pirate products believed to have originated in Malaysia

have been identified throughout the Asia-Pacific region, North America, South America, and Europe, and pirate products are sold openly in public markets in Malaysia.[23]

The harshness of copyright protection is mitigated in the United States by the doctrine of fair use. Under this doctrine, copyrighted material may be used without obtaining prior permission of the copyright owner. The most recent Supreme Court decision in 1994 involving fair use was whether a parody of the song, *Pretty Woman*, by the rap group, 2 Live Crew was entitled to the protection of fair use.[24] In holding that parody could qualify for fair use, the Supreme Court analyzed in depth the facts of the case and applied the four statutory criteria set forth in the Copyright Law:

§ 107 Limitations on exclusive rights: Fair use
In determining whether the use made of a work in any particular case is fair use the factors to be considered shall include
(1) the purpose and character of the use, including whether such use is of a commercial nature or is for nonprofit educational purposes;
(2) the nature of the copyrighted work;
(3) the amount and substantiality of the portion used in relation to the copyrighted work as a whole, and;
(4) the effect of the use upon the potential market for or value of the copyrighted work.[25]

Justice Souter stated that all of the factors must be considered and treated equally in determining the question of fair use. The case was remanded to the District Court for further analysis of these factors.

Trademarks

The essence of trademark protection is the protection of any sign that distinguishes goods or services. Although many believe trademarks are a less important form of intellectual property than either patents or copyrights, trademarks have the unique quality that they may be renewed indefinitely if they remain in continuous use. Bayer aspirin is a familiar case in point. A trademark can outlive a patent and retain its value long after the patent has entered the public domain. Trademarks need not be associated with patents. An Indian pharmaceutical company, Ranbaxy, successfully competes in the global generic market through emphasizing and marketing aggressively its global brands:

> Today, we [Ranbaxy] operate in over 40 markets. In 26 of these we market our brands through our own sales/marketing teams. This, we believe, demonstrates our commitment to brand marketing as a strategic tool.[26]

Counterfeiting trademarks and selling goods for what they appear to be, but are not, is as old as history. In the United States, the period following World War II saw large-scale introduction of counterfeit goods particularly from Japan and the Far East. Four reasons are generally given for this increase: Shortages of consumer goods, springing in part from the pent-up demand caused by World War II; status symbols in the form of counterfeiting well-known brands on often unrelated goods; improvements in technology permitting the counterfeit product to be of comparable quality as the original; and globalization of the economy where more and more goods are being marketed outside of their country of origin.[27] These observations were made in 1980. They are even more true today.

A particularly costly form of trademark abuse involves registering a mark abroad, by someone other than the true owner before a product is introduced into the country. When the true owner is ready to register the mark, he may find that it is no longer available, and that he must "buy" it back from the local owner. There is an apocryphal story about Coca-Cola having to buy back its trademarks in Brazil from an enterprising São Paulo businessman who had registered them during World War II when Coca-Cola was not marketing its products due to sugar rationing and its contribution to the war effort. Such practice is not uncommon and often occurs with the implicit support of the government as was the case with Cartier in Mexico.[28] TRIPS allows participating countries to deny or cancel trademark registrations of brands already well known in a country when registration is attempted by one other than the true owner.[29] Implementing this policy is often difficult as the local "owner" of the trademark may enjoy political protection. There is much money to be gained in "selling" the mark back to the true owner. This practice is sometimes referred to as *wholesale piracy*[30] and has become an issue in assigning Internet domain names. Unscrupulous individuals register names of well-known firms in advance and owners are forced to buy them back. WIPO has just published a report on the subject of abuse of trademarks on the Internet dealing specifically with "cybersquatting" and reverse domain name hijacking.

> *Cybersquatting* occurs when individuals register a recognized trademark as a domain name and attempt to sell it to the genuine owner of that trademark for commercial profit. So-called "reverse domain name hijacking," which has appeared as a reaction to this, involves big businesses threatening to sue legitimate domain name registrants who do not give up the right to the registration.[31]

The International Chamber of Commerce is attempting to deal with this problem by creating a ". . . Cybercrime Unit to provide advice and assistance to business companies to limit their exposure to crimes involving electronic networks and computer system."[32]

The WIPO Report makes specific recommendations as to "best practices" for certain registrations and provides for an obligatory dispute resolution mechanism.[33]

Efforts to obtain trademark protection in multiple countries through a single registration began with The Madrid Agreement concerning the International Registration of Marks (Madrid Agreement) of 1891. The Madrid Agreement has not enjoyed broad acceptance largely because the international registration is vulnerable to central attack, attacking the original, home registration any time within five years. Therefore, there is no security that the international mark will be granted until after that time. More satisfactory, although on a smaller scale has been the introduction of the Community Trademark (CTM) established in 1994. The CTM is described as:

> A Community trademark shall have a unitary character. It shall have equal effect throughout the [European] Community.[34]

The CTM provides considerable advantages to firms operating within the EU. Not only does it offer one trademark recognized in all 15 countries of the EU, but it can be obtained by filing a single application prepared in one language and payment of a single registration fee. In addition, the extension of the trademark may be achieved by the payment of a single renewal fee. Finally the "use" requirement, often essential for renewal, can be met by establishing use in any one country of the EU.[35]

An important issue was recently resolved in the EU involving parallel imports of branded goods into the EU. Although the actual case involved a trademark situation, the problem could have arisen with any form of intellectual property. An Austrian manufacturer of sunglasses, Silhouette, sold some of its branded frames to a trading company in Bulgaria with the understanding they were to be sold there or in other states of the former Soviet Union. An Austrian discount firm with whom Silhouette had previously refused to deal, obtained these frames from Bulgaria and began selling them in Austria at a reduced price. Silhouette sought an injunction and eventually prevailed when the European Court of Justice (ECJ) held that a EU trademark owner could prevent the importation of its products. In 1988, a directive on Harmonization of Trademark Laws was issued which prevented assertion of a trademark once the goods were placed in the market in a EU country, perhaps the notion of "European exhaustion." The Silhouette decision was based on the doctrine of "exhaustion" of the trademark. Once goods covered by a trademark are placed in the market by the owner of the trademark, the trademark ceases to protect future sales. The notion is widely accepted at the national level, and some of the EU member countries had even recognized the doctrine of "international exhaustion," thereby allowing the sale of cheaper parallel imports arriving in the EU countries from Asia. In these cases of parallel imports, there is no question of counterfeiting or piracy, the goods are authentic and carry legitimate trademarks. Ultimately this interpretation prevailed in the decision of the ECJ to allow Silhouette to keep "imported" branded goods out of the EU even though they were originally manufactured there. This notion of exhaustion of an international property right upon sale is followed in the area of copyrights as well as trademarks.[36]

Geographical Indications

Geographical indications are a concept only recently becoming familiar in the United States. They derive from the European practice of labeling products with the name of the geographical region where the product was originally produced or manufactured (for example, Champagne, a bubbly white wine exclusively from the Champagne region of France; Roquefort, a sheep's milk cheese produced in a distinct region of France; and more recently, Tequila, an alcoholic beverage distilled from a particular species of the Agave cactus grown in a distinct region of Mexico). Traditionally, geographic indications have been largely of European concern going back as early as the Paris Convention where ". . . direct or indirect use of a false indication of the source of the goods" could result in the seizure of the goods when they entered a foreign country.[37] Lacking the traditions where goods were identified and their quality established by place of origin, new world countries tended to minimize these requirements. They still are taken quite seriously in Europe. For example, in Spain, the company, Freixenet markets its sparkling white wine as "cava" and not "champagne."

Because of the strong protection of geographical indications provided in TRIPS,[38] this area will receive greater attention, particularly as related to wines and spirits. The United States has responded to the TRIPS requirements by amending its trademark law to provide for the cancellation or refusal to grant a trademark when the name compromises a geographical indication.[39] NAFTA also recognizes geographical indications in its chapter on intellectual property.[40] In addition, NAFTA has specifically in Annex 313 noted Distinctive Products as belonging exclusively to one of the three signatories. Bourbon Whiskey and Tennessee Whiskey (a straight Bourbon Whiskey only produced in Tennessee) are recognized ". . . as distinctive products of the United States," and Canada and Mexico have agreed not to permit the sale in their respective countries of any products with these names unless manufactured in the United States. Similarly "Canadian Whisky" is recognized as a distinct product of Canada and "Tequila and Mezcal" as distinct products of Mexico. The European Union is interested in concluding a comprehensive treaty with the United States covering the wine industry that would include geographical indications.[41]

Patents

Under most national legal systems, patent protection is granted to the inventor of a new product or process for an exclusive period of time. In the language of current U.S. law, the person who "invents or discovers any new and useful process, machine, manufacture, or composition of matter, or any new and useful improvement thereof, may obtain a patent." The nature of the grant gives the owner of the patent "the right to exclude others from making, using, offering for sale, or selling" the invention in the United States or "importing" the invention into the United States. The patent owner is also permitted to assign or license his rights under the patent.[42] There has been considerable harmonization worldwide in those countries offering patent protection, as to the scope of rights granted by a patent. The TRIPS provides that "patents shall be available for any inventions, whether products or processes, in all fields of technology, provided that they are new, involve an inventive step and are capable of industrial application."[43] Signatories are permitted to deny patents for inventions contrary to public policy, thus leaving these decisions to national law. The rights granted to the patent owner under the TRIPS are similar to those of the United States.

Historically, the period of exclusivity in the United States was 17 years from the date of the patent grant. Under TRIPS, the patent term is 20 years from the date of filing.[44] The United States has amended its patent law to reflect the TRIPS' requirement as of January 1, 1995.[45] In practice, the actual "exclusivity" provided by the patent may actually be less than the 17 or 20 years. In the highly competitive pharmaceutical industry, often a "follower" or "me-to" drug will be introduced, to treat symptoms similar to the original drug. The introduction of the follower drug under patent protection of its own during the period of the first drug's exclusivity dilutes the first drug's exclusivity in the marketplace. For example, the patent for Tagamet, a stomach acid-reducing drug was granted to SmithKlein Beecham in 1977 while Zantac, which treated comparable conditions, was introduced by Glaxo Wellcome, Inc. in 1983. Thus, the period of actual exclusivity for Tagamet was only 6 years, not the 17 years contemplated under the original patent grant. Zantac was issued a separate patent because the PTO believed it was a different and unique drug. Tagamet retained its patent for the duration of its term, but its value was clearly less because of the availability of a competitive alternative.

Just as a single worldwide trademark is unavailable, patent protection must be sought under each national law. For the global firm seeking protection in more than one country, some relief is available through the Patent Cooperation Treaty (PCT), administered by WIPO, which currently includes 98 member states, including virtually all of the industrialized countries of the world.[46] Although the PCT cannot provide patent protection in all of its member states, it does permit the filing of an "international" patent application either at a patent holder's national patent office or with the International Bureau of WIPO in Geneva. This application designates a number of countries where the patent owner believes he may want protection. The filing of the application gives rise to an international search, which results in a report providing the applicant with information that will help determine whether to pursue a patent application in a particular country. It would reveal, for example, whether a similar patent already exists or is being processed. Thus, the applicant is spared the expense and time of filing a new patent application in countries where it is unlikely he would be eligible to receive a patent. Should the applicant decide to file for a patent in a different country, he is given a period of up to 18 months to do so, a significantly longer period than the 12 months provided in the Paris Convention. This additional time has been an important factor in making the international patent application a popular one. Although there is a basic filing fee for the PCT search, it is considerably less expensive than paying multiple, national filing fees up front. National filing fees must still be paid and the requirements of full registration must be met in those countries where the applicant chooses to obtain a national patent.

Unlike the CTM, which has been in effect since 1994, the EU has been unsuccessful in creating a single European patent, despite efforts since 1973. The European Commission is so concerned over this situation that it issued a Green Paper in 1997 on the subject of the Community Patent, subtitled "Promoting Innovation through Patents." The Green Paper argues that the failure to enact a unitary patent system has stifled innovation in the EU. It states:

> However, the patent system must under no circumstances act as a further brake on the competitiveness of European companies. Ease of obtaining patents, legal certainty, appropriate geographic coverage; these are all essential criteria for the effective protection of innovation in the European Union.[47]

Although there is a high degree of harmonization between the patent laws of the industrialized, developed countries and the United States, there are two areas of important differences. The first is the question of confidentiality. In the United States, the contents of a patent application remain confidential until the patent is granted. Assuming the patent remains pending or is denied, its contents are never made public. In many parts of the world, particularly Japan and the countries comprising the EU, patent applications are made public 18 months after their filing date. The rationale behind this early disclosure policy is consistent with that part of the goal of recognizing intellectual property as set forth in the U.S. Constitution, "to promote the progress of science and the useful arts." Yet the United States has been reluctant to decrease the period of confidentiality, largely because of pressure from independent inventors, who believe that early publication will enable potential competitors to compete sooner by gaining information from their patent application. International pressure to conform to the Japanese and European approach has caused pending legislation to abolish the confidentiality requirement and requires publication of the application 18 months after filing. Exceptions may be made available for small firms, universities, and independent inventors provided their application has not been pending more than five years and there have not been any dilatory delays by the applicant.

The second issue confronting the United States in the patent area is the question of priority dates, known as the first-to-invent versus the first-to-file. Historically, the United States has recognized for patent protection purposes the *first-to-invent*. Under this approach, all the inventor has to establish to enforce his patent is the date of the invention. Once this can be proven, he can claim infringement against the subsequent issuance of a patent to a rival claimant. This system is consistent with the notion that the United States is a country of small investors, who should receive maximum protection with a minimum of cost. It enables an inventor to benefit from his invention before the patent term of 17 years from the date of grant began. Its validity today is questionable, in a world where most patent applications are filed by large corporations and where the need to know current activities in your own business environment is as great as the need for patent protection. The United States, Jordan, and the Philippines are the only countries in the world where the first-to-invent rule prevails. There is increasing pressure on the United States to abandon this practice, claiming foreign inventors are losing money perfecting patentable inventions only to be subject to infringement suits by patent owners unknown to them claiming priority on the basis of first-to-invent. This question has become an increasing issue between the United States and the EU in the business groups comprising the Transatlantic Business Dialogue where the Europeans are urging the United States to abandon its current practice. Japan has also objected to the practice and refers to non-issued, first-to-invent patents, as "submarine" patents, which surface only after a patent for a rival invention has been issued. A variation of this practice is when an inventor with a patent application pending keeps amending the application, which is kept secret, so as to delay the adjudication of the patent. The applicant will attempt to bring infringement suits based on the first-to-invent. In the United States, there is some attempt to limit this process to one year and limit amendments to essential matters thereby accelerating adjudication and publication of the patent.[48]

Different effective dates for TRIPS compliance by WTO members produces an uneven level of enforcement of patent protection throughout the world. Thus, the agenda for the United States, member countries of the EU, and other nations seeking strong patent protection worldwide takes the form of advocating:

- TRIPS compliance at the earliest possible date;
- Enactment of effective national legislation including meaningful enforcement; and
- A willingness to negotiate special issues on a bilateral level.

The United States, Japan, and members of the EU monitor international compliance against these criteria. Substantive areas that require constant attention include such issues as patent term, less than 20 years from the date of filing; compulsory licensing, including decreasing the patent term for social or political reasons and finally; pipeline protection, a mechanism to offer limited protection during the transition period.

Although the TRIPS is unequivocally clear: "The term of protection available shall not end before the expiration of a period of twenty years counted from the filing date,"[49] there are countries, even TRIPS signatories, who fail to comply with this requirement. Because TRIPS is not a self-executing agreement and requires implementing legislation, national law must be modified to conform to its terms. Implementation problems developed with, for example, Portugal a country with a shorter patent term. In apparent compliance with TRIPS, Portugal amended her law to provide the 20-year term for new patents, those granted after June 1, 1995. The Portuguese law did not include extension for the 20 years of those patents in effect prior to June 1, 1995. Several U.S. firms operating in Portugal complained to the U.S. Trade Representative (USTR) that they would lose considerable revenue by not benefiting from the longer term. The United States began an investigation of this matter and requested WTO consultation. Portugal modified its implementing legislation to comply fully with the TRIPS requirement and the United States dropped its investigation.

Even in the United States, the transitional period and change in patent term from 17 years from the date of the patent grant to 20 years from the date of filing produced an unexpected windfall for at least one pharmaceutical company. Glaxo Wellcome, Inc. The implementing legislation provided the longer term for any patent in effect as of June 8, 1995. The patent for Zantec, the largest selling drug ever at that time, with sales of $3.66 billion in 1994, was due to expire on December 5, 1995. As a result of the change in U.S. law, Glaxo Wellcome received an additional 19 months of patent protection.[50]

The practice where a country grants a patent, but permits others than the patent owner to obtain the rights to manufacture the patented product before the expiration of the term is known as *compulsory licensing*. This practice may be allowed at any time or after a minimum period of exclusivity is enjoyed. It may also be invoked if the owner of the patent does not utilize the patent. Historically, compulsory licensing has been justified as a means to stimulate manufacturing in the country where the patent has been granted, or as a way to offer competition, presumably to the advantage of the consumer. In some instances compulsory licensing is available for certain products such as food, medicines, or surgical devices. When allowed, a potential competitor of the patent owner can request a designated government agency to allow him to also manufacture the product. In some instances, a royalty will be due the original patent owner, but not necessarily at a truly fair rate.

Countries advocating strong patent protection have always restricted the use of compulsory licensing and are very critical of the practice. In recent years, there has been considerable friction between the United States and Canada, as a result of Canada's liberal use of compulsory licenses for pharmaceutical products. Although Canada was motivated by the belief that competition in the pharmaceutical sector would result in lower drug prices for the Canadian consumer, the United States argued that it was the American consumer that was subsidizing the lower cost of medicine in Canada. Because of continuing pressure from the United States and a desire to harmonize her patent law with other industrial nations, Canada amended her patent laws in 1987 and finally abolished compulsory licensing in 1992. These measures laid the groundwork for Canada to participate in NAFTA, which contains provisions for strong intellectual property protection and allows compulsory licensing only under limited circumstances. Art. 1709: Patents provides in section 6:

> A Party may provide limited exceptions to the exclusive rights conferred by a patent, provided that such exceptions do not unreasonably conflict with a normal exploitation of the patent and do not unreasonably prejudice the legitimate interests of the patent owner, taking into account the legitimate interest of other persons.

Terms and conditions for compulsory licensing are spelled out in section 10 and include such factors as: nonexclusive use; use principally for the domestic market, and adequate remuneration for the owner of the patent. Each case must be determined on its own merits. There are no over-all exclusions for all products or for specific industries. The TRIPS also limits the use of compulsory licensing under comparable conditions to those found in NAFTA (Art. 31).

The final issue of concern in the patent area is determining when new patent legislation becomes effective in a given country. This situation arises when a country currently does not offer patent protection in general, or denies coverage to certain sectors such as pharmaceuticals or chemicals. This issue has become a major problem under the TRIPS where developing countries and least-developed countries are allowed grace periods of 5 or 10 years, respectively, before they are obligated to comply with its provisions. In effect, they are provided the benefits of the TRIPS, but are not required to comply with specific requirements. Thus, a country like Argentina, which currently provides minimal patent protection for pharmaceuticals, can continue to counterfeit drugs until it must comply with TRIPS in the year 2000. The American pharmaceutical and research manufacturers estimate that their members lose $600 million a year to sale of pirated products in Argentina and another $100 million as a result of Argentine exports of these products to Brazil.[51]

This "transition" problem can also exist outside of TRIPS compliance issues. For example, a country that does not offer patent protection finally enacts effective legislation. How can protection be provided to firms that were previously denied it. Under NAFTA, firms are allowed to enjoy, in any one of the member countries, the duration of the patent term existing under the patent issued by the home country. For example, a U.S. pharmaceutical company that was issued a patent in 1984 in the United States was unable to receive any protection in Mexico at that time. Once Mexico passed an effective patent law in 1991, and participated in NAFTA, Mexico was obliged to offer patent protection in Mexico to the U.S. firm for the duration of its U.S. term. Assume a 17-year patent term from the date of the grant, U.S. law prior to TRIPS, the U.S. patent would expire in 2001. If the firm applied for a Mexican patent in 1995 as soon as it was able, Mexican protection would extend from that time until 2001, six years of protection, less than optimum, but better than none. Pipeline protection is the mechanism to provide some protection during a transition period.

TRIPS Agreement expressly rejects the notion of protection prior to membership in the WTO. Art. 70.1 provides:

> This Agreement does not give rise to obligations in respect of acts which occurred before the date of application of the Agreement for the Member in question.

This view is necessary to avoid such issues as retroactive application, which would certainly alienate developing and least-developed countries as well as any potentially new members. Yet Article 70.8

partially mitigates this result for pharmaceutical and agricultural chemical products by requiring member countries to provide a filing system for these products that will serve to establish a valid priority date during the transitional period that will be recognized at such time full protection is available. This procedure is referred to as *mailbox* applications. This filing can also establish a basis for exclusive marketing rights, during the period when patent protection is not available, for a period of up to five years once marketing permission has been granted or until the patent is finally granted (Art. 70.9).

Particularly in the area of pharmaceutical patents, the United States monitors the issue of pipeline protection closely. Even when a country may justify its implementation delays under the transitional provisions of the TRIPS, the United States may attempt to negotiate earlier compliance on a bilateral basis, and even threaten unilateral sanctions under "Special 301" provisions of the Trade Act of 1974, as amended. This negotiating strategy raises questions as to the level of compliance required. Is legislation consistent with the TRIPS minimal standards sufficient, or can the United States demand compliance on an accelerated basis as a result of damage imposed on U.S. firms due to unfair trade practices. Since the creation of the WTO, the United States has the added option of utilizing dispute settlement procedures provided under the TRIPS Agreement, which it has already utilized on several occasions effectively. For example, the United States initiated an action against India for failing to provide mail box protection as required by TRIPS to allow pharmaceutical firms to obtain priority dates pending enactment of a new patent law in India. The Appellate Body of the WTO upheld a decision on favor of the United States in December, 1997.[52]

Undisclosed Information

The final kind of intellectual property covered in TRIPS is undisclosed information.[53] The term is not a familiar one in the United States where we more commonly use "trade secrets." The TRIPS inclusion of undisclosed property derives from Article 10[bis] Unfair Competitions of the Paris Convention dealing with unfair competition, and defined as ". . . competition contrary to honest business practices in industrial or commercial matters." This Article of the Paris Convention deals with what we would call "unfair business practices." Article 39 of TRIPS extends this notion to contemporary reality, the misappropriation of all kinds of proprietary information, and confidential information submitted to government agencies. This area encompassing trade secrets is one of increasing concern as technology changes so rapidly and can so easily be transferred electronically. Adding to the theft of proprietary information are changes in personnel practices. No longer do workers or engineers take a position and remain with the firm for life. Relocating is ever more common and it is understood in the marketplace that offers are made to individuals or groups of professionals because of knowledge they have acquired in previous positions.

Perhaps the most significant instance of industrial espionage was the case between General Motors (GM) and Volkswagen (VW) growing out of the defection of a former GM executive, Jose Ignacio Lopez de Arriortua, accused of stealing GM secrets when he began his employment with VW in 1993. These items included plans; information about industry secrets, the costs manufacturers pay for parts; and secret plans for a Plant "X," a revolutionary way to manufacture and assemble automobiles and trucks. Aside from the obvious legal issues, the dispute was intensified due to GM's image in Germany, particularly as the manufacturer of the Opel, second largest manufactured car in Germany after VW. Similarly VW was concerned about its image in the United States where it was attempting to restore its market position. Lawsuits were filed both in the United States and Germany by GM. The companies ultimately reached a settlement whereby VW paid GM one hundred million dollars and agreed to purchase at least a billion dollars worth of parts from GM over the next seven years.[54] This high-profile dispute triggered a concern throughout the industrial world as to its vulnerability in the theft of trade secrets.

The reaction to this new threat was swift in the United States. Congress enacted the Economic Espionage Act of 1996 (EEA) imposing criminal penalties on individuals or companies found guilty of stealing trade secrets.[55] This law created for the first time in the United States a federal crime, which expressly includes the theft by utilizing the new technologies including such activities as ". . . photographs, downloads, uploads, alters, destroys, photocopies."[56] Prior to the EEA, trade secret enforcement was limited to the theft of physical property. It is not a coincidence that the definition of trade secrets found in the EEA is similar to that provided in Article 39 of TRIPS. In both instances, the information must be secret, have commercial value, and its owner must have taken reasonable efforts to protect the property.[57] Increasingly, employers require personnel to sign confidentiality agreements in an effort to anticipate what belongs to the company and what belongs to the employee at the termination of employment.

Conclusion

This examination of global protection of intellectual property rights results in an uneven conclusion. The failure to have a worldwide system in place, including enforcement, for any kind of intellectual property leaves protection under the control of national laws. As we have noted throughout this chapter, these differences are significant both substantively and at the enforcement level. The dispute resolution mechanism provided by the WTO and incorporated into the TRIPS Agreement is at its infancy. It is far too early to reach conclusions as to its effectiveness. The complex fabric of the underlying conventions and agreements are but guidelines for national laws to interpret according to their own priorities. The major instruments, the Paris and Berne Conventions, were conceived during the Industrial Revolution sweeping through Europe in the latter part of the nineteenth century. We are currently experiencing a new industrial revolution as new technologies emerge, and we must examine the validity of the current system and determine whether some of the assumptions are applicable today.

This is not an easy situation for corporate decision makers. Changes in laws come slowly. Given this uneven environment how do firms with significant intellectual property rights develop strategies to take advantage of globalization without losing their assets when they are sent abroad? Some strategies do emerge. They are:

- Know and understand the resources available to you in your home country. These may include familiarity with government agencies and their activities. Knowledge of the activities of the U.S. Trade Representative (USTR) is essential. Become active in a trade association that effectively protects your industry's interests. Support efforts to strengthen intellectual property laws and enforcement at home and abroad.

- Know and understand the foreign environment in which you plan to work. If the country does not protect intellectual property effectively, don't export your newest technology there. Even though India does not have pharmaceutical product patents, Glaxo Wellcome remains the largest single drug company there, obviously not by selling her newest pharmaceutical products.

- Staying home is no overall solution. Avoiding a given market at a given point in time might be a wise strategy, but it can't work as a permanent solution. Failure to enter a difficult market may preclude you from later entrance. Leaving a difficult market may make it more difficult to re-enter.

- More and more countries have intellectual property laws in place. The focus is shifting to enforcement. This really reflects progress. You can't have enforcement issues without laws.

Notes

1. Commission of the European Communities, Green Paper, *Combating Counterfeiting and Piracy in the Single Market.* 1998, p. 4.

2. Commission . . . , p. 4.

3. Lester C. Thurow, "Needed: A New System of Intellectual Property Rights," *Harvard Business Review,* (September/October 1997) p. 96.

4. General Information about WIPO. Available: www.wip.org/eng /infbroch/inbro98.htm, p. 3.

5. General. . . .

6. See for example, "Patents," *The New York Times,* (June 28, 1999), p. C13.

7. TRIPS, Preamble.

8. TRIPS, Art. 18.

9. TRIPS, Arts. 65–66.

10. NAFTA, Chap. 17.

11. Council Regulation (EC) No. 40/94 of December 20, 1993.

12. See, for example, Bilateral Investment Treaty between USA and Trinidad & Tobago. Available: www.sice.oas.org/bits/triusa_e.stm, in force enforced on December 26, 1996.

13. Bilateral, Article I.c.(v).

14. See Joseph T. Simone, Jr., "Improving Protection of Intellectual Property," *China Business Review,* (March/April 1992).

15. *Constitution of the United States of America,* Senate Document No. 170, 1952.

16. 15 U.S.C. §§ 1051–1127.

17. Art. 4.

18. F. Williams, "WIPO Aims to Reinvigorate Treaty on Design," *Financial Times,* (June 16, 1999), p. 10.

19. TRIPS, Art. 9.2.

20. Berne Convention, Article 6[bis].

21. The case is discussed in P. Goldstein, *Copyright's Highway,* (1994), pp. 165–68.

22. Stephen Spender, "My Life is Mine: It Is Not David Leravitt's," *The New York Times,* (September 4, 1994), p. 3.

23. USTR. Press Release announcing results of special 301 Annual Review, (April 30, 1999), p. 3.

24. Campbell v. Acuff-Rose Music, Inc., 114 S.Ct. 1164, 127 L.Ed.2d 500 (1994).

25. Copyright Law of the United States of America, *Library of Congress, Circular 92,* (1993), p. 13.

26. Ranbaxy Laboratories Limited, *Competing in the Global Generic Market.* Available: www.ranbaxy.com/glob9.htm

27. Jack G. Kaikati and Raymond LaGarce, "Beware of International Brand Piracy," *Harvard Business Review,* vol. 58 (March/April 1980), pp. 52–53.

28. Kaikati, "Beware . . . ," p. 54.

29. TRIPS, Art.16.1.

30. Kaikati, "Beware . . . ," p. 54.

31. "WIPO Targets Abuse of Trademarks on the Internet," Press Release PR/99/170, (Geneva: April 30, 1999), p. 1.

32. See advertisement, Executive Focus, *The Economist,* (May 15–21, 1999), p. 13.

33. Executive . . . , p. 2.

34. Council Regulation (EC) No. 40/94 of December 20, 1993, on the Community Trademark, Art.1(2).

35. Donna G. White, "International Trade-Marks: Selection and Protection," Available: www.osler.com/ip/ documents/international.htm

36. The discussion of the *Silhouette* case is based on two articles, Barbara E. Cookson, "Europe Awaits Controversial Ruling on Trademark Exhaustion," (July/August 1998) Available: www.ljx.com/trademar /0708_eutm.html and Anonymous, "European Court Says Top Brands Can Restrict Imports," *Marketing News,* (Chicago: August 17, 1998), p. 14.

37. Paris Convention, Art. 10.

38. Arts. 22–25.

39. *Report on United States Barriers to Trade and Investment,* European Commission (1988), p. 43.

40. NAFTA, Chap. 17, Art. 1712.

41. *Report. . . .* p. 43.

42. The Patent Act of 1952, 35 U.S.C. §§ 1–376.

43. TRIPS, 27(1).

44. TRIPS, Art. 33.

45. GATT Uruguay Round Implementing Legislation (PL 103–465), (December 8, 1994) Highlights of this legislation may be found in "GATT Uruguay Round Patent Law Changes." Available: www.uspto.gov/web /offices/com/doc/uruguay/SUMMARY.html

46. "Patent Cooperation Treaty Registers Record Growth in 1998," Update 99/49 Geneva (February 12, 1999). Available: www.wipo.org/eng /pressupd/1999/upd00_49.htm

47. A copy of this Green Paper is available: www.bugnion.it /green1.htm

48. Marc E. Brown, "Submarine Patents under Attack," *Electronic Business,* (December 1998).

49. TRIPS, Art. 23.

50. *Philadelphia Enquirer* (December 20, 1995).

51. Joshua Goodman, "The U.S Seeks a Cure for Argentina's Drug Piracy," *Bridge News,* (June 27, 1999), p. 1.

52. USTR, op cito, p. 8.

53. TRIPS, Art. 39.

54. E.L. Andrews, "None Prove So Stubborn as a Giant Spurned; G.M. Never Wavered in Its 4-Year Fight over Executive Who Defected to VW," *The New York Times,* (January 11, 1997), p. 37.

55. An analysis and text of the EEA. Available: www.carolinapatents.com /ts_articles/trade_secret4.htm

56. §§ 1831 (2).

57. TRIPS, Art. 39(2) A, B, C, and EEA § 1839 (3) A, B.

12

Global Strategy for Developing Cross-Cultural Competence

CHRISTINE UBER GROSSE

Cross-cultural misunderstandings are costly, but common occurrences in global business today. Executives who work with diverse cultures deal with communication problems and cultural misunderstandings on a routine basis. Daily communication with people around the world, frequent trips abroad, and overseas assignments put managers at risk of cultural misunderstandings with serious repercussions for their business and career. Managers may run into difficulties as they travel abroad on business. Many communicate daily via phone, e-mail, or videoconference with clients, suppliers, and fellow employees around the world. Overseas assignments place additional demands on managers and their families for cultural understanding and effective communication skills. Whether executives communicate across cultures within the company, locally, or internationally, they need to understand cultural differences to avoid errors that can cost them sales, clients, or even their jobs.

How are companies addressing the urgent need for their executives to work and communicate effectively with people from different cultures? This chapter explores the major strategies that companies use to build the cross-cultural competence of their managers. These strategies include travel and work experience, training, cultural informants, hiring practices, and diversity policy.[1]

Need for Cross-Cultural Understanding

Corporations recognize that cross-cultural communication skills are key to success in international markets, joint ventures, and sales. The Rand Report on global preparedness and human resources[2] identifies strong intercultural communication skills as essential for success in international markets. The Human Resources experts who participated in the Rand study defined cross-cultural competence as a manager's global perspective and ability to interact smoothly with members of other cultures.

Others have studied the impact of cross-cultural communication skills on business. Cross-cultural communication played an important role in the success of joint ventures between culturally diverse groups.[3] With respect to sales across borders:

> ... the impact of culture in any sales setting is not only subtle, it's a dangerous thing to ignore ... cultural differences can make or break your deal. To add to the challenge, if you're not paying attention you may never even know why you lost the sale.[4]

Almost 80% of midsize and large companies send personnel overseas, and 45% have plans to send additional professionals abroad.[5] There are many difficulties and high costs for companies sending professionals abroad and a low success rate, as measured by turnover and attrition. The turnover rate on overseas assignments is twice that of managers who stay in the United States. In addition, one-fourth leave their companies within one year after returning home.

One study investigated the practices of companies that successfully manage their expats and identified three effective strategies:[6]

1. Sending people for the right reason,
2. Sending the right people, and
3. Finishing the right way.

The right reasons included sending people to generate and transfer knowledge and/or to develop global management skills. The "right people" to send on overseas assignments had "technical skills [which] are matched or exceeded by their cross-cultural abilities . . . companies with a strong track record with expats put a candidate's openness to new cultures on an equal footing with the person's technical know-how." Effective companies used a variety of means to identify the following characteristics useful to evaluate people to post overseas: a drive to communicate, broad-based sociability, cultural flexibility, cosmopolitan orientation, and a collaborative negotiation style. When expats returned from an overseas assignment, successful companies helped to prepare them for the personal and professional changes they experienced.[7]

In spite of the widely recognized need for cross-cultural competence, many companies still do not prepare executives for overseas postings. While international managers freely admit the need for training, and the advantages of developing employee cultural awareness and understanding, they mention that their companies provide little if any cross-cultural training and assistance to executives and their families assigned overseas. The former marketing manager for Europe of a U.S. multinational remarked that global companies often talk about the problem, but actually do little about it. The vice president in charge of the international division of a large U.S. company commented that while the company was very concerned with developing cross-cultural understanding among employees, it did not have a formal strategy in place to deal with the training issues.

Confirming this widespread lack of executive preparation for doing business across cultures, "it's a fairly common practice to send expatriate families overseas with little or no preparation for the tremendous transition companies expect them to make."[8]

Cost of Cultural Misunderstandings in Business and Failed Assignments

Companies widely recognize that overseas assignments often fail due to an executive's inability to adapt to the new culture. These mistakes come at a high cost to companies. Depending on the country, the direct cost of a failed expatriate assignment ranges between

$250,000 and $500,000, according to the National Foreign Council and SRI Selection Research international. Motorola, Inc. estimates the cost to be even higher for a failed mid-level $75,000 a year employee. The company calculates the loss at $600,000 to $1.25 million for a three-year assignment.[9] Linda Kuna, global assignment manager for Motorola's two-way radio division, points out that money is not all that is lost with a failed assignment. "By sending the wrong kind of individual you can damage your relationships with the host country, you can lose business opportunities, and damage career paths for individuals who probably should not have been sent overseas."[10]

A survey by the Conference Board showed that the cost of an expatriate manager was 4 to 4.9 times the salary for nearly one-fifth of the companies, 3 to 3.9 times the salary for half of the companies, and 2 to 2.9 times salary for almost one-third of the companies.[11]

Some developing countries prefer to see nationals hold management positions, and limit the number of expatriate managers in foreign-owned businesses. Europe, for example, limits the numbers of work permits for expatriate managers.

Today more companies realize the importance of preparing managers for difficult overseas assignments. Given the high failure rate (early departures) of expatriate managers and the high cost to the company, more companies are investing in training for employees going on overseas assignments. The mistakes have cost companies far too much to ignore. Richard Smith, president of Prudential Relocation's intercultural service says that "too many executives are unaware of the culture shock awaiting them, causing employees to be dissatisfied and costing corporations 50 percent of their investment when the assignment fails."[12]

Even when a manager has completed an overseas assignment, the cost to companies can still escalate. A survey by the Conference Board of Asian, European, and North American manufacturing and service companies showed that twice as many former expatriate managers in North American-based companies leave the company as those who stay home. Prudential Intercultural indicates that companies lose up to 40% of returning managers.[13] As a result, more and more companies are investing in repatriation assistance and career planning.

Corporate Strategy for Cross-Cultural Communication

As companies enter new global markets, executives face strenuous demands trying to adapt to an unfamiliar culture. Most executives agree on the importance of learning how to interact with different cultures. However, companies are divided on the best corporate strategy for developing cross-cultural expertise. They typically employ a combination of one or more of the following strategies:

1. *Travel and work experience.* On-the-job experience is accomplished through:
   - Travel overseas
   - Expatriate assignment
   - Multicultural teams
2. *Training initiatives.* Build employees' cross-cultural communication skills through training conducted in-house or through outsourcing:
   - In-house training
   - Outsourced training
3. *Cultural informants.* Use cultural informants from the target culture, or knowledgeable about it, to guide employees through potential problem areas.
4. *Hiring and selection practices.* Use careful selection procedures in order to choose the right person for the overseas assignment to ensure a higher rate of success on the assignments.
5. *Diversity policy and corporate culture.* Follow a diversity policy within the corporate culture to develop cross-cultural communication skills among employees and externally.

Strategy 1: Travel and Work Experience

The most commonly cited corporate strategy for developing cross-cultural communication skill is travel and work experience, where the employee develops expertise dealing with people of diverse cultures through work and travel. Used alone or in combination with other strategies, many companies believe that this is a very effective way to build intercultural competence. In contrast, others consider that travel and work experience alone isn't a strategy at all. They equate it with a company doing little or nothing to provide assistance to the executive who must work with a variety of different cultures. This contrasts with the opinion of other executives who insist that the "learning by doing" experiential approach is very effective.

Companies who use this strategy believe that employees will gain expertise dealing with other cultures through on-the-job experience and travel. This strategy includes daily contact with multicultural business associates, work on multicultural teams, business travel, and overseas assignments.

Many companies are convinced that employees will develop cross-cultural expertise through travel and work experience and direct interaction with people from different cultures. This strategy resembles the "sink-or-swim" approach used in the school system to immerse students in a new language and culture, with no special assistance. Some executives realize that the "sink-or-swim" approach can be painful, as the manager struggles to cope with cultural issues. A Mexican executive commented that "this method logically produces many misunderstandings at first between cultures, but finally it should trigger a learning process. This process is slower and more painful."[14]

It also can be dangerous and costly, if executives have trouble understanding and functioning effectively in the new business culture. Without training or other strategies to assist them, executives immersed in the target culture may make costly mistakes while they are learning to do business in the strange business environment. Worse yet, executives may think that they understand the culture and have no problems, when in fact they are misreading indications that things are not going well at all.

Daily Contact

Some executives consider daily contact with people from other cultures within the company, suppliers, clients, and other business associates as a good way to develop intercultural competence. Employees and business associates communicate and do business via e-mail, phone, fax, videoconference, or face-to-face meetings. A Mexican executive wrote that managers "develop cross-cultural communication skills on the job mostly." Another commented, "At my company we develop cross-cultural communication skills by day-to-day experience. We usually talk in English with people in other countries. In the offices, you can find people from England, United States, India, Japan, Venezuela, Argentina, Panamá, and so on."

Multicultural Teams

Executives cited working on multicultural teams as another effective strategy for developing cross-cultural understanding among employees. Global companies increasingly use multicultural teams to work on projects. In the process, companies have discovered that working on these teams gives managers valuable insight into working with people from different cultures. As employees work together on a common project, they learn to work out their differences, and overcome misunderstandings. Multicultural teamwork can build trust, new understanding, and respect for members of different cultures.

Another Mexican exec commented that at a certain level of management, the bosses belong to a central business unit that is generally located at the headquarters. The central unit is comprised of people from all over the world, and the managers interact and learn indirectly how to get along with colleagues from different cultures.

Some executives see on-the-job experience as insufficient preparation to deal with cultural differences. Several managers equated it with no corporate strategy at all to prepare employees for intercultural communication. A Mexican executive believes that most companies are doing little in the area of cross-cultural communication training. He comments, "In my experience, I have not seen an effort on global companies' to develop cross-cultural skills. Global companies rather make people from different countries work together. For example, in my office in Mexico I have partners from Russia, Israel, and Hong Kong. Several Mexicans have been transferred to Brazil and South Africa. We then use our own criteria to develop cross-cultural skills." This passive strategy, which could be considered no strategy at all, is used by many companies.

Travel Overseas

Travel abroad receives high marks from some executives as an effective strategy to develop employees' cross-cultural communication skills. Companies send executives to travel or live for short periods of time in the country to gradually get accustomed to the new culture. A young German executive in Mexico believes in using a combination of strategies but that " the best way to train people culturally is to send them to the country." Another Mexican executive agreed that the best way for a company to develop cross-cultural communication skills is by sending its employees abroad to get in touch with other cultures. Kemper believes that "personal and business relationships with people from other cultures and countries are perhaps the most effective way to develop an in-depth understanding of those cultures."[15]

Expatriate Assignment

Many companies interchange people among their offices around the world with the intent to improve the cross-cultural communication skills of their employees. In this sink-or-swim immersion approach, executives face the complex challenge of life and work in a perplexing new culture without special corporate training. They may or may not develop cultural understanding as a result of living and working overseas, without specific training. For this reason, many managers recommend the combination of several strategies such as work experience and training to help people work more effectively across cultures.

Research on firms with a successful track record in international assignments concludes that "an executive cannot develop a global perspective on business or become comfortable with foreign cultures by staying at headquarters or taking short business trips abroad.[16] Such intangibles come instead as a result of having spent more than one sustained period working abroad. Indeed, the only way to change fundamentally how people think about doing business globally is by having them work abroad for several months at a time."[17]

Strategy 2: Training Initiatives

In-House Training

In some instances, companies provide in-house cross-cultural training programs for employees. These involve seminars, courses, language training, books, web sites, discussions, role-plays, and simulations. Human Resources departments may provide cultural training through trips to other locations, special courses, videos, informative booklets, and the intranet.

Some companies encourage managers to role-play encounters with clients from other cultures to anticipate differences or misunderstandings that might arise. One Mexican manager described how his company role plays cross-cultural encounters. "Every time a new customer from a different country is coming, we define a 'strategy' that we call 'a play.' Every person of our team has a role, and we work on the basics of how to treat people from that country."

An international banker working at Citibank in Mexico City believes that the best way to deal with cross-cultural communication issues is to have people take courses in different countries with participants of different nationalities. Working together in the classes, people eventually start talking about cultural differences, how things are, and how they should be.

Global companies develop cross-cultural skills through courses on doing business with the other culture, and about general cultural differences. Some companies, such as Vitro, offer in-house courses that include reading materials on cross-cultural communication skills, and ways to deal with intercultural differences.

In another form of in-house training, companies encourage employees to open up about their cultures in an effort to educate each other about their diverse cultures, through discussion of cultural differences and ways of working. Another popular training method involves group activities that open employees' eyes to cultural differences among the people they do business with.

The informal, but potentially effective, strategy of employees training other employees has considerable backing among global firms. One Mexican executive says, "I think it is important to make sure that employees open up their culture to each another. Just because they may not see each other face-to-face does not mean that they cannot help each other to learn the culture. Also, the companies could have cross-cultural training sessions involving people in the same positions but from different countries getting together to learn about each other."

The Cemex International Management Program has a course designed specially to develop executives toward higher positions within the organization in the global business arena. One of the subjects of the course is precisely multinational culture, and it is offered to shape the cultural skills of executives in order for them to easily adapt to the different countries where the company operates.

Some Mexican managers advocated combining two strategies, training and travel to give employees critical exposure to the new culture. Others recommended complete immersion in the new culture, language courses, and visits to the foreign country. One manager also encouraged giving employees access to information from the foreign media as invaluable support for the employee who is preparing to interact with another culture.

Outsourced Training

Given the specialized nature of cross-cultural training, many companies outsource their training needs to the group of companies providing this service. They provide a wide range of services for companies, expatriates, repatriates, and their families. Training for expatriates can be arranged pre-departure or on-site. Some companies outsource their cross-cultural training to an executive education unit at a university, such as Thunderbird's Executive Education unit. Others send employees to training centers such as Window on the World or Berlitz for courses where they can learn about the language and customs of a country or region. Companies like Procter & Gamble, Microsoft, Motorola, and Hewlett Packard have mandated extensive cross-cultural training courses for their overseas teams.[18]

Companies should make initial and ongoing cross-cultural training a priority. Programs include several days of "intensive awareness training and many hours of discussion about specific situations that can spark conflicts and problems."[19] Other topics might be attitudes toward communication styles, time management, conflict resolution, productivity and cooperation.

Some global companies like Andersen Consulting and Citibank have a one-year trainee program before the executives begin their responsibilities. During this program they travel to the countries and regions where they will be working. At this time, part of their training deals with business and cultural differences.

One Mexican manager commented that his company sends employees for a few weeks ahead of time to the country where they will be posted to receive training to help them adjust to the new culture.

According to one report, 61% of companies provide at least one day cross-cultural preparation for employees assigned abroad.[20] Of that number, 35% provide training for the whole family, 23% offer training to employee and partner, and 3% offer training to the employee alone. However, fewer than one-third of the employees who received training were satisfied with it.[21] Most were frustrated with the following aspects of their training: cultural self-awareness, adaptation processes, working within the culture, routine survival tips and understanding the background issues. Cultural adaptation difficulties was cited most frequently by expatriates as the hardest part of their international assignment.[22] The business challenge cited second most often was "finding expat candidates."[23]

Typically, companies provide a two-day training session for an employee and partner a few weeks before departure. Other options for training include post-arrival culture programs and language programs that last one to three months. Some providers offer long-distance learning or involve local training centers in the new country. In designing a program, many companies first assess the family's experience living overseas and with a particular culture with a written questionnaire or telephone survey. Then the trainer tailors the program to the family's background and knowledge. Most programs consist of:

1. *Culture profile:* A comparison of the home and host cultures.
2. *Cultural adaptation:* Theory of the culture shock curve, symptoms of culture shock, and how to deal with them.
3. *Logistical information:* Business and social etiquette, practical information about the living in the country.
4. *Application:* Close examination of the executive's job requirements and the family's role in the new situation, anticipating problems that might arise and applying the new cultural awareness to these situations.[24]

Lucent Technologies Microelectronics Group developed an innovative, cost-effective training program designed to address cultural diversity and key business issues. The technology-based program consisted of "a half-day country-specific seminar delivered simultaneously to all employees by video; a half-day business-cultural immersion program delivered to interested employees with immediate needs or problems, and a company intranet site that captures country-specific culture and practical travel information."[25]

The cost of training programs ranges from $50 (for a CD-ROM for language learning) to $10,000 (for a two-day cross-cultural training program and eight days of intensive language training for the executive and spouse.) Typically a company will pay $4,000 to $5,000 for a two- to three-day cultural orientation program.[26]

Program formats for language training vary among the providers from self-study language materials (CD-ROM for $50), group language training course ($275 per person), CD-ROM and 12 interactive lessons with a teacher over the Internet ($475), to private lessons. Cultural training also comes in many forms. For example, a two-day predeparture program for the manager and spouse costs the company between $3,500 and $5,000. For the children, the program costs an additional $1,375 to $2,500. Onsite, a one-day course costs $1,050 to $3,000 for the family. A more extended onsite training program, consisting of one training class per week for the first six months, costs roughly $3,500 to $5,000 per family member.

Other courses combine language and culture instruction, such as a five-day predeparture course which costs $5,500 for manager and spouse. A 10-day course with two days of cross-cultural training and eight days of language immersion costs $10,000.

Cross-Cultural Training Programs for Global Companies

To get an idea of what corporate training is offered by the companies, we will look at the example of Window on the World, Inc., a Minneapolis-based company that has designed cross-cultural communication training programs for multinational corporations with the goal of increasing individual and organizational effectiveness worldwide. Over 650 panelists and consultants, from countries around the world, are utilized for culture-specific orientations. The company's worldwide network can deliver service in over 165 countries.[27]

Providing comprehensive cross-cultural training services for global company employees and their families, they offer services that include pre-assessment testing, expatriation training for employee and family, and on-site orientation.

Strategy 3: Cultural Informants

Another corporate strategy consists of the hiring of cultural informants to guide managers as they navigate unfamiliar cultural territory.
Some companies use "culture interpreters" to help people from different cultures resolve their problems.[28] Chinese and U.S. companies
sometimes use unofficial culture interpreters to help explain the
meaning of each side's behavior. Some companies employ full-time
training specialists to work on cultural interpretation problems between Chinese and employees from other nationalities.

Several of the Mexican managers described the corporate policy
of finding a specialist who knows the other country, whether within
the firm or hiring someone from without. The culture interpreter
can help mediate in negotiations, and explain any misunderstandings
that occur.

Strategy 4: Hiring and Selection Practices

Hiring and selection practices are another way that corporations can
fill their need for managers with the desired cultural competence. By
hiring new employees from diverse cultural backgrounds, or who
possess extensive international experience, companies can increase
the number of employees with the desired skills. They can actively
search for new managers who have knowledge about the cultures
they will be working with. The companies can then rely on the new
people to informally train others in management. Companies should
select executives who are sensitive to cultural differences.[29]

A manager in Thunderbird's MIMLA program, comments on
this corporate strategy: "more and more companies try to hire bilin-
gual people and people with international experience to relate better
to their foreign clients. Also, now global companies try to hire foreign nationals to work in management positions rather than send
their own people to another country where they may not be as successful."

A Mexican manager also discussed this strategy, "companies develop the cross-cultural communication skills of their employees by
hiring open-minded and international executives. These employees
transmit to others the customs of different cultures, and try to resolve conflicts that may arise." Another young manager reflected

that "it is very important that individuals with cross-cultural experiences at different levels be incorporated into the organization as soon as possible so that they can provide immediate hands-on experience" to avoid costly mistakes that result from cultural misunderstandings.

For Ford Corporation, being a global company is basic to the way the company works. The Ford corporate web site explains that "wherever your work may be, you are part of an international organization and can be in daily contact with Ford colleagues all over the globe. Plants supply parts for vehicles on six continents, engineers coordinate changes with colleagues in almost every time zone. In addition, many salaried Ford employees have an overseas assignment at some point in their careers." In the careers section of its corporate web site, Ford actively seeks to hire international employees, saying "as a global company, Ford values your command of languages and your understanding of different cultures. We encourage you to apply in your home country."

Selection Practices for Overseas Postings

To minimize the risk of failure, some companies are trying new strategies to assist with the selection of employees for overseas posts. In a typical situation, a company needs to fill a posting abroad fairly quickly, and the business-unit manager decides who is assigned to the post. Joint-venture managers may not have been "chosen because of their cultural sensitivity or skills, receive training or assistance in developing these skills, or even have had any previous experience in China"[30] (or their assigned country). In fact, managerial competence rather than cross-cultural expertise normally plays a much greater role in the decision who goes abroad.

In an effort to reduce the high number of costly failed assignments, Motorola and Hewlett Packard use different methods to assist in the selection of managers for overseas assignments, based on input from employees. Linda Kuna, global assignment manager for Motorola's two-way radio division, builds a pool of candidates for overseas assignments through self-selection. She asks employees who are interested in international work to send their resumes and other relevant information via the company intranet.[31] Interested employees and their partners participate in an expectation exercise. This is a self-selection tool that allows employees the opportunity to get a more realistic picture of some of the cultural differences and adjustments they will need to make overseas. Her pool of candidates offers management additional information that helps them to select an appropriate candidate for a posting. Once the candidate is chosen, he or she takes a cultural adaptability instrument that is meant to raise employee awareness of potential problems living abroad. Motorola offers a two-day cultural orientation to employees and their partners, focusing on living and doing business in the other environment.

Hewlett Packard does not have a formal selection process for overseas assignments. Like many companies, HP managers pick candidates to fill the positions, and the general managers review their choices. However, Tee Hitchcock, corporate relocations manager, says that they "use cross-cultural training as an opportunity for candidates to deselect themselves. The training gives them an understanding of what it's like living in the country and working there. Then they can say, 'you know, this isn't right for us' because of the family situation or whatever reason."[32] Involving employees more directly in the overseas assignment promises a higher rate of success in placement, and greater employee motivation for the transfer.

Strategy 5: Diversity Policy and Corporate Culture

Companies such as Ford, Hewlett Packard, and Motorola incorporate cross-cultural training within their diversity policy. Diversity has become an important aspect of corporate strategy as a means of bringing diversity into the workforce and a way to encourage employees to value cultural differences in the workplace. These companies view diversity as an important competitive advantage in the global economy. Their strategy is to build a diverse workforce that reflects and understands the diverse customers served by the company.

The corporate culture and diversity policy affect the companies' globalization efforts. The company can encourage cross-cultural understanding and positive attitudes toward cultural differences by a strong corporate policy on diversity. If the corporate culture clearly values and rewards diversity, employees are more likely to have an open mind toward cultural differences, more awareness of those differences, and tolerance for them. Cultural understanding derives more from a mindset than a knowledge base or list of facts about a country.

Companies like Ford, Hewlett Packard, and Motorola are making diversity a priority by formally incorporating diversity policy within their corporate mission. They develop employees' cross-cultural communication skills with in-house programs on diversity, and programs in the target country to help their employees perform better on the job.

For example, Hewlett Packard (HP) considers diversity a vital part of its business strategy. "At HP, we don't just value diversity because it's the right thing to do, but also because it's the smart thing to do," says Lewis E. Platt, CEO of HP. HP's reasons for valuing diversity reflect the position of many global companies. In a business strategy section in its web site, HP cites the following reasons as to why diversity is essential to its success:

- Our customers, suppliers, and strategic partners are increasingly global and multicultural. *We must be positioned to relate to them.*
- Our customers are changing—their needs and expectation for products and services are diverse. *We must be able to understand, interface, and respond.*
- Our competitive advantage is to become the leader in innovation, creativity, problem-solving and organization flexibility. *We must have diverse perspectives, talents, and teams to meet this global challenge.*
- The workforce demographics are changing in most countries. The labor pool is shrinking and labor shortages are projected. The competition to attract and retain top talent is increasing. *To ensure our business success, we must be the best place to work for everyone.*[33]

Ford also has a strong policy for valuing diversity and a diversity initiative. Like HP, it sees its global workforce as a competitive strength. From Ford's point of view, "diversity in our employees, dealers, and suppliers helps us understand our customers and serve them better. It also helps us create the best team possible. For this reason, we strive to attract, develop, and retain employees from all backgrounds."[34] Ford spends significant money each year on training and development of its global workforce. The corporate goal is to provide at least 40 hours of training a year for every employee.

Motorola does business on six continents and employs over 140,000 people around the world. Globalization is a driving force at Motorola, where almost half the employees work outside the United States. The company provides wireless communications, semiconductors, and advanced electronic systems and services. Its corporate culture emphasizes empowerment, "drawing on the creativity of all the cultures represented in our workforce."[35] One of two key beliefs are "constant respect for people" and "uncompromising integrity." Motorola's Global Diversity Philosophy Statement states that "Motorola is committed to constant respect for its culturally diverse workforce and customers and to fostering global leadership qualities in its employees." Company policy is "diversity is every manager's and employee's responsibility."[36]

Motorola places a great emphasis on training, and requires at least one week (40 hours) of training for each employee every year.[37] The company's Motorola University has 14 training delivery centers around the world, in addition to training operations in each business unit. Vince Seratela, director of planning, quality, and communications at Motorola University comments that Motorola recognizes that training—no matter how and where it's delivered—is a key competitive advantage." They use an integrated, strategic approach to training. "We've been religious about measuring quality, cycle time, and customer satisfaction. We've kept the discipline and rigor of training, not just in Motorola University, but also across the company. And that has helped build a companywide appreciation for how critical training and education are to this company's success." He attributes this to the strategic vision of the son of Motorola's founder, Bob Galvin, who keeps asking "What are you learning? Are you learning the right things?" Finally, he comments on the great payoff of training. "Every time we put a dollar against training to drive one of our quality initiatives, we get enormous benefits."

Conclusion

Global companies are applying five basic strategies to deal with the urgent need for managers who possess strong cross-cultural communication skills: Strategy 1 travel and work experience through travel overseas, expatriate assignment, and multicultural teams; Strategy 2 in-house or outsourced training; Strategy 3 cultural informants; Strategy 4 hiring and selection practices; Strategy 5 diversity policy and corporate culture.

Costly mistakes occur when managers miscommunicate, make mistakes in doing business due to cultural misunderstandings, have problems adjusting to life abroad, or have problems readjusting upon return from an overseas assignment. More and more companies place value on their managers' ability to communicate effectively across cultures. In the twenty-first century, the global economy and diversity in the workplace will continue to grow. These trends will fuel the need for cross-cultural competence. To develop managers who work effectively across cultures, companies will have to apply a combination of strategies.

The current strategies of travel and work experience, training initiatives, cultural informants, hiring and selection practices, and diversity policy help to develop managers' intercultural competence. Many companies still have not addressed the need to prepare managers to work successfully with different cultures. New strategies will develop as companies continue to gain expertise in conducting international business.

The demand for executives with the ability to interact successfully with diverse cultures will continue to grow and drive corporate strategy to address this concern. The need for cross-cultural competence is clear. In the twenty-first century, companies will continue to search for effective strategies to meet the need to prepare managers who are comfortable and competent doing business across cultures.

Notes

1. Information on corporate strategy was provided by corporate web sites, interviews with HR executives, and comments by international executives in Mexico. These executives participated in a business communication class taught by the author, and provided information on intercultural training in their companies. The web sites of Cargill, Ford, Hewlett Packard, and Motorola gave valuable insight into corporate strategy for diversity and cross-cultural training. In addition, the web sites of cross-cultural training companies (in particular, Window on the World, Inc.) provided further information about the training strategy for developing cross-cultural understanding and communication skills.

2. College Placement Council Foundation/Rand Foundation, *Developing the Global Work Force: Insights for Colleges and Corporations* (Bethlehem, PA: College Placement Council, Inc., 1994).

3. Linda Beamer, "Bridging Business Cultures," *China Business Review,* vol. 25, no. 3 (May 1998), pp. 54–58.

4. Cynthia Kemper, "Global Sales Success Depends on Cultural Insight," *World Trade,* vol. 11, no. 5 (May 1998), pp. S2–S4.

5. J. Stewart Black and Hal B. Gregersen, "The Right Way to Manage Expats," *Harvard Business Review,* vol. 77, no. 2 (Boston: March/April 1999), pp. 52–63.

6. Black, "The Right. . . ."

7. Black, "The Right. . . ."

8. Valerie Frazee, "Send Your Expats Prepared for Success," *Global Workforce Supplement to Workforce,* vol. 3, no. 3 (May 1998), pp. 15–16, 21.

9. Edward M. Mervosh and John S. McClenahen, "The Care and Feeding of Expats," *Industry Week,* vol. 246, no. 22 (December 1, 1997), pp. 68–72.

10. Mervosh, "The Care. . . ."

11. Mervosh, "The Care. . . ."

12. Brenda Paik Sunoo, "Inbound Executives Need HR's Help," *Workforce,* vol. 77, no. 3 (March, 1998), p. 23.

13. Mervosh, "The Care. . . ."

14. The comments of Mexican executives cited in this chapter come from students enrolled in a joint international management masters program run by Thunderbird and ITESM. The program, called "MIMLA"—Master of International Management for Latin America, is offered via distance learning to executives in four locations in Mexico—Monterrey, Guadalajara, and two campus sites in Mexico City. Instruction is delivered through a combination of satellite videoconferencing and high-speed ISDN telecommunications lines. MIMLA students in Mexico participate in classes televised live from Thunderbird's studio in Glendale, Arizona.

15. Kemper, "Global. . . ."

16. Black, "The Right. . . ."

17. Black, "The Right. . . ."

18. Kemper, "Global. . . ."

19. Beamer, "Bridging. . . ."

20. *The Global Relocation Trends 1996 Survey Report* (New York: Windham International and the National Foreign Trade Council, 1996).

21. *1996-1997 International Assignee Research Project* (Princeton, NJ: Berlitz International, 1997).

22. *The Management of Internationally Mobile Employees* (London: William M. Mercer Ltd., 1997).

23. *The Global. . . .*

24. Frazee, "Send Your. . . ."

25. Bernard Schmidt and Bella Poborets, "Developing the 'Global' Engineer," *Electronic Engineering Times,* (August 31, 1998), p. 138.

26. Frazee, "Send Your. . . ."

27. For further information, please contact Window on the World, Inc., 100 N. 6th St., Suite 300A, Minneapolis, MN 55403, USA Tel: 612-338-3690 Fax: 612-338-3037 e-mail: wowintl@isd.net web site www.windowontheworldinc.com

28. Beamer, "Bridging. . . ."

29. Beamer, "Bridging. . . ."

30. Beamer, "Bridging. . . ."

31. Mervosh, "The Care. . . ."

32. Mervosh, "The Care. . . ."

33. Hewlett Packard web site, 1999.

34. www.ford.com

35. www.motorola.com

36. www.motorola.com

37. Jane Goldenberg, "Distance Learning Cuts Training Costs, Boosts Skills," *Crain's Chicago Business,* (August 31, 1998), pp. SR12, 13.

13 | This Is Not Your Father's International Business

JOHN C. BECK

The 1990s was the decade of globalization. For U.S. interests, the threat of Japanese dominance in the world market, coupled with recession at home, convinced U.S. firms to look abroad—particularly to emerging markets—for growth. Later in the decade, financial crises in Mexico, Thailand, Korea, Russia, and Brazil challenged the wisdom of relying on international opportunities. By the end of the 1990s, the unrealized potential of globalization was expressed by 300 U.S. CEOs in a Baldrige Award Foundation survey. They named "the ability to think globally" as their most significant challenge—not strategic thinking, not cost cutting, not innovation, not competition—just thinking globally. As we enter a new decade, the Internet promises not only to change the way we have conducted international business in the past, but to redefine radically the concept of globalization itself.

In the 2000s, the World Wide Web is expected to begin to live up to its name. In 1999, 57% of Internet users were located in North America, with another 33% in Europe and Japan; in a few years these demographic concentrations will change dramatically. Averaging the predictions of a handful of electronic industry forecast companies, we expect that by 2003, nearly two-thirds of Internet users (67%) will be from non–North American locations. As the Internet helps to create a global business culture, it is also creating new ways of doing international business—and new obstacles.

Anyone who has studied or conducted business internationally in a traditional bricks-and-mortar world knows that critical differences exist between the way business is practiced in the United States and in the rest of the world. Commerce on the Internet will reduce or remove some of the traditional obstacles to international business. However, in certain cases, e-commerce will actually form new barriers to global business. Growing reliance on the Internet as a predominant mode of communication and commerce has created new areas of concern in international business, particularly in regard to buyer trust-anxiety, government regulation, buying and selling behavior, and the rather chaotic evolution of a shared language-based culture.

Trust-Anxiety

For centuries, lack of trust has been the biggest impediment to cross-border business. Fear of international deceit is hardly new; it's been several centuries since Virgil wrote: "Do not trust the horse, Trojans! Whatever it is, I fear the Greeks, even though they bring gifts." In traditional bricks-and-mortar international business, executives boarded trains and planes specifically to meet their customers and alliance partners face-to-face, establishing a higher level of trust. Doing business on the Internet has not reduced the trust-anxiety of international buyers. If anything, we are more afraid of potential fraud on the Internet than in any other form of commerce. For one thing, we can't see our counterpart's eyes. We can't even hear their voices.

Stefano Grazioli, of the University of Texas, has conducted research on U.S. domestic Internet fraud. Student participants in his study were asked to buy a product on the Internet by going to one of two web sites. One of the sites was real, while the other was designed for the purposes of the experiment. On the real site, the student could buy a product and actually expect to have it shipped to his or her home. On the fake site, the student could expect site operators to take his or her credit card number and buy themselves some badly needed products for their own households. The fake site was carefully designed to elicit feelings of trust and legitimacy; it contained a fake Better Business Bureau button (one that would actually take you to the BBB site, but you wouldn't find the phony web site name listed if you searched that far), testimonials from bogus customers, and fantasy reviews from real magazines like *Wired* and *Newsweek*. Not surprisingly, the students who used the fake site were more likely to buy than those using the real site.

Studies show that one of the main factors limiting Internet commerce is concern about security. In international e-commerce, users are even more fearful of potential fraud. Twenty-five percent of business respondents to a 1998 KPMG study claimed that security was the most significant barrier to Internet transactions. In reality, fraud on the web is much less prevalent than most people seem to think. For example, the auction site e-Bay claims it receives only 27 fraud complaints for every 1 million sales. With some of the technological improvements on the horizon, the Internet may actually make international business more trustworthy and less fraudulent.

Product Reviews

Companies such as Amazon.com use the Internet to invite customer comments on their products. The web page of any book being sold by Amazon includes reader ratings (0- to 5-star scale) and comments. Controversial books may attract hundreds of comments, allowing a buyer to assess the product not only based on the opinions of professional critics, but also on that of the average reader.

The auction site e-Bay, unlike Amazon, is not a direct purveyor of goods. Instead, it acts as an intermediary between buyers and sellers. Like Amazon, however, it accepts and posts "reputation" critiques of products and vendors in a "Feedback Forum," a voluntary track record of buyers and sellers who have used the auction service.

Notably, Amazon does not solicit opinions from customers about the company itself. Customers can use the web site to e-mail comments to Amazon customer service, but this is not a public forum—no other users may read those messages. Amazon management, not surprisingly, does not want its customers to calculate such input into their decision to use Amazon or a competitor (e.g., Barnes and Noble.com or Buy.com).

ihatemicrosoft.com

It is little wonder that companies have not wanted their "office web sites" used as a source of negative customer comments. The firms owned their ".com" addresses and were about as eager to let the average site-visitor post negative customer satisfaction messages as bricks-and-mortar retailers would be to put a huge bulletin board with negative customer feedback in front of their stores. But on the web, it does not matter that a company won't *give* customers their freedom of speech—Internet users can just *take* it. Using the most democratic of all technologies, deeply dissatisfied consumers can buy URL names that readily express their dissatisfaction (e.g., "ihatemicrosoft.com" or "ihatebillgates.com").

Web Graffiti

Current technology can make even the "official" site of a given company the target of negative commentary. Three Singaporeans have developed a "graffiti system" for the Internet. After these developers moved their company's operations to Silicon Valley (to more easily access venture capital or to avoid the "long stick of the law" in Singapore?), they began offering a system that allows users to write notes over the top of current web pages. Only users with their "Third Voice" software are able to read the comments, but it gives an outlet to the "little person" who has been ill treated or otherwise peeved by the company in question.

Now that anyone is able to complain or criticize, it is up to the buyer to beware. It also benefits companies who use the Internet—and therefore know that they may be very publicly criticized—to exercise special caution in avoiding any black marks. The traditional retailing "rule of thumb" is that only 1 in 10 dissatisfied customers complain in the first place (the other 9 simply stop using the product or services). If a company can satisfy a complaining customer, that company may gain life-long loyalty; if it doesn't, that customer is likely to boycott the company and take up to ten other customers along with him. In the Internet world, a dissatisfied buyer is likely to spread the mutiny to many more than 10 loyalists. Analysts estimate that on e-Bay, a single negative evaluation in their comment section leads to dozens less people buying from that vendor.

This system has some inherent ironies: for example, more experienced e-Bay buyers understand that the more a vendor has sold on the web, the more likely that vendor is to have accumulated bad marks along the way. Meanwhile, a seller who has only completed one or two transactions can show a "perfect record" and not, in actuality, have nearly as much of a proven track-record as the frequent seller. As customers become more savvy to the realities of e-commerce, the average person's interpretation of posted comments is likely to grow more sophisticated and accurate.

In .Com We Trust

Electronic payment systems are being developed to allow for easy, safer "one-click" transactions on the web. Such automatic debits to accounts at first seem strange and potentially unsafe to many Americans, but "cybercash" will actually do away with the need for the human interface that is usually the source of embezzlement and credit card misuse.

In most current cross-border consumer interactions, buyers are required to fax or phone their credit card numbers to international destinations, where employees have the opportunities to use the information for a variety of nefarious purposes. The electronic cash system, by contrast, would simply inform merchants that the appropriate money had been transferred to their accounts and that the products could now be shipped. No more credit card verifications, credit card refunds, or faxed signatures. And in the future, electronic cash may even replace letters of credit as a way to hold money (or even a credit line) in escrow pending the delivery of international shipments. The secured payments systems now in development may be enormously advantageous for international business. With the click of a mouse, buyers will be able to send payments in any currency around the world by credit card, smartcard, or direct debit to their bank accounts. The Internet allows sellers to confirm the receipt of money.

Reference Checks

A reference check of a first-time buyer or seller is easier to perform on the web than by any other means currently available. Especially when doing business in foreign countries, it is difficult to assess the reputation and trustworthiness of a firm with which you are considering doing business.

For example, consider how a consultant during most of the 1990s might have investigated a potential Chinese partner for a U.S. firm. Doing this effectively was next to impossible: there was no local Better Business Bureau, and few international companies who might have dealt extensively with Chinese firms in the past. When asked for references, the typical practice for Chinese companies was simply to send inquirers to meet with firms they knew were "friendly," and would give laudatory reports. The Commercial Attaché in the U.S. Embassy tried to keep up with it, but didn't really have the time or resources to keep tabs on most potential partner firms.

This situation resulted in many hopeful beginnings, unpleasant surprises, and costly bailouts for Western companies that tried to penetrate the Chinese market during the early 1990s. That was the old days, when the only available reference information came from "middlemen" with their own agendas. That was before everyone had a voice in the world.

Taking a Bite Out of the Middleman

As the web becomes a trusted source of feedback on corporate behaviors around the globe, one of the most revered positions in international business will become obsolete. The people who performed this function in the past went by several monikers: the Deal Maker, the Local Expert, or a number of culture-specific titles (the China Hand, for example). Whatever the person was called, he or she was likely to have the same list of priorities: remain intimately familiar with the local flavor of a country, foster a large set of contacts, and sell one's knowledge to foreigners who don't trust their own ability to evaluate a particular market.

Nowadays, intercultural middlemen are facing some uncomfortable questions. What if all that knowledge is on the web, readily accessible to anyone, anywhere, any time? What if an exporter is able survey potential foreign partners, get a quick read on their reputation and reliability, do a credit check, and assess their ability to deliver product to the right segment of customers—all with a single click of a mouse button? Suddenly, every domestic businessperson becomes an internationalist, and the middleman's margin is gone.

Naturally, there will always be some use for middlemen in international business. While advice on the Internet is more democratic than the traditional model, the anonymous and often random nature of company reviews on the web will never be able to fully replace the face-to-face interaction with a trusted individual who has a larger view of a particular foreign market. Middlemen can help cement relationships with governments and key customers, solve unanticipated problems in the local environment, and service as the local "face" for a company that prefers not to incur the cost of a wholly-owned local staff.

Nevertheless, the input from middlemen—and the inordinate power and control that often went with it—will increasingly be tempered by data from other sources. In international business as in every other pursuit, the more intelligence we gather, from a wider variety of sources, the more informed our decisions. The role of e-commerce in supplementing flesh-and-blood middlemen is to add as much reliable knowledge as technology can muster.

Internet-based advice is already the topic of considerable concern in the medical field. Healthcare professionals fear that web users who log into sites like WebMD.com may put off a visit to the doctor. Those who dispense medical advice over the web do it without the help of physical exam or a clear sense of the patient's medical history. Doctors' advocacy groups, not surprisingly, have warned the public that such sight-unseen medical advice may be hazardous to their health. Companies looking to the web for inexpensive international business advice should heed the same warning. Middlemen may be used to validate information accrued through the Internet, rather than as the ultimate source of all data about a given business environment.

Government Regulations

Interacting with the government has been one of the main headaches of international businesses since the merchants started traveling the Silk Route. To oil the wheels of international business, merchants plied emperors, lords, and shahs with gifts. Once the local powers were on their side, they could conduct business more or less as they wished—at the price of continued homage to the crown.

Even today, most countries rely on a similar system. In emerging markets, finding favor with the local war baron, governor, or mayor is often a matter of bribes and obeisance (the recent scandals over the use of expensive "gifts" to woo the Olympic Games to different locations highlighted this practice). Developed countries generally have developed a rule-of-law to regulate transaction of business across borders. While the "face time" and "gifts" required for success in emerging countries are done away with, the alternative—miles of red tape and years of bureaucratic minutia—is sometimes even more time consuming and expensive. Most companies hire (or outsource) a cadre of lawyers, accountants, and consultants to keep them on the right side of the law in foreign countries.

The virtual trader does not have to give so much thought to local governments. Without a physical presence in a country, the Internet businessperson has no need to fear nationalization, is not nearly as likely to be sued, and runs virtually no risk of ending up in prison (not an unrealistic concern in traditional international business). Bribes to overzealous immigration officials or even customs inspectors are unnecessary, especially if it is a "weightless" product (information, computer software, music or video files) that is crossing the borders.

Free at Last

Most countries have not yet decided how to deal with the issue of Internet commerce regulations. Most regulations that do exist are haphazardly enforced. One e-commerce buyer in Chile reported that shipments of Internet-bought goods usually appeared at her home directly without the assessment of duties. Sometimes she was called to the customs office to pay a fee on a particular shipment, but the assessment of fees appeared to be almost random.

Extremely strict unilateral regulation of Internet business or information is unlikely, given most governments' laissez-faire attitude toward it thus far. Policymakers know that to impose rules and regulations too late in the game is to risk causing a revolt (a case in point being the British government's belated decision to extend tax laws to tea sold in the American colonies). Once you've let the genie out of the bottle, it would rather fight than go back in.

Regulations and taxes that do emerge on Internet commerce are likely to be of a bilateral or multilateral nature. The country (and locality) bricks-and-mortar commercial laws that govern most of our business transactions today emerged over many centuries, and were designed for local municipalities buffered from the rest of the world.

The taxes and regulations on the Internet are now being discussed at multinational conferences, to ensure that the rules are fair and to preserve the untethered aspects of the Internet that have fostered its tremendous growth.

The few examples of differentially harsh Internet regulation suggest that it is better to leave well enough alone. Until late 1999, the U.S. carefully regulated the encoding systems that could be shipped outside of its borders. The most secure Netscape and Internet Explorer versions could not be shipped off American soil. Web developers mounted a lobbying campaign to U.S. legislators to get some of these rules changed. They explained that the strictures virtually ensured a "world-standard" security system developed outside of the United States. In September 1999, the U.S. government relaxed its standards to encourage export of U.S.-developed security systems around the world. In an Internet universe, control lies in market share, not in laws and regulation.

Big Bad Bullies

Incumbent brick-and-mortar multinationals have the potential to do real harm to startup Internet companies as they attempt to go abroad. Multinational firms have already established governmental and regulatory-body relationships around the world. Those that fear startups stealing their market share are likely to lobby these governments to more carefully monitor their borders. If such border-protecting legislation is enacted and enforced, the already established firms may benefit.

This is not a matter of barriers to entry. Internet companies will probably be able to sell *some* product across borders. A trickle of sales is always possible without detection. Nevertheless, bricks-and-mortar-instigated laws and regulations could erect barriers to *volume* that make global selling unprofitable for companies "born on the web."

Buying and Selling Behavior

In 1998, only about 26% of the total Internet commerce originated from non-U.S. sources, according to a report from the International Data Corporation. In contrast, by 2003 almost half of the world's e-commerce transactions will be occurring outside of the United States. In Europe alone, e-commerce spending will increase from

$5.6 billion in 1998 to $430 billion by 2003. Consumer and business spending in Europe has only been increasing at the rate of two percent a year. So most of the $430 billion is money that would have been spent in traditional channels in the past—now it will be going to merchants and corporations that are selling on the web. Foreign web sales may increase even faster than domestic transactions because of the perceived ease of doing business by Internet instead of by traditional means.

Setting a Standard

Many believe that the web will be the great equalizer of the twenty-first century, making sales and buying techniques ever more standardized and rational. During the globalization decade of the 1990s, even businesspeople with the most domestic mindsets became at least somewhat aware of the differences in the way consumers react around the world. The Japanese like high-priced designer goods, the Germans are known for their interest in highly stylized designs, the Chinese will buy anything they can get their hands on, but only if it *looks* like a bargain. Selling behaviors have also varied wildly. The Japanese auto manufacturers sold most of their products door-to-door. In countries like Germany "blue laws" kept shops from opening in the evening and on Sundays. And a handful of foreign retailers in major cities around the globe did a good business in servicing the "expatriate" communities with products they traditionally bought at home, often at tremendous markups from the base price.

Analysts predict that the Internet will change all of that—and shareholders believe it. Many expect that selling behavior will increasingly move to an "order-deliver" model (not popular since the hey-days of the Sears catalog), shops will be open 24-hours-a-day, 7-days-a-week, and products will be relatively easy to come by anywhere on the globe. Pokemon-obsessed pre-teens are already able to find Japanese retailers happy to sell them exotic Japanese-language trading cards shipped within a couple of days to their mailbox (if the targeted customer can get a credit card number from mom or dad).

Haggling for Dollars

Western cultures are known for their reserve when it comes to bargaining; in many other cultures, haggling is a highly developed and respected art. When Singaporean housewife Doreen Lim first took a trip to London in the early 1980s, she was confused to see fixed prices at Harrods. She offered the sales clerks 30% of the marked price. They were not amused. Lim's method of buying seemed archaic and culturally alien to the British—as theirs did to her. She thought every child understood that "the fun of shopping is in getting a good price."

Historically, most buyers and sellers would agree with Doreen Lim's position. Fixed-price buying has been a defining characteristic of the "modern" world, first introduced around the turn of the twentieth century. Increasingly, "bargaining" (in auction form) is the most common form of transaction on the Internet, both in business-to-customer and customer-to-customer selling. Even Westerners seem to feel that this is a better way to price goods than fixed-price methods.

Business-to-business or business-to-government relationships that depend on "transparency" will also be well served by the advent of the Internet. Bids for contracts can be solicited from a larger and more diverse group of vendors than could ever be handled in the old paper-based system. And increasingly, closed-bidding systems may be replaced by auction systems that allow governments and businesses to get even lower contract prices than they were ever able to get in the traditional system.

Language and Culture

The most important barriers to cross-border commerce are not physical, but linguistic and cultural. Today, 90% of the 400 million web pages are written in English and accessed by the 80% of web users who are native English speakers. But by the year 2005, according to IDC, 700 million of the 1 billion Internet users will not claim English as their native language. Internet page content will have to change accordingly. A report from Allied Business Intelligence indicates that the language translation market (machine, human, and software and Internet site localizations) is expected to almost double over the next five years, from $11 billion in 1999 to almost $20 billion 2004.

Lingua Internetica

Web-based translators now offered on some of the more popular portals have the potential to make international business less costly and more efficient. One of the most popular and highly rated of these is the Alta Vista's Bablefish. According to Seth Socolow, the director of this service, the site receives a half-million translation requests each week. Bablefish initially offered translation between English and the most common European languages, but has plans to expand this to Russian, Japanese, and Chinese as well. When a user enters a word, phrase, or web site address, a translation appears on the screen in a matter of seconds—a pleasant surprise for a business practitioner who is accustomed to waiting days, or even weeks for human translators to turn out interpretations of foreign-language letters or business intelligence.

Even without translations, the text-base nature of computerized interaction actually makes cross-border communication and business dealings more exact and understandable. For years, Japanese managers have relied on fax communication not only with their Japanese colleagues, but with customers and suppliers as well. Writing out requests and receiving requests back in written form allows less room for confusion. Moreover, many of the non-native English speakers who try to do international transactions in English read and write more proficiently than they can speak or listen. Finally, Internet transactions leave a detailed "cyber trail" that can be consulted should disputes or misunderstandings ever arise.

The technological advances of the Internet (over fax) allow for real-time, long distance, written conversations that can ameliorate some of the potential downsides of doing international business. Chatroom technology is not new, but it can be more ubiquitous now there is a net. "Internet culture" is creating a generation of computer users around the world who are comfortable communicating across distances with unseen colleagues in written form. English speakers benefit enormously from this trend, since English has become the default "common language" of cross-border Internet business.

The Culture of Language

Language isn't the only issue to consider in international commerce. Other cultural differences are more important than one might expect—particularly when dealing with countries we think of as similar to our own. When Jorden Woods, CEO of Global Sight, asked U.S. executives to relate stories of epic cross-cultural misunderstandings, they rarely come from "exotic" cultures. According to Woods, "the stories usually come from Australia." The problem is that Americans and Australians think they understand each other—after all, they speak the same language. In communicating with Japanese, Russians, or Sri Lankans, Western business people will take great pains to understand and be understood. When the language seems identical, except for the occasional "G'day, mate," the fear of foreignness is assuaged, and business people expend less effort on understanding nuance.

Slight misunderstandings about nuance can result in strange marketing campaigns and advertising copy, which might confuse customers. For instance, Clean Grape Toilet Tissue, a brand sold in South East Asia, boasted in colloquial English of qualities we all want in our toilet paper: "Clean Grape," the label read, "is sturdy and tenacious."

As English becomes more and more popularized on the web, Internet businesspeople may increasingly rely on products like the Encarta Worldwide English Dictionary. Most business people in the United Kingdom and United States are familiar with the different local terms for particular items: elevator = lift; car trunk = boot; toilet = loo. But lesser-known word use differences magnify the potential for trouble. Take the word "similar" which means "resembling" or "almost the same" in both British and U.S. English. In Malaysia it means "identical." This slight but crucial difference could engender chaos in a business negotiation.

The very structure of Internet commerce ensures that business must be conducted in more universal and exact terminology. For example, buttons in web pages ask for a simple "yes" or "no" before a user can continue gathering information. In a face-to-face or fax relationship, there might be a longer, subtler explanation that could be interpreted as *either* a "yes" or "no." The simple "tree design" of most web sites forces a level of clarity and common understanding between users that is rare in traditional cross-border business transactions. Over time, Internet technology itself may forge a new international decision-making culture.

Conclusion

Sales practices, language, trust, and the regulatory environment are only three of the myriad aspects of doing business abroad that will be affected by the increasing importance of the Internet in cross-border commerce. Other topics, such as contracts, supply and delivery chains, managerial styles, labor relations, currency, and finance are equally important. The effect of all of these must be examined in much greater detail than is possible in this chapter.

Certainly, in the next decade traditional brick-and-mortar companies will need to change both their high-level strategies and their marching orders to the troops because e-commerce will significant alter the "rules of international business engagement." Incumbent firms should expect to use their installed global infrastructure and tried-and-true government, buyer, and supplier contacts to keep their newfound cyber-competitors at bay. Brick-and-mortar firms that have never had a significant international presence in their histories have the chance to become preferred global vendors by using the web. In the next decade the race will be to the swift, and companies, particularly traditional firms, that first capture the eyeballs (and then the hearts) of Internet users will be the most likely to thrive. And while we can be sure that International Business (as we have known it) will change, a pure black-or-white view of the role of the web in its integration or collapse would be ill advised.

What can be said without doubt is that the web will obliterate the need for some practices and services in international business, while creating new, often profitable opportunities. The Internet, like any new communication device, makes the world smaller; and like any new transaction tool, it creates areas of concern and unfamiliar perils. Companies that are able to skillfully navigate these uncharted waters are those most likely to reach their desired international business destination.

14 Conclusions

Thunderbird on Global Business Strategy has provided a wide-ranging view of the challenges and opportunities facing companies at the global level in the new millenium. While there is no single model or theory that captures all of the wealth of perspectives offered here, there are a few common threads that run through these chapters.

One central theme is that business is global, whether we like it or not. Competing successfully in the twenty-first century requires fending off (or allying with) rivals from other countries, even if a firm operates only in a domestic market. The old examples of the corner store, or the local restaurant, as purely domestic businesses are fading away, as the stores are exposed to competition not just from Wal-Mart and Kmart, but also from Carrefour and Tesco, and the restaurants are facing entry from chains from several countries along with McDonalds, Friday's, and other U.S. chains.

The global nature of business is not necessarily a threat; rather it can be seen as an opportunity, for example, to realize economies of scale by selling products over a broader market. Likewise, looking at business from a global perspective reminds us to look for inputs from any source around the world where new ideas may originate, where production may be cheaper, and where allies may offer to jointly carry out activities and reduce each partner's costs and risks.

The other cornerstone of the analyses presented here is the need for rapid action in corporate strategy for the twenty-first century. Whether competition is on the Internet or simply realized through global telecommunications and transportation, the speed of action and response to changes in the competitive environment must be much faster than before. To survive in such competition requires managers to utilize the technology that exists to put their products in front of potential customers through the media that are now available, and it also requires managers to look forward and look across national borders for opportunities. Rapid response does not mean just copying the leaders, but anticipating the changes that are coming. This does not require one to know the future—always an impossibility—but it does require the capable manager to envision the implications of current technology for near-future competition—and to act on it.

Our goal in writing this book is to provide insights into the kinds of issues that managers should be considering in their attempts to forge global strategy in this radically changed competitive environment. Never has it been more true that 'the future is today'; and our strategies must be changed to deal with the speed and globality of the competition.

About the Authors

The authors whose works are compiled in this volume are all present or former members of the Thunderbird faculty. Their biographical sketches are given here in alphabetical order.

Raj Aggarwal's professional interests include finance, international business, and strategic analysis. He currently holds the Mellen Chair at John Carroll University and has taught at Harvard, Hawaii, Michigan, South Carolina, Thunderbird, and Toledo Universities. He has lived and worked in Japan, Singapore, India, Australia, Sweden, and the United States and has traveled extensively in other European and Asian countries. Aggarwal is the author of twelve books and over fifty scholarly papers, serves on the editorial boards of scholarly journals such as the *Journal of Multinational Finance Management, Financial Review, Journal of International Business Studies, International Business Review,* and is the editor of *Financial Practice and Education* and *Corporate Finance Review.*

He is a corporate board member and has been a consultant to the United Nations, World Bank, Finance Ministers, Securities and Exchange Commission, NASA, and the boards and senior managements of banks and Fortune 100 multinationals. He is a highly regarded speaker and seminar leader and has been the graduation speaker at John Carroll University and Pacific Asia Management Institute and a keynote speaker for groups such as the National Association of Accountants and the Associates of Japanese Business Studies. He has received many university and college teaching awards and has been elected an officer of civic and professional organizations such as the Financial Management Association, Financial Executives Institute, Council of World Affairs, and the Academy of International Business. He is a Fellow of the Academy of International Business, has been a Senior Fulbright Research Scholar in Southeast Asia, and is listed in Who's Who in Finance and Industry.

John C. Beck is an Associate Partner and Senior Research Fellow at the Andersen Consulting Institute for Strategic Change where he has led research projects on the following topics: global e-Commerce, the internationalization journey of large firms, the Asian Financial Crisis, economic development in emerging nations such as the Czech Republic and Cambodia, global team building, and a model of large-scale change and integration known as The Change Cycle.

He is also a Visiting Professor at the Anderson School of Management at the University of California at Los Angeles (UCLA) where he teaches courses on Globalization and Leadership. Dr. Beck has also taught courses in multinational management, strategy, management consulting, group psychology, organizational behavior, and management in emerging economies at Harvard University and at Thunderbird, The American Graduate School of International Management.

Dr. Beck served as the Senior Strategic Advisor to the First Prime Minister, Prince Ranariddh, and other top officials in Cambodia during the first three years of democratic government in that nation. In conjunction, he also served as a member of the Board of Advisors to Royal Air Cambodge (the national airline of Cambodia).

Previously, Dr. Beck was Co-Director of the "Project on Strategies of the World's Largest 50 Companies" for the United Nations. Additionally, he served as the Far East Advisor with Monitor Company, a Boston-based strategy consultancy, and oversaw the start-up of their operations in Korea and Japan. He was also President of Asian Business Information Co. and Publisher of *The Asian Century,* a newsletter specializing in strategic analysis of Asian companies and industries.

Dr. Beck earned his bachelor's degree *summa cum laude* (an honor given to only 50 graduating students a year) from Harvard University, in East Asian Studies and Sociology. The University awarded him the Hoopes and Thornton Prizes for a thesis on juvenile delinquency in Japan. Professor Beck completed his Ph.D., also from

Harvard, as the first graduate in a new integrative Ph.D. program in Business Studies. He has published over 100 books, articles, and business reports on topics of business in Asia, strategic management, globalization, leadership, and organizational behavior.

Michael Bradley is F.M. Kirby Professor of Investment Banking at the Fuqua Business School at Duke University, and Professor of Law at the Duke University Law School. Prior to Duke, he was at the University of Michigan Business School, and at the faculties of the Universities of Chicago and Rochester. Professor Bradley's research interests lie at the intersection of corporate finance and corporate law, spanning such areas as corporate capital structure, mergers and acquisitions, takeover defenses and tactics, fiduciary duties of corporate managers, and corporate bankruptcy. His work has been published in the leading journals of finance and law.

Charles Chun is an Associate Partner with Andersen Consulting's Strategy Practice in Los Angeles. He specializes in developing competitive and marketing strategies for clients in the electronics and high-technology industry. Prior to Los Angeles, Mr. Chun spent several years in the Asia–Pacific region working with both MNCs and Asian conglomerates on resolving strategic and operational issues. Mr. Chun holds a Bachelor of Science degree from UCLA, a Master of Science degree from the University of Southern California, and a Master of Business Administration from NYU.

Christine Uber Grosse is Professor of Modern Languages at Thunderbird. She teaches Advanced Business Communication in the regular master's program and in the MIMLA (Masters in International Management in Latin America) distance learning program for Latin American executives. She received her doctorate in Romance Languages (Portuguese, French, and Spanish) from the University of North Carolina at Chapel Hill. Prior to that, she received the MA in Portuguese, with a minor in Arabic from UNC. She earned a B.A. in Geography (double major in Spanish) from Mary Washington College, graduating Phi Beta Kappa with honors.

Before coming to Thunderbird, she worked at Florida International University in Miami as director of graduate programs in the

Teaching of English to Speakers of Other Languages (TESOL) teacher education and modern language education. She also has taught Spanish at the University of Michigan, Eastern Michigan University, and Miami-Dade Community College.

She has published several books (*Speaking of Business* and *Case Studies in International Business*), and numerous articles on teaching languages for business, the economic utility of foreign language study, and distance learning in leading professional journals. She has served as President of Florida TESOL and Chair of the Video Interest Section for TESOL.

Robert E. Grosse holds a B.A. degree from Princeton University and a doctorate from the University of North Carolina, both in international economics. He has taught international finance in the MBA programs at the University of Miami, the University of Michigan, and at the Instituto de Empresa (Madrid, Spain), as well as in various universities in Latin America. As a consultant in international business, he has worked for the U.S. Commerce, State, and Treasury Departments, the Organization of American States, and the United Nations. Among the many companies he has served are: American Express, Anaconda, Banco Ganadero, Chase Manhattan Bank, EXXON, IBM, Raymond James, Texaco, and YPF.

Professor Grosse has published numerous studies on financial and managerial strategy of international firms, including his article on "The Privatization of YPF" (with Juan Yañes) *Academic of Management Executive* (Spring 1998), and his textbook on *International Business* with Duane Kujawa (Irwin, 3rd ed., 1995). He has been examining the phenomenon of privatization of state-owned companies in Latin America, and has written articles about the sale of Aerolineas Argentinas and about the success of such firms after privatization.

In the past few years, Professor Grosse has worked as Chair in Capital Markets at the Instituto de Empresa (Madrid), and as Visiting Professor of International Finance at ICESI (Cali, Colombia) and at the Universidad Gabriela Mistral (Santiago, Chile). He has taught executive programs in international finance and global business strategy in Argentina, Chile, Colombia, Costa Rica, Ecuador, México, Perú, Puerto Rico, Spain, Trinidad, Uruguay, and Venezuela.

Professor Grosse functions as Director of the Thunderbird Center for International Business Education and Research, which is launching major research projects on the subjects of "Developing Global Leaders for Global Firms," "Thunderbird on Global Strategy," and "The Future of the Financial Services Industry," among others. He was Director of the University of Miami's International Business & Banking Institute from 1986–1993.

Andrew C. Inkpen is an Associate Professor of Management at Thunderbird, The American Graduate School of International Management in Glendale, Arizona. He holds a Ph.D. in Business Policy and International Business from the University of Western Ontario. He has also been on the faculties of Temple University and the National University of Singapore. His research and teaching deal with the management of multinational firms, with a particular focus on strategic alliances. He is the author or co-author of more than 30 articles in journals such as *Academy of Management Review, Academy of Management Executive, California Management Review, Strategic Management Journal, Journal of International Business Studies,* and *Organization Science.* He is actively involved in international executive education and has consulted with a variety of organizations.

Alan I. Murray is Clinical Professor of Management at Thunderbird, The American Graduate School of International Management, in Glendale, Arizona. Prior to joining the Thunderbird faculty, Dr. Murray was an Associate Professor in the Department of Organizational Analysis at the University of Alberta (1983–1992). He has held visiting professorships at INSEAD and at the University of Auckland.

Dr. Murray's primary research and teaching interests lie in competitive strategy, organizational change, and knowledge-based competition. He has made numerous converence presentations and his articles have appeared in *The Academy of Management Review, Strategic Management Journal, Journal of Experimental Social Psychology, The British Journal of Industrial Relations,* and *Handbook of Business Strategy 1991/92 Yearbook.* He is a member of the Academy of Management and the Strategic Management Society.

Dr. Murray holds a Ph.D. from Stanford University's Graduate School of Business (1985) and a Bachelor of Commerce Degree from the University of Auckland, New Zealand, Faculty of Management Studies (1979). He is a citizen of both Canada and New Zealand and is married with three children.

Sundaresan Ram is Associate Professor of Marketing at Thunderbird, The American Graduate School of International Management in Glendale, Arizona. He holds a Ph.D. in Business Management (Marketing) from the University of Illinois at Champaign-Urbana, and is an alumnus of the Indian Institute of Management, Calcutta, and Indian Institute of Technology, Madras. Ram has also been on the faculty of UCLA, University of California at Irvine, and University of Arizona. His research and teaching deal with global product development, with a particular focus on telecommunications. He is the author or co-author of several articles in the areas of expert systems for new product screening, usage of high tech products, corporate and customer barriers to new product development, and innovation resistance. Ram is also a multiple winner of the teaching excellence award at Thunderbird. He is actively involved in executive education—he is the Academic Director of the Global Telecommunications Program and has consulted with a variety of organizations. He is the Chair of the U.S. Western Region of the Academy of International Business.

D. Lance Revenaugh is currently serving as Visiting Assistant Professor at Arizona State University-West. He has previously served on the information systems (IS) faculty of Thunderbird, City University of Hong Kong, the University of Idaho, and Biola University. He has published papers in the areas of IS Strategy, measuring information worker productivity, Business Process Re-engineering, and implementation of major change within organizations. For the past five years he has also chaired the IS Strategy and Implementation track of the Americas Conference on Information Systems.

Cindy A. Schipani is Professor of Law at the University of Michigan Business School. Professor Schipani's primary research interests are in the area of corporate governance, with a focus on directors' and officers' duties. She has numerous articles on these topics in the leading law journals. Prior to her academic career at the University of Michigan, she served as a law clerk for Justice Charles L. Levin of the Michigan Supreme Court, and practiced law as an associate with two major commercial law firms.

Anant Sundaram is Associate Professor of Finance at Thunderbird. Prior to Thunderbird, he was at the University of Michigan Business School and the Tuck School of Business at Dartmouth College. Professor Sundaram's primary research interests are in the areas of cross-border mergers and acquisitions and comparative corporate governance. He is the author of numerous articles in such diverse areas as finance, international business, corporate strategy, and law.

Robert S. Tancer received his B.A. and LL.B from the University of Michigan and a LL.M from Harvard University. He has practiced law in Washington, D.C., Buenos Aires, Argentina, and Phoenix, Arizona. He has also worked for the Department of State. Currently, Mr. Tancer is a Professor of International Studies at Thunderbird, The American Graduate School of International Management in Glendale, Arizona. He teaches courses in intellectual property, legal problems of international business, competition policy, and the pharmaceutical industry. Mr. Tancer has contributed articles to various journals in the areas of intellectual property in world trade, foreign investment, and the pharmaceutical industry. He has recently published an article, "The Pharmaceutical Industry in India: Adapting to TRIPS," in *The Journal of World Intellectual Property*. Mr. Tancer is also active in the community, where he serves as President of the Arizona Opera and Trustee of the Desert Botanical Garden.

Shoshana B. Tancer is Director of the NAFTA Center and Professor of International Studies at Thunderbird, The American Graduate School of International Management. Dr. Tancer is also "Of Counsel" to Ryley, Carlock and Applewhite, P.C., a prestigious Phoenix law firm. Dr. Tancer received her Ph.D. from Columbia University, her LL.B. from the University of Michigan Law School and her A.B. from Barnard College.

Dr. Tancer has lived and worked in Argentina where she was Chief of the Translation Department of Allende & Brea, a law firm in Buenos Aires; and in the Dominican Republic where she taught at the Universidad Nacional Pedro Henriquez Urena in Santo Domingo. She has written on various topics related to Latin America, the Canada–U.S. Free Trade Agreement, and the North American Free Trade Agreement.

In addition, Dr. Tancer is a member of the Board of Directors of The FINOVA Group, a NYSE company, and a former member of the Board of Directors of Xantel Corporation and Mountain Bell (now a subsidiary of US West) Corporation.

James P. Walsh is the Gerald and Esther Carey Professor of Business Administration at the University of Michigan Business School. He has a long-standing research interest in the area of corporate governance. He is currently examining the substance and symbolism of corporate social responsibility initiatives. His work has been published in the leading journals of management, strategy, and finance.

William E. Youngdahl is Assistant Professor of Operations Management in the World Business Department of Thunderbird. He received his Ph.D. in Business Administration from the University of Southern California. Dr. Youngdahl was an engineer at Xerox and a project manager at Hughes Aircraft, Ground Systems Division. He is an Associate Editor for *The Journal of Operations Management* and conducts research in quality management, global supply chain management, and service operations management. Additionally, he has delivered a variety of executive education programs to clients including General Motors Asia Pacific, Phelps Dodge, Motorola, Allied Signal, Dow, IBM, Avon, and Honeywell.

Index